Rev

Advanced PE for
Edexcel

Tim Barry
Dee Crawford
Mike Hill
Gavin Roberts
Jon Spence

Edexcel
Success through qualifications

Heinemann Educational Publishers
Halley Court, Jordan Hill, Oxford OX2 8EJ
Part of Harcourt Education

Heinemann is the registered trademark of
Harcourt Education Limited

First published 2002

07 06 05 04
10 9 8 7 6 5 4 3

British Library Cataloguing in Publication Data is available
from the British Library on request.

ISBN 0 435 10045 9

Designed by Wendi Watson
Typeset by TechType, Abingdon

Original illustrations © Harcourt Education Limited 2002
Photograph on page 165 reproduced with permission from Colorsport

Printed in Great Britain by Bath Press Ltd

Cover photographs: © Male gymnast on rings – Alan Edwards
                   Women's Rugby World Cup – Allsport/Dave Rogers
                   Women's 800m wheelchair race – Actionplus/Neil Tingle
                   Original Olympic Stadium (Greece) – Corbis

Acknowledgements
Every effort has been made to contact copyright holders of material reproduced in this book. Any
omissions will be rectified in subsequent printings if notice is given to the publishers.

Tel: 01865 888058 www.heinemann.co.uk

Contents

General introduction/how to use this book

In order to assist with the revision process this book is laid out in a manner that corresponds to the student textbook, 'Advanced PE for Edexcel'. Units 1, 3, 5 & 6 are covered, these being the Units that are directly addressed in the theory examinations.

The revision material for each Unit is preceded by a short introductory or explanatory text highlighting particular issues or points that should be borne in mind when revising that Unit. The material for each Unit also includes a 'reminder' or 'do you know about' section, which serves as a means of reminding you of topics in each Unit with which you should be familiar. At the end of each Unit there are a small number of 'exam tips' written by examiners, to act as further reminders and help you approach examination questions more directly.

It should be remembered that revision is an on-going process and not something that can be done simply by going through the material in each Unit once and ticking it off as 'done'! Nor is it a good idea to wait until the taught element of your course is finished before beginning revision. You will not have sufficient time to do it thoroughly.

Revision should begin almost as soon as you have completed any work at all. It is a process of constantly refreshing what you have learned so that it stays at the forefront of your mind. The material in each Unit should be reviewed several times over an extended period – not just in the few days immediately prior to the examination!!!

Thorough revision should raise questions and these should be addressed by referring to this text, the student text, your own notes and in discussion with your teachers.

The key to scoring well in any examination lies in the following process.

*   Look at the mark allocation for each question as this gives an indication of the extent and detail required in your answer.
*   Do you understand what the question is actually asking of you?
*   Do not get hung up on a few key words that you have read before. Try to work out exactly what is being asked.
*   Are you actually answering the question that is set?
*   Look for important phrases such as;
    'and' — this means that you have been asked to do at least two things e.g. *"Identify **and** describe...."*
    'Using an example' — quite often if you fail to provide the example that is asked for you might fail to score any marks at all.

UNIT 1: The social basis of sport and recreation

Section A: UK and the European context

Overview

1. Cultural background
- Social analysis and mainstream values
- Attitudes to sport, leisure and recreation
- An overview of sport before 1800
- The development of combat sports
- Class and collaboration
- Venues for recreation and sport
- The role of the Church
- Types of recreational activities
- Sport after 1800
- The urban revolutions
- The pace of industrial change
- Social change
- Mass transport

2. The development of physical education
- Sport and public schools in the nineteenth century
- Physical education – by military intent?
- Sport and Oxbridge
- Further developments
- The diffusion of the new concept
- Diffusion through the Empire
- European and military influences
- Sport and physical education in the twentieth century
- The early syllabuses
- Broadened interest and provision
- The 1944 Education Act
- Outdoor apparatus
- Outdoor education
- Movement and dance
- Current and future policies in school sport and PE

3. Social influences on performance and participation
- Cultural setting
- Resources
- Lifestyles in contemporary society
- Access, opportunity and provision
- Other factors affecting participation
- Stacking, centrality and self-fulfilling prophecy
- Target groups
- Reformative policy
- Geographical factors

4. Professional (élite) sport
- Practice of exclusion
- Increased free time
- Mass spectator sport
- The rise in status of the professional
- National governing bodies of sport
- European and international governing bodies
- The nurture of talent in the UK
- School sport
- Club sport
- National sports centres and academies
- UKSI in Sheffield and network centres
- Other initiatives
- Sport England
- European models of sports excellence
- Commercialisation and Americanisation of UK and European professional sport

5. Recreative sport (mass participation)
- Commitment to Sport for All
- The impact of sport for all in Europe
- The role of national agencies
- Grass-roots programmes
- Concept of target groups and reforms
- Amateur sports and the voluntary sector
- Wilderness and alternative sports

Explanatory notes

Physical activity

Terms such as 'sport', 'recreation', 'leisure', 'physical education' and 'outdoor education', as well as other associated terms, occur regularly in the units throughout this book. It is important that context is clearly understood. We are concerned here with physical activities and how they are perceived or 'classified'.

- 'Sport' is highly structured and organised. It requires a specific commitment from participants and places a high significance on 'outcomes', or results.

- 'Recreation'/'leisure' activities are often less stringently organised than sport and require only a level of commitment that is appropriate to the particular activity, e.g. an individual keen on rambling need make no commitment other than that which s/he feels inclined to make, whereas members of a local five-a-side soccer group make a commitment to each other. Outcomes, or results, are only as important as participants wish to make them.

- Some leisure activities may be almost entirely passive in the physical sense, e.g. reading or going to the theatre. Therefore, the term 'recreation' tends to be associated with more active forms of leisure.

Whether physical activities are seen as 'sports', 'recreations' or part of physical education programmes depends on the purpose for which they are used. Football, for example, is an activity that can be a recreation (a friendly kick-about), a sport (playing in a local league) or educational (as part of a PE programme). It is not the activity itself that determines how it is classified, but the context in which it is performed.

PE programmes should embrace a number of aims, including:

- educational
- recreational/enjoyment
- physical/developmental.

The activity used at any given time is merely a vehicle, not an end in itself.

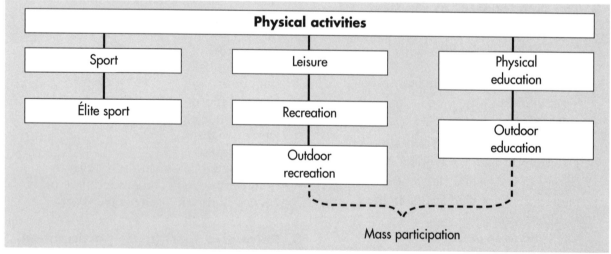

Physical activities and their different contexts

1. Cultural background

Fact:
Sport and recreation do not take place in a vacuum. They are just as much influenced by cultural change as by any other aspect of life.

Fuller information on these themes can be found in *Advanced PE for Edexcel*, pages 5–14.

Social analysis and mainstream values
- The move to the towns
- The social context
- The urban middle class

Attitudes to sport, leisure and recreation
- The influence of the Church
- 'Base and evil pastimes'

An overview of sport before 1800

The development of combat sports
- Recreations of the peasantry
- Recreational characteristics

Class and collaboration

Venues for recreation and sport
- The coaching inn
- The racecourse
- The fairground
- The river
- The road
- The baiting pit

The role of the Church

Types of recreational activities
- Festival activities
- Court games
- 'Mob' activities

Sport after 1800

The urban revolutions

The pace of industrial change

Social change

Mass transport
- The effect of transport on sport

 **points**

Social analysis and mainstream values
Before the Industrial Revolution:

- there was a clear unbridgeable distinction between the gentry and the peasantry (although there were some exceptions in larger towns, where the legal, clerical and other professions bridged the social gap)
- the UK had a largely rural population
- everyone knew his or her place in the social order.

The move to the towns
- This occurred largely between 1750 and 1850.
- The mechanisation of agriculture forced labourers to seek work in the rapidly growing towns.
- The process of industrial change had a major influence on recreational patterns, previously governed by religious and rural calendars.
- Regulated factory hours allowed little recreation time.

The social context
- Rural recreations were replaced by those of the town.
- Many former recreations were lost as space was given over to industrial development and housing.
- The public house became one of the few places of recreation for the labouring classes.
- Wives and children were forced into the factory in order to 'make ends meet'.

The urban middle class
- The most significant instrument of change was the newly emerging urban middle class.
- This class assumed responsibility for the moral/social welfare of its communities.

Attitudes to sport, leisure and recreation

- Attitudes to recreation changed in the second half of the nineteenth century.
- Many former rural recreations died out and church wakes were closed down.
- Recreation had to be seen to be purposeful rather than pleasurable.
- Many blood sports were curtailed and eventually banned (Blood Sports Act of 1834).
- Those that survived were forced underground.
- Many former 'Sabbath day' recreations were discouraged as 'base and evil pastimes'.
- Propriety was valued above everything and church attendance conferred social acceptability.
- Recreation was available only to those with time and money.

An overview of sport before 1800

 **points**

Sport grew out of the activities used by man to:

- survive
- defend himself and his allegiances
- perform rituals and celebrations
- fulfil a need to recreate, invent and 'contest'.

The development of combat sports

- Combat sports were part of training for war and the preparation of knights.
- Jousts/tournaments were part of this preparation.
- The broadsword and lance were 'knightly' weapons.
- The freeman had the long bow and the peasant relied on the quarterstaff.
- The knight hunted as sport, whilst the peasant hunted for food.
- The countryside was a place of recreation as well as a source of food.

Recreational characteristics

These included:

- a localised cultural focus
- occupational activities
- a seasonal and church calendar
- problems with lawlessness
- rituals/festivals
- limited codification (rules)
- the gentry utilising their estates for their recreations, whilst the lower classes patronised the inn, the river and common land.

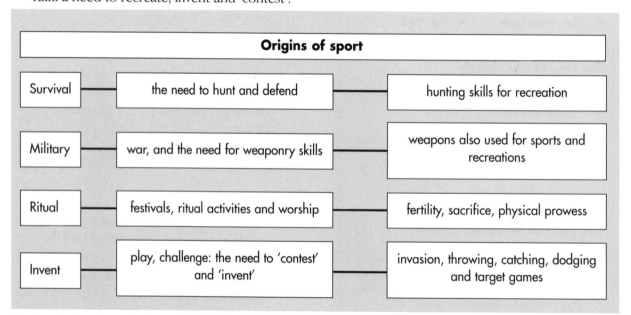

A simplistic view of the origins of sport

Class and collaboration

- The clearest example of this was cricket, where it was common for both ordinary people and upper classes to make up a team.
- In horse racing, the upper classes retained jockeys to ride on their behalf.
- This patronage also occurred in pedestrianism and the prize ring.

Venues for recreation and sport

These included:

- the coaching inn
- the river
- the racecourse
- the road
- the fairground
- the baiting pit.

In addition:

- venues were often frequented by both the upper and lower classes
- the feudal knight became the country gentleman
- social status also required a mastery of fencing, gymnastics and sparring.

The role of the Church

- Church precincts had often provided recreational space for ball games.
- Some over-zealous clergyman caused the closure of many local festivals and pastimes.

- Young men crossed into parishes where Sabbath restrictions were less diligently enforced.

Types of recreational activities

These could be classified as:

- aquatic games
- athletic games
- combat games
- country pursuits
- court games
- invasion games
- target games.

Court games such as Real (or Royal) tennis were designed to be strictly 'exclusive', whilst the drinking and gambling associated with the recreations of ordinary people caused them to be discontinued. Some traditional activities – such as the Ashbourne football game, the Hallaton Bottle Game and the Haxey Hood Game – did survive and continue today as tourist attractions.

Sport after 1800

The change from rural to industrial/urban society also brought changes to patterns of recreation.

 **Key points**

The urban revolutions

- The recreational patterns of the labouring classes changed markedly.
- There was much delay between urban population growth and municipal provision for recreation.
- The old 'rowdy recreations' disappeared slowly, reflecting the change in social attitudes.

The pace of industrial change

- 'Saint Monday' was a result of the reluctance of the labouring classes to give up their recreations. Workers simply took the day off to attend prize-fights and other entertainments as they always had.

- The spread of steam power eventually dictated regular hours of work.
- Recreational space made way for factories and cheap housing as towns mushroomed in size.
- Municipal parks were often placed between slum and middle-class areas.
- These parks were closed on Sundays, the only day the labouring classes were free from work.

Social change

- The lower classes lost two recreational assets – time and space.
- The new middle class had two primary aims – the creation of capital and good Christian living.
- Only recreations that were seen to be 'purposeful' were acceptable.
- The YMCA played a crucial role in broadening access to sport.
- Gaining the Saturday half day and shorter working hours made it possible for ordinary working men to return to recreation.
- The development of rationalised sport began in public schools, and was spread by 'old boys', clerics and schoolmasters working in local communities.
- Sports governing bodies were set up to ensure uniform rules and middle-class control.
- The grandstand and the members' enclosure separated the lower classes from their 'betters'.
- The control of sport had passed from the parson and the squire to the new middle class.

Did you know?
The Fairs Act of 1871 empowered magistrates to close down any activity they considered harmful to the morals of the people.

Mass transport

- Cheap rail excursions allowed ordinary people access to the countryside or the seaside.
- Mass transport allowed regular fixtures for those who had the time and money to enjoy them, and the growth of professional leagues in cricket, rugby league and football.
- Interest in sport amongst ordinary people was accelerated by the speed with which results could be spread around the country.
- The growth of literacy also meant that information could be spread much more effectively.

Did you know?
Robert Dover's Cotswold Olympicks closed down in 1851 due to rowdy day-trippers on rail trips from Birmingham.

Do you know about...?

1. The mass exodus of people from the countryside to the towns in the eighteenth and nineteenth centuries?
2. Why there was such a gulf between the upper and lower classes, and how it was filled?
3. The nature of social change that resulted from filling this gulf?
4. How these social changes affected sports and pastimes?
5. The ways in which sport originated?
6. The influence of the medieval knight, combat and war on the nature of recreation?
7. The typical characteristics of recreations prior to 1800?
8. The activities that were common to both upper and lower classes, and why this was so?
9. The venues used for sports and recreations prior to 1800?

Do you know about...?

10. The part played by the Church in constraining and/or supporting recreation?

11. Life in the towns and how it restricted the freedom of the lower classes to enjoy recreation?

12. The mechanisation of industry and how this affected recreation – both negatively and positively?

13. Which group of people had the greatest influence on social change?

14. The importance of the Church, the school and the workplace in the development of sport in the UK?

Exam tips

Make sure you understand the reasons why people moved from countryside to town in such large numbers and how the Industrial Revolution created a new 'middle class'.

It is important that you understand and can give examples of a range of 'popular recreations' other than 'mob football' and can explain why it was that some activities were class orientated whilst others were not.

You must be able to say why life in the industrial towns resulted in ordinary people being excluded from recreations.

The church, industry, schools and municipal authorities all played a significant part in gaining access for ordinary people to sport and recreation. Make sure you can give examples where a question requires you to.

In trying to explain a particular development, remember: 'who', 'what', 'where', 'when', 'how' and 'why?'

2. The development of physical education

Fact:
Physical training and physical education are not the same thing.

Fuller information on these themes can be found in *Advanced PE for Edexcel*, pages 14–27.

Sport and public schools in the nineteenth century
- The 'right to play'
- Harsh environment
- Channelling excess energies
- Christian virtues
- The introduction of rules

Physical education – by military intent?
- Archibald MacLaren

Sport and Oxbridge

Further developments

The diffusion of the new concept

Diffusion through the Empire

European and military influences

Sport and physical education in the twentieth century
- The beginnings of out of school clubs

The early syllabuses
- An improved syllabus
- Primary and secondary provision

Broadened interest and provision

The 1944 Education Act

Outdoor apparatus

Outdoor education

Movement and dance
- Circuit and weight training
- Towards the National Curriculum
- Reduced curriculum time

Current and future policies in school sport and PE

Sport and public schools in the nineteenth century

 **Key points**

- There was an urgent need for order and discipline.
- Masters took no interest in the boys' recreations.
- Public schools were spartan environments.
- Most boys accepted beatings and fagging because one day it would be their turn.
- Thomas Arnold was instrumental in the development of recreations for a purpose.
- Arnold recognised that the boys' interest in games meant they could be used as instruments of social control.
- Athleticism was used as a way of promoting muscular Christian values through 'manly' games and sports.
- Outcomes of athleticism were:
  - social control
  - physical preparation
  - character development.
- This promoted loyalty, obedience and fair play.
- Experiences on the playing field were seen as good preparation for later life.
- The subjugation of oneself to a greater cause was seen as essential training for Christian young men.
- The new 'proprietary' schools and many of the older grammar schools copied the public schools.
- Team games remained the central plank of athleticism, along with gymnastics and rowing.
- The best-known image of the Victorian public school is portrayed in *Tom Brown's Schooldays'* (1857).

Physical education – by military intent?

- The military campaigns of Queen Victoria's reign produced an alarming shortage of fit recruits.

- This triggered the development of the Officer Training Corps in public schools.
- At some military recruiting stations, almost half the would-be recruits were rejected out of hand as being unfit for military service.
- Archibald MacLaren was influential in physical training for the military and for schools.
- Many Army Gymnastic Staff instructors (Aldershot 1861) took up posts in the public schools and independent schools.
- MacLaren's gymnastics remained popular until it was displaced by Ling's Swedish gymnastics.

> **Did you know?**
> During Queen Victoria's reign the British military was involved in twenty-eight military campaigns in different parts of the Empire.

Sport and Oxbridge

- Many of the early 'national' rules developed in the Oxbridge 'melting pot' – for example:
  - the Football Association (1863)
  - the Rugby Football Union (1871).
- Oxbridge athletes figured largely in the formation of rules and national associations.
- Many of Britain's early Olympic competitors came from Oxbridge and the public schools.
- The University Boat Race and other 'varsity' fixtures were highlights of the British sporting calendar.

Further developments

- Increased participation by ordinary people led to a questioning of middle class control of sport.
- The growth of professionalism led to a series of rifts between middle-class and working-class sporting interests.
- With the exception of a small number of sports, the amateur/Olympic ethic held sway until relatively recently.

The diffusion of the new concept

- Some former public schoolboys returned as masters to their old schools or to others nearer home.
- Others promoted sports and athleticism as:
  - members of the clergy
  - members of the professions
  - captains of industry
  - civil servants
  - military officers.

Diffusion through the Empire

- Former public schoolboys were significant in taking British sporting values round the world as:
  - missionaries
  - colonial officers
  - military officers
  - merchants.
- By the end of Victoria's reign, 'the message' had been spread throughout the Empire.

European and military influences

- Baron de Coubertin developed his ideas on Olympism whilst visiting English public schools and the festivals of Much Wenlock and Dover's Hill.
- Also important were the European influences of Gutsmuths, Jahn and Ling.
- Martina Österberg was appointed to the London School Board in 1882 and opened her own college at Hampstead in 1885.
- Österberg's first students subsequently founded other women's PE colleges.
- There were no facilities for men, with the exception of cities such as Birmingham and London and in some of the Church of England's teacher-training colleges.
- With a few exceptions, qualifications could only be gained in Europe or by becoming a military instructor.
- Military instructors were often the first to provide instruction in schools.
- Swedish gymnastics was very popular in girls proprietary schools before a wider adoption in state elementary schools.

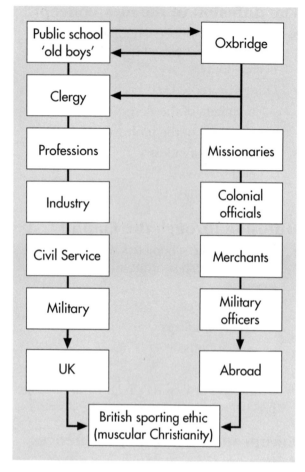

Public school 'old boys' and the process of diffusion

Sport and physical education in the twentieth century

 **points**

- The Forster Education Act of 1870 contained no statutory provision for physical training or games.

- Drill was approved of, but was included for disciplinary rather than educational reasons.

- A national system of physical training was not implemented until 1902 (the Model Syllabus).

- Some school boards had made earlier provision, but this was unusual prior to 1902.

- However, there were football, cricket, athletics and swimming associations run by teachers in their own time from the mid-1880s onwards.

- Swimming galas were held in a growing number of towns with public baths (made possible by the Baths and Wash-houses Acts of 1847).

The early syllabuses

- Girls were not initially included in these provisions, although some local school boards did so.

- The poor health of military recruits was a major factor, but the findings of the Inter-departmental Enquiry into Physical Deterioration (1904) was also significant.

- The 1902 Model Syllabus was accompanied by claims of 'militarism gone mad'.

- With the 1904 Syllabus there were distinct moves away from militarism.

- The 1909 Syllabus required local authorities to provide for the training of teachers and discouraged the use of former drill sergeants.

- The 1919 Syllabus came just after the First World War (1914–1918), and introduced team games and the concept of 'enjoyment'.

- The Hadow Report of 1926 re-established the importance of state grammar schools, and recognised the need for PE at primary and secondary levels.

- The 1933 Syllabus was the first to include sections for primary and secondary age groups.

The Fisher Act of 1918 had also made provision for:

- holiday and school camps
- centres for physical training
- playing fields and school baths.

> **Did you know?**
> The 1933 Syllabus is generally regarded as the first real PE syllabus.

Broadened interest and provision

- A one-year course for women PE specialists opened at Reading University in 1918.
- The only course for men (Sheffield Training College) was closed in 1923.
- The YMCA expanded its programmes of physical recreation, as did the National Association of Boys' Clubs.
- The YHA increased its provision for young people in the post school-leaving age groups.
- 1925: National Playing Fields Association formed.
- 1929: Women's League of Health and Beauty was formed.
- 1933: Carnegie College opened a PE course for men.
- 1935: the Ling Association and the National Association of Organisers of Physical Education created the Central Council of Recreative Physical Training; this became the Central Council for Physical Recreation (CCPR) in 1944.
- 1935: Loughborough College offered PE courses for men.
- 1937: Goldsmiths College, London, also offered courses for men.
- 1937: the Board of Education produced *Recreation and Physical Fitness for Youths and Men*, with a companion volume for girls and women.

The 1944 Education Act

- The Act had no specific PE syllabus, but required the provision of playing fields and gymnasia.
- It raised the school leaving age to fifteen and gave PE teachers the same status as other teachers.
- It recognised seventeen specialist or 'wing PE courses'; ten of them were for men and seven for women.
- Birmingham was the only university offering a degree course in PE (from 1946).

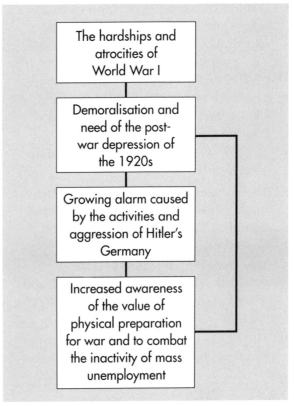

Social and political context of PE

Outdoor apparatus

Another post-war initiative was the development of a range of outdoor apparatus at, for example:

- Bristol
- Halifax
- Darlington
- Manchester
- Southampton.

Outdoor education

There was a growing focus on outdoor education, which included:

- cycling and the YHA
- continued development of the scout and guide movement
- Outward Bound Trust
- Kurt Hahn's 'county badge scheme' of the 1930s at Gordonstoun School, which eventually became the Duke of Edinburgh's Award Scheme

- continued expansion of youth clubs and boys' clubs offering outdoor trips and expeditions.

Movement and dance

- The work of Rudolph (von) Laban and Lisa Ullman had a major impact (modern educational dance and gymnastics).
- The Art of Movement Studio opened in 1953 near Weybridge.
- There was much antagonism from many teachers towards the new 'movement education', and the PE profession was divided into two camps.
- The years 1952 and 1953 saw the publication of 'Moving and Growing' and 'Planning the Programme', for primary age pupils.
- The loss of games and formal gymnastics was regretted by many PE professionals.

> **Did you know?**
> Rudolph (von) Laban was originally an expert in the study of time and motion in industry in his native Germany.

Circuit and weight training

- There was a trend in secondary PE towards a wider range of 'options', including water and outdoor activities.
- This trend resulted in the 'inch thick – mile wide' syndrome, with accusations of poor levels of supervision and instruction at the hands of non-PE trained instructors.

Towards the National Curriculum/Reduced curriculum time

- The 1970s and 1980s has been referred to as a period of teachers 'wandering in the wilderness'.
- The Education Reform Act (ERA) was passed in 1988, leading to the present National Curriculum.
- There was a subsequent 'watering down' of PE allocation, affecting both primary and secondary PE.

- Additional time has since been found for GCSE and 'A' level PE.
- Positive developments include increased student involvement in the learning process, and in the evaluation of outcomes.

Current and future policies in school sport and PE

These include:

- the selling off of valuable playing field space
- the growth of sporting alternatives outside of school
- whether increasing teacher workloads are detracting from the time that might be given to school sport
- the demise of traditional Saturday morning fixtures
- CCPR Sports Leaders Awards adding to the 'tools' available to teachers
- the development of sports colleges, which should help to raise skill levels
- TOP Start, TOP Play and TOP Sport programmes, which are innovative – although there is a question as to whether they are educational or simply about early talent identification
- BT TOP Sport (Sport England and the Youth Sports Trust), which is intended to support the National Curriculum.

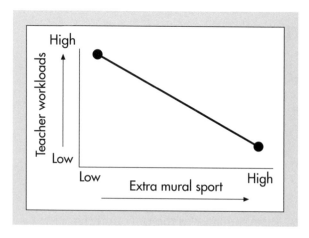

The impact of teacher workloads on PE

The Sport England programme for schools also includes:

- Active schools programme
- Activemark/Activemark Gold
- Active schools co-ordinators
- Coaching for teachers
- The Panathlon Challenge
- Running sports for schools
- Sporting Ambassadors
- Sportsearch
- Sportsmark/Sportsmark Gold.

Do you know about...?

1. The reasons why sport became accepted in nineteenth-century public schools?
2. Why physical education in the form of 'drill' became a priority towards the end of the nineteenth century?
3. The Oxbridge 'melting pot' and its role in the development of organised sport?
4. Why Oxbridge athletes dominated early international sport?
5. The term 'process of diffusion' in connection with sport in the late nineteenth and early twentieth centuries?
6. How the British Empire was significant in this process?
7. European influences on the development of PE in the United Kingdom?
8. Military influences in the development of early forms of physical training?
9. The early PT syllabuses and how each differed from its predecessor?
10. Particular developments in PE in the mid-twentieth century?
11. Organisations and other factors that contributed to the growth of outdoor education?
12. The 1944 Education Act and its influence on facilities for PE in state schools?
13. The major influences on the growth of movement and dance?
14. Criticisms that were levelled at PE in the period prior to the setting-up of the National Curriculum?
15. The issues surrounding the growth of PE colleges and national sports body initiatives?

Exam tips

Remember that in almost all cases 'drill' had a military rather than educational purpose.

Remember that there were notable exceptions to those sports that were 'rationalised' in the 'Oxbridge melting pot' – e.g. cricket, horse racing and golf.

Many of the early influences of 'English' or 'British' PE in fact came from Europe.

Make sure you can gives examples of how each of the early PT/PE syllabuses differed from its predecessor.

Remember that the 1944 Education Act did not contain any specific PE syllabus – but it did require the building of gymnasia and the provision of playing-field space for state schools.

3. Social influences on performance and participation

> **Fact:**
> The essential requirements of physical activity are time and space.

Fuller information on these themes can be found in *Advanced PE for Edexcel*, pages 28–35.

Cultural setting

Resources

Lifestyles in contemporary society
- Health concerns

Access, opportunity and provision
- Opportunity and provision
- Discrimination

Other factors affecting participation
- Self-discrimination
- Stereotyping
- Esteem

Stacking, centrality and self-fulfilling prophecy
- Stacking
- Self-fulfilling prophecy

Target groups

Reformative policy

Geographical factors

Cultural setting

 **points**

- The freedom of individuals and groups to participate freely is a reflection of the culture in which they live.

- Constraints on physical activity can be:
  - enforced, e.g. political, gender-based, religious or economic restrictions
  - natural, e.g. limits on activity due to natural or unavoidable economic limitations.

Resources

- All activities utilise resources. Some occur naturally, whilst others have an economic cost.
- The cost of resources is a reflection of the technology and/or resources involved in their provision.
- In emergent cultures, activities utilising the fewest economic resources are chosen in an attempt to build a national identity (nation-building; role-models).
- In technologically-advanced societies, recreation is less restricted by economic considerations than it is by political philosophies.

Lifestyles in contemporary society
Health concerns
Increasingly sedentary lifestyles give rise to concern over health, adding weight to arguments that access to recreation should be available to all, e.g. mass participation programmes.

> **Did you know?**
> There are fewer coronary deaths due to improved medication, but the incidence of heart disease is unchanged.

Access, opportunity and provision

 **points**

- There is no access without opportunity and provision.
- This is controlled by the dominant institutions/agencies in any culture.

- Where religious or political influences dominate, the nature of access reflects those philosophies.
- Most 'free' societies embrace a range of provision.

Discrimination

The most common bases for denial of access include:

- age
- class
- disability
- education
- ethnicity
- gender
- poverty.

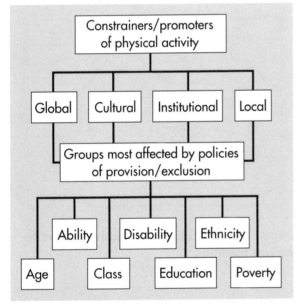

Opportunity and provision

Other factors affecting participation

Self-discrimination

- Some groups of people believe that recreation 'is not for them'.
- Some women are discouraged or prevented from participating by their own communities.
- Some activities are thought to be too élitist for participation to be considered a possibility.

Stereotyping/Esteem

- Stereotyping can be split into negative and positive.

Negative stereotypes

- Negative stereotypes include, for example, women as tennis players or gymnasts, but not as rugby players or boxers.
- They also include some minority groups who are often perceived as being 'non-active'.
- Such views are sometimes held by those in influential positions.
- Negative stereotypes can detract from esteem.

Positive stereotypes

- Positives stereotypes include those images that challenge negative stereotypes and promote positive/desirable images.
- Positive stereotypes add to esteem.

Stacking, centrality and self-fulfilling prophecy

- Stacking occurs where there is a multi-cultural presence.
- The dominant culture 'stacks' other cultures in order of acceptability.
- The centre of power remains with the dominant cultural group.
- Until recently, minority groups have believed that the status quo could not be changed (self-fulfilling prophecy).

Target groups

Targeting identifies specific groups for whom provision is not being made. Each may contain several 'sub-groups' – for example:

- ethnic women
- disabled women
- older women
- mother and baby groups.

Reformative policy

Reformative policies are aimed at creating/improving access to recreation for targeted groups and to encourage the creation of 'interest groups' – for example:

- the Women's Sports Foundation (WSF)
- the British Sports Association for the Disabled (BSAD).

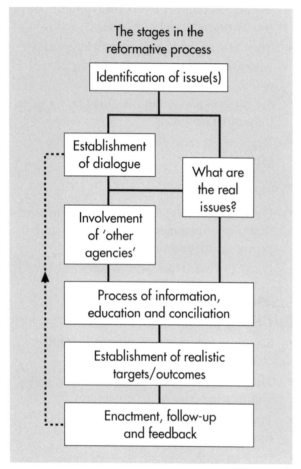

The stages in the reformative process

The reformative process is:

- a means by which issues are identified, differences rationalised, informed opinion sought and realistic outcomes agreed
- not necessarily solely aimed at ethnic minorities; other 'targeted groups' might include rural communities, inner-city groups or deprived urban areas.

Geographical factors

 **points**

- Geographical factors can influence the natural provision for recreation and sport.

- Large landmasses have a climate range and varied topography, which support a wide range of activities.
- Britain has a wide range of topography, but not the extremes of climate for all summer/winter sports.
- Some environments can be artificially created, but this requires both sophisticated technology and economic wealth.
- The combination of limited natural resources and a poor economy can be severely limiting in terms of levels and range of recreational provision.
- Access to existing facilities can be hampered by poor communication/transport systems.

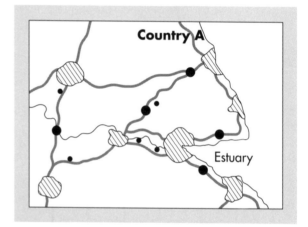

Good communications maximise access to limited facilities

Do you know about...?

1. What the presence (or otherwise) of the essential components of physical activity can tell us about the nature of a culture or society?

2. How economic wealth can help in overcoming limited natural resources for recreation and sport?

3. Why it is that modern-day lifestyles give rise to concerns about health?

4. The way that culture and politics influence levels of access to and funding for recreation?

Do you know about...?

5. The differences between discrimination and self-discrimination?

6. The differences between a 'stereotype' and a 'role-model'?

7. Positive and/or negative stereotypes, and how they can affect esteem?

8. Stacking, why it occurs and how it limits access to ethnic/minority groups?

9. The reasons why it is necessary to identify target groups?

10. Reformative policies and what they are meant to achieve?

11. The influence of physical topography/climate on recreational patterns?

12. How the use of technology can overcome some topographical/climatic limitations?

Exam tips

Remember that there is a relationship between economic wealth, politics and the nature and level of provision for sport and recreation. This can often help in answering questions about the nature of provision in a particular country. e.g. 'rich or poor'; 'central provision' or little or no central funding.

Do remember that 'stereotypes' and 'role-models' are not necessarily the same thing.

Can you identify a number of 'target' groups' and say why they have been 'targeted'?

The relationship between 'Access', 'Opportunity' and 'Provision' is significant. Do be clear on what is meant by each one and how each affects the other.

Can you explain what is meant by the term 'stacking'?

4. Professional (élite) sport

Fact:
Professional sports people are no longer the wage-slaves of club owners.

Fuller information on these themes can be found in *Advanced PE for Edexcel*, pages 35–48.

Practice of exclusion

Increased free time
- Boxing – the birth of an 'acceptable face'

Mass spectator sport

The rise in status of the professional

National governing bodies of sport
- The global sports arena

European and international governing bodies
- Changing perception

The nurture of talent in the UK

School sport
- Sports education initiatives

Club sport

National sports centres and academies

UKSI in Sheffield and network centres
- UKSI in Northern Ireland
- UKSI in Scotland
- UKSI in Wales

Other initiatives

Sport England
- How Sport England works
- World Class programme

European models of sports excellence
- France
- Finland

Commercialisation and Americanisation of UK and European professional sport
- The American college system
- Franchise

 **Key points**

The history of professional sport in Britain centres on three main aspects of development:

- the employment of 'paid retainers' by the upper classes
- the increase of time free giving rise to the growth of mass spectator sport
- the growth of commercial links.

Practice of exclusion

- The exclusion clauses of amateur sporting bodies left many with little alternative but to turn to professionalism.
- People were excluded in many cases simply because they had manual jobs (mechanics clauses).
- In cricket, however, able bodies were needed for the 'sweaty aspect' of the sport (not an upper class forte).
- In horse racing, the risk of injury and the development of handicap events forced upper-class owners to engage professional jockeys.

Increased free time

- Increased free time helped to create the British sporting Saturday afternoon.
- It produced huge crowds at sporting occasions, which generated a level of income that could sustain professional sport.
- It also helped to establish a mutually advantageous link between sport and commercial goods and services.
- In soccer, the game's massive popularity forced the Football Association (FA) to sanction the professional game.

Boxing – the birth of an 'acceptable face'

- Professionalism was traditional, but had attracted an undesirable element.
- The formation of the Amateur Boxing Association in 1880 was an attempt to generate a more acceptable image.
- The National Sporting Club (1891) was also an attempt to do this.

- The patronage of Lord Lonsdale did much to help in this respect.

> **Did you know?**
> The Broughton Rules were a forerunner of boxing's Queensbury Rules.

Mass spectator sport/The rise in status of the professional

- Huge crowds gave professional footballers the collective confidence to argue for better terms.
- Ordinary people did not object to men earning a living doing what they did best.
- The 1960s saw professionals at Wimbledon, the abolition of the distinction between 'gentlemen' and 'players' in cricket, and between military officers and other riders at Hickstead.
- The more recent growth of broadcasting and commercial interest has encouraged professional sport.

National governing bodies of sport

 **points**

- The majority of sports governing bodies were created in the last thirty-five years of the nineteenth century.
- All were based on the middle-class ethic of gentlemanly recreation.
- They were created so that uniform rules and codes of conduct could be applied nationally.
- Eventually, middle-class control was challenged by the growth of mass sport and professionalism.
- Today, sports governing bodies promote and develop their own sports, with professional rather than amateur sport representing the élite level of performance.
- Many are also members of the CCPR.

European and international governing bodies

- The globalisation of sport has forced national sporting bodies to accept the authority of European and World bodies.
- FIFA (*Fédération Internationale de Football Association*) and the International Olympic Committee (IOC) are probably the two most influential sports bodies.
- Britain is no longer always at the forefront of developments.
- The formerly 'British' interpretation of the term 'sport' is now subject to much broader influences.
- The 'Bosman ruling' has established the right of sports performers to 'ply their trade' freely.
- Professional rather than amateur sports bodies are now mainstream organisations.
- The sporting world must now be perceived in a global as well as a national context.
- The IOC is distinct from other global sporting authorities in that it is a 'multi-sport' body.
- There is some resentment (e.g. 'Superleague' in Rugby league and the Premier League in soccer) that newly formed bodies divert income away from traditional sporting infrastructures.
- Much of this is to do with 'media money' and the degree of independence it confers on a small number of élite clubs.

The nurture of talent in the UK

- Traditionally this has been a 'hit and miss' affair.
- The traditional divide between amateur and professional limited any attempts to co-ordinate talent identification policies.
- There is a traditional British 'reluctance' to take sport too seriously.
- There is also a question of the morality of subjecting young people to serious training at an early age.

School sport

- Britain's teachers have traditionally

provided a wide range of sporting opportunities for pupils.

- This provided a mass participation base and a potential framework for talent identification.
- Modern school sport began in nineteenth-century public schools.
- By the 1890s, elementary schools were providing opportunities for athletics, cricket, football, gymnastics, rugby and swimming.
- The English Schools' Football Association was formed in 1904.
- The first schools' football international was played in 1907.
- Many state schools lacked facilities; this was not addressed until after the 1944 Education Act.
- Facility provision then expanded rapidly but has recently become an issue with the selling-off of playing field space.
- Most schools' sports governing bodies promote award schemes in conjunction with sports' governing bodies.

The broadening of opportunity outside of school sport has implications for the identification and nurture of talent. The primary concern of educationalists will always be the well-being of young people. This cannot always be said to be the case in the wider sporting context.

Club sport

- The public schools of the nineteenth and early twentieth centuries have left their mark on British sport.
- Old boys' and old girls' clubs have stood the test of time.
- Factory and church clubs have also contributed to a the development of a vast sports network.
- The 'recreative' ethic is still important at all levels for those who take part simply because they enjoy it.
- Recreational sport does prioritise talent identification.

- Many young people never have their potential recognised, but this situation is now slowly changing.
- April 2000 saw the founding of the Football Foundation – with the aim of assisting with the provision of pitches and changing rooms in local parks and in schools.

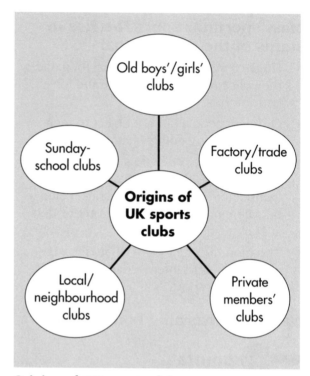

Origins of UK sports clubs

National sports centres and academies

- National Sports Centres sports centres are situated at:
  - Bisham Abbey
  - Lilleshall
  - Plas-y-Brenin
  - Crystal Palace
  - Holme Pierrepont.
- Sports academies have been in place at Premier League football clubs, rugby and county cricket clubs for some time, the intention being to identify and nurture talent in order to meet future needs.
- Sports governing bodies now also operate regional and national centres of excellence for junior and senior development squads.

UKSI in Sheffield and network centres

- The United Kingdom Sports Institute (UKSI) will have a network of ten regional centres throughout the UK.
- This network is under the centralised control of the UKSI.
- 'National squads' will work at the centre with the most appropriate facilities for their particular sport – for example:
  - swimming: University of Bath
  - water sports: Holme Pierrepont
  - gymnastics: Lilleshall
  - cycling: Manchester.
- UKSI in Northern Ireland is based at the University of Ulster.
- UKSI in Scotland is based at the University of Stirling.
- UKSI in Wales is based at the University of Wales Institute.

Network centres	Based at
East	University of East Anglia
East Midlands	Holme Pierrepont
North	Gateshead
North West	Manchester
South	Bisham Abbey
South Coast	Southampton University
South East	Crystal Palace
South West	University of Bath
West Midlands	Lilleshall
Yorkshire	Sheffield

Network centres and their locations

Other initiatives

- The Elite Coach Education Programme is a joint venture between Sportscoach UK and the British Olympic Association.
- Its purpose is to provide for the needs of coaches at the very highest level.

- The ACE UK (Athlete Career and Education Services) programme helps to develop career and educational opportunities for athletes both during and after their time in sport.

Sport England

- Sport England is the new name for the former English Sports council.
- Sport England's current slogans are:
  - more people involved in sport
  - more places to play sport
  - more medals (in élite sport).
- A series of panels also advises on:
  - lottery issues
  - women and sport
  - local authority issues
  - disability
  - racial equality
  - governing body investment.
- The UK Sports Council (UK Sport) replaced the former GB Sports Council in 1997. Sport England is accountable to Parliament through the Secretary of State for Culture, Media and Sport, and is responsible, through the Sport England Lottery Fund, for the distribution of funds earmarked for sport in England.

World Class programme

- The World Class programme developed by Sport England has two major components:
  - 'World Class' events
  - 'World Class' performance.
- These programmes finance the infrastructure necessary for the staging of major sporting events and the preparation of athletes for top level competition.
- Funding of the above programmes and infrastructure development is now possible because of a combination of National Lottery funding and commercial sponsorship.
- It is also apparent that comparative study has been made of systems and funding models employed in other countries, e.g. France and Australia.

European models of sports excellence

 **points**

France

- INSEP (*Institut National du Sport et de l'Education Physique*), founded in 1976, is part of the Ministry of Youth and Sport, which has responsibility for the development of French sport.
- Young athletes in residence receive a normal education.
- There is provision for more than 25 sports on site.
- French sports federations provide 90 per cent of funding.
- Public companies must invest a small part of their profit in sports development.
- Regional INSEPs operate at a more local level, but do not have athletes in long-term residence.
- The Ministry of Youth and Sport maintains a sports development fund (FNDS) for sport at grass-roots level.
- France is the best European example of an acceptable, modern, centralised approach to funding élite sport.
- A population of over 50 million can support such a system.

The figure entitled 'Model of sporting excellence: France' is not typical. There are many variants throughout Europe. For example, the Czech Republic does not have a national sports academy but does have regional sports schools.

The national sports governing bodies also run Centres of Young Talents. Some of this is government funded, but income from major lotteries goes directly to identified athletes.

Finland

- Élite sport in Finland does not have a government arm.
- Finland is much smaller than France.
- Sports bodies run their own élite sports.
- The majority of Finnish professional athletes live abroad.
- Government funding focuses on local/minority groups.
- The objective of the Finnish Sports Federation (FSF) is to promote the health of the whole population – not élite sport.
- Finns consider exercise to be very important.
- Sport attracts a high level of corporate sponsorship.
- Lotteries provide a large proportion of public sports funding.

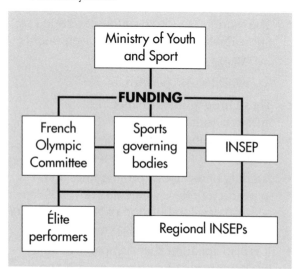

Model of sporting excellence: France

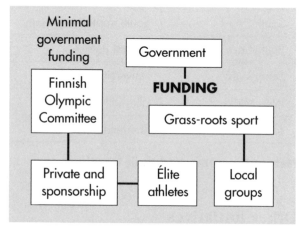

Model of sporting excellence: Finland

Commercialisation and 'Americanisation' of UK and European professional sport

- The decline of amateurism and centralist socialism have seen a growth of American-style commercialisation of sport.
- Sport provides the market for business.
- Business provides the finance for sport.
- The athletic scholarship system in US colleges was seen as a form of professionalism.
- The popularity of sport on TV meant that professional sport and TV became inseparable.
- The 'win-at-all-costs' ethic has spread around the world – in the USA this refers not just to sport but is an approach to life.

Franchise

- The franchise is a commercial and media innovation – sport just happens to be a convenient vehicle for big business.
- The up-rooting of a team from its 'home' city became fairly common practice.
- This has not yet spread significantly into European sport.
- Grand Prix athletics and Champions League football are examples of European televised sporting events that utilise satellite television to maximise viewing audiences.

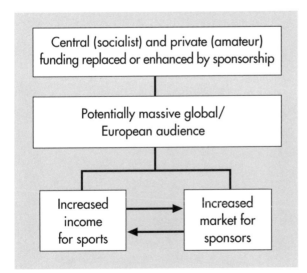

UK and European professional sport: commercialisation and 'Americanisation'

Do you know about...?

1. The major influences in the development of professional sport?
2. What is meant by the terms 'practice of exclusion' and the 'mechanics clause'?
3. The relationship between the growth of professionalism and free time for working men?
4. Why it was that boxing needed to adopt an 'acceptable face'?
5. How the growth of mass spectatorism helped professional sport?
6. The origins of today's national governing bodies of sport?
7. Why European and international sports governing bodies have major influence on sport in the UK?
8. Why the nurture of talent in the UK has traditionally been rather haphazard?
9. The origins of school sport in the UK and how it is organised?
10. The different influences that contributed to the development of club sport in the UK?
11. Why national sports centres were created?
12. The purpose of sports academies attached to top sports clubs?
13. The purpose and structure of the UKSI and its network centres?
14. The four 'home' sports councils and their relationship to UK Sport?
15. The purpose and funding of World Class programmes?
16. Models of sports excellence from other European countries, including 'centralised' and 'de-centralised' programmes?
17. The ways in which UK and European professional sport has been Americanised and commercialised?

Exam tips

Remember that modern professional sport developed for three main reasons:

As a reaction to the practices of exclusion by amateur sports bodies

As a result of increased free time for ordinary people

Because the growth of 'mass spectatorism' provided the income that allowed professional sport to develop independently of 'middle class' control.

In dealing with questions about the expansion of professional sport in recent times it is important to remember that the commercial association between sport and television has been particularly significant. Remember the meaning of terms such as 'franchising' and 'Americanisation' and how they apply to professional sport in both the UK and Europe.

5. Recreative sport (mass participation)

Fact:
The European Sports Charter views sport as an important factor in human development.

Fuller information on these themes can be found in *Advanced PE for Edexcel*, pages 48–52.

Commitment to Sport for All
- Improving performance and supporting élite and professional sport
- Sport and the environment
- The wider picture

The impact of sport for all in Europe
- Democracy and sport

The role of national agencies
- UK Sports Council
- Other European examples

Grass-roots programmes

Concept of target groups and reforms

Amateur sports and the voluntary sector

Wilderness and alternative sports

Commitment to Sport for All

 **points**

- The European Sports Charter acknowledges:
  - the freedom of individuals to participate in sport safely
  - having the opportunity to receive instruction in at least basic sports skills
  - that those who are able to should have the opportunity to improve their ability.
- The charter makes a commitment to:
  - protect the morals and ethics of sport
  - legislate against commercial exploitation and drug-taking.
- It defines sports as activities that 'aim at expressing or improving physical fitness and mental well-being, forming social relationships or obtaining results in competition at all levels' (Article 2).
- Article 4 also states clearly that: 'No discrimination on the grounds of sex, race, colour, language, religion, political opinion or nationality shall be permitted in the access to sports facilities or activities.'
- Article 5 requires that:
  - steps be taken to develop physical fitness and basic sports skills
  - sport for young people is encouraged and opportunities should be available to all pupils
  - appropriate time should be set aside for this, including participation after school
  - sport is for all sections of communities.

Improving performance and supporting élite and professional sport
The European Charter asserts that sport should be encouraged through provision of:

- talent identification and counselling
- provision of suitable facilities
- sports medicine/science support
- scientific coaching and education
- other leadership functions
- appropriate infrastructures
- competitive outlets
- support for élite performers – including education and career opportunities.

Sport and the environment
The Charter requires that limited resources and the environment should be considered, including:

- environmental considerations in the planning and building of facilities
- supporting sports organisations in environmental conservation

- increased awareness of the relationship between sustainable development and sport.

The wider picture

There should be wider co-ordination between national agencies and the public/voluntary sectors in each member country.

The impact of sport for all in Europe

 **points**

- The European Parliament has no wish to interfere in the direct control of sport – either on a European scale or within member countries.
- The philosophy of Sport for All is embodied in the European Charter for Sport.
- It provides an avenue of redress for those who are denied legitimate access to sport and/or recreation.
- Two policies, under a heading of 'Democracy and sport', have a high priority:
  - sport and the law
  - sport as a democratic movement.
- The European administration wishes to encourage more sports participation amongst all age groups and cultures.

> **Did you know?**
> Gender equality issues are amongst those most commonly referred to the European Court of Appeal.

The role of national agencies

These fall into three categories:

- government departments charged with responsibility for 'open access' to sport
- 'national' bodies whose purpose is to encourage participation at all levels, e.g. Sport England

- organisations such as national associations of boys' clubs, girls' clubs and youth clubs, who promote sport within their own membership.

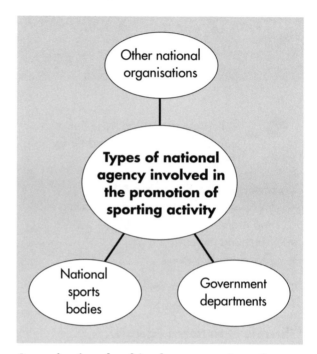

Agencies involved in the promotion of sporting activity

Other organisations raise funds, promote or provide for recreation – for example, in the UK:

- the National Playing Fields Association
- Sports Aid
- British Heritage
- the National Trust
- the Countryside Commission.

UK Sports Councils

There are four of these:

- Sport England
- The Northern Ireland Sports Council
- 'sportscotland'
- The Sports Council for Wales.

The above organisations are responsible for:

- the promotion of opportunities at all levels and across communities

- training and education of coaches and officials in partnership with the Coaching UK, UK Sports Institute and UK Sport
- working with school sports governing bodies and the Youth Sports Trust.

Other European examples
- Many aspects of European sport are derived from 'Olympian' philosophies.
- A strong military presence runs through the history of sport and PE.
- Many European cultures have traditionally valued physical activity.
- Topography and climate are influential in European countries as elsewhere.
- In Scandinavia, for example, recreational skiing grew out of its everyday importance.
- In many European countries, natural forests and mountains support a tradition of hunting, shooting and fishing.

Grass-roots programmes

 **points**

- Youth sports programme are not always created simply to identify potential élite performers, e.g. Austria, Finland.
- In France, de Gaulle's 'five-star plan' developed facilities both for excellence and for mass participation.
- 'Sport pour Tous' was established in France long before 'Sport for All' in the UK.
- Most national governing bodies in the UK now run grass-roots programmes, e.g. 'Hi-Fives' rugby and 'Quick-Cricket'.
- TOPS, 'Active Sports' and 'Active Schools' programmes are funded by Sport England.
- The Sport Aid Foundation is now known as SportsAid. Its three major aims are:
    - to further the education of young people through sport
    - to encourage the socially or physically disadvantaged
    - to enable those living in poverty to take advantage of sport.

Concept of target groups and reforms
- Target groups are those groups identified as being in need of specific funding/provision.
- Target groups might be identified as a result of either 'local' or 'national' initiatives.

Amateur sports and the voluntary sector
- The demarcation between amateur and professional sport no longer exists in most sports.
- The term 'amateur' now tends to be associated with sport below élite level.

Wilderness and alternative sports

 **points**

The increase in wilderness and alternative sports is a reflection of:

- a desire to return to nature
- an indication that previously remote areas are now easily accessible
- a rejection of traditional sports and values.

Ironically, these new activities are now attractive to the establishment they were set up to oppose.

Do you know about...?
1. The influence played by the European Charter for Sport in defining and legislating for sport and recreation?
2. The commitment the Charter requires from sports event organisers and facility providers in terms of the environment?
3. The attitude of the European parliament to the concept of 'Sport for All'?
4. The likelihood of the European Parliament interfering in the direct control of sport – either on a European scale or within member countries?

Do you know about...?

5. The different agencies involved in the promotion and provision of sport and the nature of their contribution (e.g. statutory/non-statutory)?

6. The mandate/responsibilities of the UK Sports Councils, both individually and collectively?

7. The work of the Youth Sports Trust?

8. Influences on recreation in other European cultures (e.g. military, topographical, climatic, cultural)?

9. Grass-roots programmes in France and at least one other European country?

10. SportsAid and its major aims?

11. The concept of 'target groups' and their intended purpose?

12. The current place of amateur sports and the importance of voluntary contributions in recreation?

13. The factors that have contributed to the growth in 'wilderness' and 'alternative' sports?

Exam tips

Remember that 'Sport for All' is a broad concept and does not apply only to sport in the UK - or exclusively to élite sport.

Do ensure that you understand the relationship between UK Sport and the four 'home' sports councils and are aware of the regional network centres in England.

Have the names of several 'grass-roots' sports programmes to give as examples if asked.

Make sure you understand the meaning and can give examples of 'wilderness and alternative sports'.

Practise your exam technique

(a) Many of the early programmes of physical training in the UK were based on military drill and placed little importance on pupil enjoyment. Why was this? (3 marks)

(b) Many of the above programmes also initially excluded girls from participation. Why do you think this policy eventually changed to include girls? (3 marks)

(c) Can you identify THREE characteristics that were seen as important in team games in the Victorian public school? (3 marks)

(d) Most of the governing bodies of sport in the UK were formed in the last half of the 19th century. What were the values promoted by these organisations and how have they changed ? (4 marks)

(e) What social changes outside of the field of sport contributed to the growth of professional sport in England in the early years of the twentieth century? (6 marks)

(f) Outline the structure and function of UK Sport and describe its relationship with the Sports Councils of the four 'home countries'. (6 marks)

UNIT 1: The social basis of sport and recreation

Section B: Issues in sport: The Olympic case study

Overview

1. History of the modern Olympics
- The Games of the ancient world
- The Games before the modern Olympics
- De Coubertin and the establishment of the modern Olympics
- Amateurism and the myth of the recreational ethic
- The Avery Brundage years
- The rise and reforms of Samaranch

2. Race and ethnicity within the Olympic movement
- Race and sport
- IOC Commissions
- Stacking and centrality
- Stereotypes and myths
- Non-white athletes in the Olympic games
- South Africa, apartheid and the IOC

3. Commercialisation and the Olympics
- An 'amateur' philosophy
- Uberroth and Los Angeles
- The globalisation of sport
- The influence of sponsorship
- Corruption

4. Women and the Olympics
- The rise of women in sport
- Discrimination against women
- Women's involvement in the IOC
- The modern sporting female

5. Political uses of the Olympics
- An overview
- Ping-pong diplomacy
- Shop-window policy
- Apartheid
- The Olympics as a political tool

6. The political nature of Olympic bidding
- How the Olympics are awarded
- Why cities bid for the Olympics
- The Manchester bids of 1992 and 1996
- Atlanta not Athens – the controversy

7. Deviance and the Olympics
- Deviance and cheating in sport
- The concept of sportsmanship
- Sportsmanship replaced by gamesmanship
- Deviant behaviour
- The IOC and international drug control

8. Paralympics
- History of the Paralympics
- Impairment classifications
- IOC support of the disabled movement?
- Links with the Olympic movement

Explanatory notes

This section of Unit 1 addresses several critical issues in sport using the Olympic Games as a case study. Many of the issues, such as those focusing on racial minority groups, women in sport and drugs in sport, are relevant across the socio-cultural spectrum and also occur in Unit 1A, both parts of Unit 4 and in the synoptic section of Unit 6.

In this unit, these and other similar topics are addressed in the context of Olympic competition – both historically and in the context of present-day Olympic scenarios. However, it is important that students are aware of the relevance of such topics to their revision of the other units referred to above.

Remember that Olympic sport is just one example of global sporting activity. There are other global multi-sport events (such as the Commonwealth Games) in which these issues also arise as well as major single sport events such as the FIFA World Cup, and the World Track and Field Athletics Championships.

Your studies in Unit 4A should also identify many of these issues in the focus culture(s) of your choice, so be prepared to relate to them in a number of different contexts – for example:

- Olympics
- UK/Europe
- selected 'global culture'.

Major global events

The above are particularly relevant in the manifestation of political activity associated with various Games – particularly in the period spanning the 1960s to the early 1990s. Although reported and generally held to be 'Olympic issues', they also manifested themselves in different ways both here in the UK and in other cultures in the form of boycotts and other economic sanctions.

1. History of the modern Olympics

Fact:
Modern Olympiads were inspired by the ancient Games, but they are not a re-creation of them.

 Fuller information on these themes can be found in *Advanced PE for Edexcel*, pages 55–64.

The Games of the ancient world
- The Games of Olympia
- The Pythian Games
- The Isthmian Games
- The Nemeean Games
- Prizes at the Games
- In the beginning
- Stade
- Stadium

The Games before the modern Olympics
- Robert Dover
- Other early Olympics
- Wenlock Olympian Games
- The founding of the National Olympian Association

De Coubertin and the establishment of the modern Olympics
- English public schools
- The first modern Olympic Games

Amateurism and the myth of the recreational ethic
- Class and the early Olympics

The Avery Brundage years

The rise and reforms of Samaranch

The Games of the ancient world

Known collectively as Panhellenic Games, they combined religion, sport and music, but began as religious ceremonies – in honour of a god – or as funeral games, held in honour of Kings or great warriors.

The Games of Olympia
There were four major 'Games':
- the Olympic Games – at Olympia in honour of the god Zeus
- the Pythian Games – at Delphi to celebrate the festival of Apollo
- the Isthmian Games – at Corinth in honour of the god Poseidon
- the Nemean Games – at Nemea in honour of Zeus.

The Olympic Games:
- are believed to be the oldest and certainly the best known Games
- were first reliably dated at 776 BC, but were believed to have begun as early as 1300 BC
- were festival Games, part of everyday Greek life held all over the Hellenic world.

The Pythian Games:
- were second only to the Olympic Games, believed to have begun in the seventh century BC
- were originally held every eight years, but every four years from the early sixth century BC
- comprised a music festival followed by three days of athletic and equestrian competition, with a final day devoted to the worship of Apollo.

The Isthmian Games:
- were held near the Isthmus of Corinth
- became a multiple day festival by the sixth century BC, attracting as many competitors as the Olympic and Pythian games
- comprised events similar to those at Olympia – including running, wrestling, boxing, the pankration and pentathlon. There were also equestrian (probably chariot) events and a festival of music.

The Nemean Games:
- began in the first quarter of the sixth century BC, and were held towards the end of the summer

- also included equestrian and music contests, with athletic events following the pattern at Olympia.

Prizes at the Games

- Originally the prizes were 'crowns', or garlands of leaves:
  - Olympia – wild olive leaves
  - Delphi – laurel leaves
  - Isthmia – pine leaves
  - Nemea – wild celery leaves.
- Other Games had their own awards, which ranged from shields and cups to leather jerkins (at Pellene).
- Victors were handsomely rewarded on their return home – dispelling the common myth that they were 'amateur' Games.
- Victory at a major Games normally assured the athlete a prosperous living thereafter.

> **Did you know?**
> The major Games, giving prizes of crowns or garlands of leaves, were known as 'Crown Games'.

In the beginning

- As the Games evolved, the 'sporting' element came to overshadow the 'sacred'.
- By the fifth century BC, the two aspects were almost separated, and by the sixth century BC, competitors travelled from much further afield in order to compete.
- As well the spread of athletics, this age also heralded the spread of Greek culture across the ancient world.

Stadium

- 'Stadium' is based on the word 'stade' – a distance of approximately 200 metres – meaning 'building around the stade'.
- There was a curve only at one end, with the gymnasium and training area at the open end.
- Competitors ran up and down the centre of what we now call the 'infield', not around its perimeter.

- Races of more than one stade in length involved negotiating a turning post at either end of the stadium.

The events included:

- the stade – a foot race of that distance
- the diaulos – a foot race of approximately 400 metres
- the dolichos – a long-distance race of between seven and twenty-four stades (approximately 1,500–5,000 metres)
- the hippolite/hoplite (race in armour) – this may originally have been an equestrian event ('hippo' implies horse, or 'horsey')
- the pankration – a form of no-holds barred fighting, often to the death
- the pentathlon – which consisted of the stade, the long jump, the javelin-throw, the discus and the wrestling events.

> **Did you know?**
> Only Greek citizens were allowed to compete in the major Games. However, records show that Coroebus of Ellis – winner of the Stade in 1776 at Olympia – was in fact a cook.

The nature of throwing implements and technique in jumping has changed over the centuries:

- some long jumps may have been two jumps in succession
- some discoi have been found measuring almost twice the diameter and several times the weight of modern implements.

> **Did you know?**
> Phaylus of Croton is reputed to have long jumped over 55 feet – nearly 18 metres.

Event	Date
Stade	776 BC
Diaulos	724 BC
Dolichos	720 BC
Wrestling and Pentathlon	708 BC
Boxing	688 BC
Pankration	648 BC
Boys' running and wrestling	632 BC
Race in armour (Hoplite)	520 BC
Boys pankration	200 BC

First known events at Olympia. A boys' pentathlon was held in 628 BC but was immediately discontinued

The Games before the modern Olympics

 **points**

- The most notable Games were:
  - the Cotswold Olympick Games, first mentioned in 1636, founded by Robert Dover, a lawyer
  - the Wenlock Olympian Games, founded in 1850 by Dr William Penny Brookes.
- The 'folk', or popular, tradition was highly valued in both Games.
- This was quite distinct from the Games of Ancient Greece and the early modern Olympics, where class was a key to entry.
- The National Olympian Association (NOA) was formed in London.
- The NOA held several Olympic festivals in:
  - London
  - Liverpool
  - Birmingham
  - Wellington
  - Much Wenlock
  - Shrewsbury.
- Brookes did not succeed in persuading the King of Greece to stage a modern version of the Olympics (1859).

- Baron Pierre de Coubertin had greater success, possibly because of his aristocratic connections.

> **Did you know?**
> Over 50 'Olympic Festivals' took place in England during the nineteenth century – before 1896.

De Coubertin and the establishment of the modern Olympics

 **points**

- Baron Pierre de Coubertin had a great interest in education and sport, and attended the Wenlock Olympian Games in 1889.
- He was delighted with the literary and artistic competitions, and this influenced his own vision of a re-born Olympics

English public schools
- De Coubertin visited several English public schools, including Rugby.
- He was most impressed with the English approach to 'manly sports'.
- He saw muscular Christianity and athleticism as the way to re-build the youth of France following that country's defeat in the Franco-Prussian War.
- He also visited the United States, and by the early 1890s had formulated his 'Olympic Dream'.
- He saw the Ancient Greek ideals and those in English sport as being the greatest forces for good.
- The International Olympic Committee (IOC) was established by de Coubertin in 1894.

The first modern Olympic Games
- On Easter Sunday 1896, 311 athletes from 13 nations entered the first modern Olympic Games. The nations were:
  - Austria
  - Australia

- Bulgaria
- Chile
- Denmark
- France
- Germany
- Great Britain
- Greece
- Hungary
- Sweden
- Switzerland
- United States.

- Events that survived from ancient times included:
  - javelin
  - discus
  - running races
  - wrestling.
- The rest of the programme consisted of acceptable nineteenth century middle-class élite sports.
- The ancient Olympic tradition of a laurel wreath for the victor was, however, retained.

Athletics	Cycling
Fencing	Gymnastics
Lawn Tennis	Shooting
Swimming	Wrestling
Weightlifting	

Sports at the first modern Olympiad

Amateurism and the myth of the recreational ethic

- Professionalism became an issue in Olympic sport as it did elsewhere.
- An amateur was not simply someone who did not compete for money; it was also necessary to be a gentlemen.
- De Coubertin's vision of a 'Games for the world' was not realistic at that time.

Class and the early Olympics

- Amongst the British entrants to the Games of 1896, two would not have been regarded as 'gentlemen':
  - Edward Battell – footman to the British ambassador – cycling
  - Frank Keeping – butler to the British ambassador – cycling.
- Their entry in the cycling events caused the first such confrontation of principles in modern games history.
- De Coubertin had open views on the issue of class and sport, but they were clearly not shared by his peers.
- The banning of Harold Abrahams' professional coach Sam Mussabini from the stadium during the 1924 Games in Paris is an example of class-based exclusion.
- It would be some time before Coubertin's dream embraced all classes, colours and creeds.

> **Did you know?**
> During this period, one of the requirements of 'gentlemanly status' was not having to work to make a living.

The Avery Brundage years

 **Key points**

- Brundage was President of the IOC from 1952 to 1972.
- His presidency spanned the political problems of:
  - a divided Germany
  - Korea and China
  - the Hungarian uprising of 1956
  - Northern Ireland
  - the Middle East
  - Vietnam.
- He believed that politics and sport were entirely separate affairs.
- He was also uncompromising in his rejection of professional sport.

- He was instrumental in convincing both the US and the rest of the world that the Games of 1936 in Berlin should go ahead.
- He was duped by Hitler's assurances that there would be no vendetta against Jewish athletes in selection of the German team.

Brundage was succeeded in 1972 by Lord Killanin, whose eight-year tenure was beset by the boycotts of 1976 and 1980, and his own serious illness. He was criticised by many for being weak, but he simply had a quieter way of getting things done.

The rise and reforms of Samaranch

- Juan Antonio Samaranch began his presidency in 1980, and had to contend with boycotts and the growth of professional sport.
- He also presided over the return of South Africa to the Olympic movement after many years of isolation.
- However, he will probably be remembered because of the accusations that questioned the IOC's integrity, his own conduct and that of several IOC Commissioners.
- Ten commissioners were removed following allegations of fraud and dishonesty, and limitations have since been placed on the activity of those remaining.

Name	Years of presidency
Demetrius Vikelas	1894–1896
Pierre de Coubertin	1896–1925
Henri de Baillet-Latour	1925–1942
J Sigfrid Edström	1946–1952
Avery Brundage	1952–1972
Lord Killanin	1972–1980
Juan Antonio Samaranch	1980–2001

IOC Presidents since 1894

Did you know?
The current IOC President is Jaques Rogge, of Belgium.

Do you know about...?
1. The origins and purpose of the ancient Hellenic Games and Crown Games?
2. The nature of events at these ancient Games?
3. Prizes, professionalism and the origin of the word 'stadium'?
4. Robert Dover's Cotswold Olympicks and the Much Wenlock Olympian Games?
5. Baron Pierre de Coubertin and the influences that gave him the idea for a 'modern' Olympics?
6. How the Olympics of 1896 differed from those of ancient times?
7. Issues concerning amateurism and social class in the early modern Olympiads?
8. Avery Brundage's attitude to politics and sport and the question of professionalism?
9. Brundage's involvement in the 1936 Olympics in Berlin?
10. Lord Killanin: a weak president or simply a quiet operator?
11. Samaranch and the Olympic boycotts of 1976 and 1980?
12. Samaranch as peacemaker for Seoul in 1988?
13. The IOC and its growing disrepute during the Samaranch years?

Exam tips
The ancient Olympics are important because they provided the basis on which de Coubertin modelled certain aspects of the modern Games.

The contributions of de Coubertin, Brundage and Samaranch as IOC presidents were both controversial and significant. You may be asked to say what these were.

2. Race and ethnicity within the Olympic movement

Did you know?

Ethnic minority participation has increased dramatically.

Fuller information on these themes can be found in *Advanced PE for Edexcel*, pages 64–68.

Race and sport

IOC Commissions

Stacking and centrality
- Ranking social groupings
- Bar to advancement

Stereotypes and myths

Non-white athletes in the Olympic Games
- The first black competitors
- Jim Thorpe
- Jesse Owens
- Cassius Clay
- More black Olympians
- The Games as a political stage

South Africa, apartheid and the IOC

Race and sport
- The level of mass access to sport is a reflection of political and cultural values.
- In some instances, constraint is imposed from within, e.g. some Muslim women are excluded from participation by their own culture.
- The exclusion of racial groups is no longer acceptable.

IOC Commissions
- Olympic Solidarity was founded in 1961.
- Its aim is to organise aid for those Non Olympic Committees (NOCs) in the greatest need.
- It was initially targeted at developing countries granted independence as a result of de-colonisation.
- Funding is derived from a share of the IOC income from television rights.
- IOC Commissions are responsible for education, provision and organisation in specific areas.

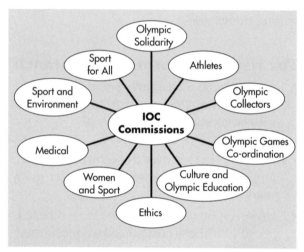

IOC Commissions

Stacking and centrality
- Stacking and centrality are reflections of the cultural values within dominant groups.
- The WASP culture was very much reflected in early Olympics.
- Stacking and centrality stem from the inclination of dominant cultures to perpetuate their own well-being and values by excluding those of a dissimilar background.
- Such exclusions are mainly based on race, colour or religion.
- The glass ceiling is the invisible barrier to advancement for members of ethnic/minority groups.
- Despite the increase in performers from ethnic groups, few teams have black or coloured owners.

Stereotypes and myths

Racial stereotypes take many forms – for example:

- naming sports teams as 'the Chiefs', 'the Braves' or 'the Savages'
- 'white men can't jump'
- 'black men can't swim'.

> ### Did you know?
> The term 'white flight' refers to the disappearance of the white sprinter at international level as the black sprinter rose to prominence – but it increasingly applies to other sports.

Non-white athletes in the Olympic Games

 points

- The St Louis Games of 1904 saw two Zulu tribesmen become the first black African Olympians.
- George Poage was the first black American to win an Olympic medal.
- Jim Thorpe, an American Indian, was the star of the 1912 Games.
- Thorpe was later stripped of his medals because he had played baseball for money.
- Jesse Owens incurred Hitler's displeasure in Berlin (1936), winning four gold medals against the best of the 'Fatherland'.
- Owens, the star of the Games in 1936 was later banned from amateur competition.
- The black Africans arrived in 1960 with Abebe Bikila winning the marathon, a feat he repeated in 1964.
- Kipchoge Keino heralded the arrival of the Kenyans, winning the men's 1,500 metres in 1968 and the 3,000m steeplechase in 1972.
- Further opportunity was given to black and Asian athletes following the independence

of former British colonies and the passing of equal opportunities legislation in the USA in the 1960s.

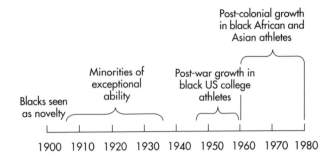

The history of non-whites and the Olympic Games

South Africa, apartheid and the IOC

 points

- South African was excluded from the Games from 1964 until 1992 because of its policy of Apartheid.
- This was done only after other countries threatened to withdraw from the Games.
- The South African National Olympic Committee (SANOC) was itself a non-racial body, but it was impossible for them to be effective in a hostile political environment.
- Avery Brundage – who mistakenly considered sport and politics to be entirely unrelated – was consistent in his view that South Africa should not have been expelled.
- It was not only expulsion from the Games that forced South Africa to change its policy on Apartheid, there was also increasingly widespread political and economic pressure.

Do you know about...?

1. The origins and purpose of Olympic Solidarity Programmes and IOC Commissions?

2. The terms 'stacking', 'centrality', 'stereotypes' and 'myths'?

3. Events that have subscribed to the increased participation of non-white athletes in the Olympics?

4. The reasons for South Africa's expulsion from the Olympic Games from 1964 until 1992?

Exam tips

Remember that the growth of racial equality in the USA and the independent states of former European colonies in Africa and Asia have contributed to the growing number of female participants

3. Commercialisation and the Olympics

Fact:
Commerce and élite sport are now almost inseparable.

Fuller information on these themes can be found in *Advanced PE for Edexcel*, pages 69–72.

An 'amateur' philosophy

Uberroth and Los Angeles

The globalisation of sport

The influence of sponsorship
- The Olympic Programme (TOP)

Corruption

 **points**

An 'amateur' philosophy

- Amateur status depended as much on social standing as it did on not competing for money.
- In the nineteenth and early twentieth centuries, most national sports governing bodies interpreted the laws of amateurism very strictly.
- This excluded would-be participants on the basis of how they earned their living.
- Finding the time and money to train and compete at the highest level was impossible for all but the wealthy and privileged.
- IOC presidents such as Brundage refused to accept that clinging to amateur principles was no longer a realistic option.
- The US scholarship system gave athletes from that country an unfair advantage, as did the (later) state funding of athletes from Communist bloc countries.

- The huge financial loss incurred by the city of Montreal also made it clear that an 'amateur' Games funded by a single host city was no longer viable.
- The Soviet government funded the Moscow Games of 1980, but a solution had to be found by 1984.

Uberroth and Los Angeles

- The Los Angles organising committee gave Peter Uberroth the task of making the 1984 Games viable.
- He was so successful, this set the pattern for future Games.
- He persuaded private enterprise to build the major facilities, and charged everybody for just about everything else he could.
- For the first time, an Olympic Games (and the IOC) made a profit.
- The IOC could then hardly object to athletes doing the same.

Did you know?
The Games of 1984 made a surplus of US$50 million. The surplus for 1996 was US$250 million.

The globalisation of sport

 **points**

- Following the financial success of the LA Games, Olympic sport had become financially secure almost overnight.
- New communications networks, based on satellite technology and funded by subscriptions, broadcast Olympic (and other sporting) competition to global audiences.
- Each Games now sees potential sponsors queuing up to part with their money in order to buy a piece of the global market.
- This phenomenon is sometimes referred to as the 'Sale of the Five Rings'.
- For sponsors and other commercial interests, global television means a global

market-place in which to advertise their goods and services.

- It also means that sports themselves can now cross cultural boundaries.

The influence of sponsorship

- Major sponsors and franchise-holders (e.g. TV networks) exert considerable influence on the IOC in return for their huge investment.
- The alteration of schedules to fit in with prime-time broadcasting or the delaying of an event until the news broadcast finishes is now fairly commonplace.
- Sponsorship is now seen as a back door to the control of sport.

The Olympic Programme (TOP)

- TOP ensures that main sponsors are unchallenged in their category of merchandise.
- TOP sponsors for the Games in Sydney included:
  - Coca-Cola
  - IBM
  - John Hancock
  - Kodak
  - McDonald's
  - Panasonic (UK)
  - Samsung Electronics
  - Swatch
  - Time International
  - UPS
  - VISA.
- America's NBC paid US$705 million for the rights to the 2000 Games in Sydney and the 1998 Winter Games in Nagano – in advance!
- The size of the potential market audience for advertisers has been estimated as being in excess of 1.5 billion people per day.

Corruption

- Allegations against the IOC have included:
  - commissioners accepting cash and/or material rewards in return for their vote
  - business and/or political interests influencing decisions on the venue of future Games
  - corrupt awarding of contracts without a proper tendering process
  - the 'buying' of medals
  - drug test results 'lost' or 'misplaced'.
- When faced with accusations regarding his own conduct, President Samaranch saw no reason why he should not accept personal gifts.

Do you know about...?

1. How the original amateur philosophy of Olympic sport restricted commercial activity?
2. The part played by Peter Uberroth in changing the IOC's attitude to commercialism?
3. How the demands of sponsorship influences the presentation of Olympic sport?
4. The issues surrounding allegations of corruption levelled at the IOC?

Exam tips

Two 'key' points:

There has been a vast increase in the spread of communications technology (global)

The fact that 1976 produced a huge deficit for Montreal (and the IOC) led to the IOC being forced to entertain the notion of commercial sponsorship in order to run the Games on a viable basis (Peter Uberroth)

4. Women and the Olympics

Fuller information on these themes can be found in *Advanced PE for Edexcel*, pages 72–78.

The rise of women in sport

Discrimination against women
- Equal access for women
- The early involvement of women

Women's involvement in the IOC

The modern sporting female
- The power of the sporting female
- Marketability
- Overcoming resistance

The rise of women in sport

 **points**

- A Greek woman (Melpomene) ran the marathon unofficially in the 1896 Games.
- The first official women's participation came in 1900 with golf and tennis, and in 1904 with archery.
- There had been no women at the ancient Greek Games and this was used initially as an argument against their inclusion.
- Britain's Charlotte Cooper was the first female victor (tennis singles, 1900).
- Women were allowed to enter the athletics event in 1928 but only after Alice Milliat (France) had threatened to stage a women's event in opposition to the Games.

- The first female 'star' of the Games was the USA's Mildred 'Babe' Didrickson, who won two gold medals in the 1932 Olympiad.
- The first purpose-built athletes village housed 1,300 male competitors – and 120 women!
- The first female to catch the attention of the media was Fanny Blankers-Koen, who won four gold medals at the 1948 Games.

Discrimination against women

- Whether or not women have access to sport is a reflection of the culture in which they live.
- Some fundamentalist Muslim countries do not allow women to appear in public; hence they are not able to participate in sports.
- There were only four sports for women at the 1936 Games; by the 1996 Games, this had risen to twenty-four.

Did you know?
There were only nine countries that did not send female competitors to the Games of 2000.

Gender discrimination is as indefensible as racial discrimination. The Olympic community has a responsibility to highlight such issues and legislate against member countries that do not encourage open access.

Women (and other groups) have been denied equal access to Olympic sport on four levels:

- global
- institutional
- cultural
- domestic (local or sub-cultural).

Women competitors as % of men		Women's events as % of men's	
1980	21%	1980	24%
1984	23%	1984	28%
1988	25%	1988	30%
1992	28%	1992	33%
1996	34%	1996	35%
2000	38%	2000	40%

Source: www.sportnet.com.au
'Active Australia' website

The growth of women competitors and women's events in the Olympics from 1980 to 2000

Women's involvement in the IOC

 **points**

- The involvement of women in the IOC at administrative/Commissioner level is a relatively recent development.
- The first women's IOC delegate was not appointed until 1981 – 85 years after the first modern Games!
- Dame Mary Glen-Haig (1982) and HRH the Princess Royal (1984) were the first British women delegates.
- The recent IOC Review (2000) has established that there shall be more women delegates.
- The IOC also decreed (1996) that by 2005 at least 20 per cent of senior posts in National Olympic organisations should be held by women.

Did you know?
Piru Hagnu of Finland was the first woman IOC Commissioner.

The modern sporting female

 **points**

- The traditional constraints placed on sporting women were no different to others – those of modesty, propriety and restraint.
- A 'flirtatious' Olga Korbut changed all that in Munich in 1972.

The power of the sporting female

- It suddenly became acceptable for the sporting female to be attractive.
- Other women gymnasts helped women's sport out of the age of the gymslip and into the world of fashion.
- The media became very interested in promoting this new, more feminine image.
- Some women are reluctant to accept that 'image' and not ability has advanced their cause.

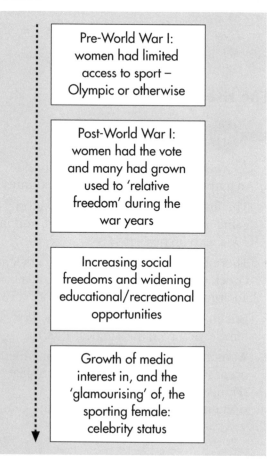

Changing perceptions of women in sport

- The fact that some women may choose not to exploit the market-place should not mean that others are not free to do so.
- Although institutionalised resistance has been overcome, some women athletes have to break down local/cultural barriers before they can have the freedoms enjoyed by other women.
- The fact that there is now debate on such topics means that some progress has been achieved.
- TV networks are now keen that the Olympics should contain a wide range of events that appeal to male, female and family viewers.

Exam tips

Significant points:

'early pioneers' (e.g. Alice Milliat)
emancipation
eastern bloc women
independence of former British/European colonies

Do you know about...?

1. The limitations placed on early women competitors and the reasons for this?
2. How and why women have slowly begun to gain 'parity' with male Olympic competitors?
3. Why women have only relatively recently been involved as IOC Commissioners?
4. The influence of the Eastern Communist bloc countries and the African nations in the rise in numbers of female Olympic participants?
5. The reasons for the creation of the modern powerful sporting female?

5. Political uses of the Olympics

Fuller information on these themes can be found in *Advanced PE for Edexcel*, pages 78–82.

An overview
- 'Hitler's Games' in 1936
- World events on the Olympic stage

Ping-pong diplomacy

Shop-window policy

Apartheid

The Olympics as a political tool

An overview

 **points**

- International sport is now a powerful political tool and the IOC finds it increasingly difficult to avoid political confrontations.
- In some cases this is unavoidable, whilst in others the IOC has been proactive:
  - invitations to the Games of 1920 were withdrawn from Austria, Bulgaria, Germany, Hungary and Turkey because of their role in the First World War
  - invitations were not extended to Germany and Japan for the 1948 Games following their part in the Second World War
  - the IOC did respond (belatedly) to the political situation in South Africa, but made no response to New Zealand's continued sporting association with that country during the 1970s and 1980s.

- The IOC also failed to respond to:
  - the politicisation of the Berlin Games of 1936, despite strong pressure from several countries – particularly when Jewish athletes were excluded from the selection process
  - the withdrawal of Egypt, Iraq and Lebanon over the 1956 Suez crisis, or that of Spain and Switzerland in protest at the invasion of Hungary by the USSR.
- The IOC:
  - was also seemingly unable to prevent the participation of the deviant East German and Soviet systems of the 1960s, 1970s and 1980s
  - seemingly preferred the mass boycott of Moscow in 1980 to the alternative of moving the Games to another venue.

Did you know?
The Olympic Games was used for ideological purposes by the Eastern bloc countries in the 1960s, 1970s and 1980s.

World events on the Olympic stage
- In the 1968 games in Mexico, John Carlos and Tommy Smith used the victory ceremony of the 200 metres to demonstrate their resentment of the poor treatment of black Americans.
- Lee Evans and the 4 × 400 metre squad repeated this gesture of defiance after their victory in that event.
- The 1972 Olympiad witnessed the horror of terrorism, when Arab terrorists killed eleven Israeli athletes. Security at subsequent Games has become a major issue.
- There were mass boycotts of the 1976 and 1980 Olympiads.
- President Carter directed the withdrawal of US athletes from the Moscow Games of 1980 following the USSR's invasion of Afghanistan. Britain faced much opposition over its decision to attend.

Did you know?
Cassius Clay (later Muhammad Ali) was the first black Olympian to use his fame in order to engage in political and civil rights debates.

Ping-pong diplomacy

 **points**

- This was so named after the visit of US table tennis players and swimmers to China as part of the USA's attempts to re-open diplomatic relations with that country and its re-admittance to the IOC.
- China had refused to recognise the right of Taiwan to compete as an independent nation.
- Taiwan is the last remaining independent territory that formerly belonged to mainland China.

Shop-window policy

- This involves the use of sporting success to show off a political system.
- It is used by former Eastern bloc countries for propaganda purposes but now also by many Western governments for political and economic reasons.
- Most nations now recognise that impressive performances at an Olympics produce 'spin-off' effects for business as well as a boost national pride.
- The Olympic Games has become the world's most effective shop window.

Apartheid

 **points**

- This is the system of exclusion of blacks and coloureds from mainstream life in South Africa – including representative sport.
- The IOC was strongly criticised for the delay in responding to calls for the exclusion of South Africa over its policy of Apartheid.

- New Zealand's insistence on maintaining sporting links with South Africa led directly to the African boycotts of the Games in 1976 and added to the absences from Moscow four years later.
- The Gleneagles Agreement on sporting contacts with South Africa (1977) had called on all Commonwealth nations to refrain from any sporting contact with that country.
- Zola Budd (a white South African) aroused much controversy by adopting British citizenship to allow her to run in Olympic competition for Britain in 1984.
- SANOC was a non-racial organisation, but had no influence on its government.

The Olympics as a political tool

Many Olympiads have become associated with political incidents. They can be categorised as tools of:

- reconciliation
- recognition
- global non-systematic protest
- global systematic protest
- propaganda
- devolution
- corruption.

Many governments now fund the Olympic preparations of their national teams and national sports institutes, and their associated infrastructure are becoming the norm rather than the exception. Previous assertions that politics and sport have no connection have now been discarded.

Do you know about...?

1. Olympic Games that have been specifically used for political purposes?
2. The origin and use of the terms 'ping-pong diplomacy' and 'shop window' policy?

Do you know about...?

3. The meaning of the term 'Apartheid' and its origins, and how it led to the various boycotts and politicisation of the Olympics during the late 1960s, 1970s and 1980s?

4. The reasons for South Africa's expulsion from the Olympic Games from 1964 until 1992?

5. The various ways in which the Olympic Games have been used as a tool of political protest?

Exam tips

First recent example was Hitler's (Berlin) Games of 1936

More recently, the eastern bloc communist countries used the Games for political advantage (shop window)

6. The political nature of Olympic bidding

Fact:
It seems that shopping, politics, local business interests and evening entertainment have had more influence on successful Olympic bids than the sporting facilities on offer.

Fuller information on these themes can be found in *Advanced PE for Edexcel*, pages 82–85.

How the Olympics are awarded

Why cities bid for Olympics
- The change to commercialisation

The Manchester bids of 1992 and 1996

Atlanta not Athens – the controversy

How the Olympics are awarded

 **Key points**

- The bidding procedure identifies future Olympic venues six years before a Games takes place.
- Any number of cities may bid, but only one will be accepted from each country.
- National Olympic Committees oversee multiple bids and decide which one will go forward.
- In the final bidding process, the city with a clear majority is awarded the Games.
- If there is no clear majority, the least successful city drops out and the IOC identifies four leading contenders from the remaining cities.
- Bids have been far more plentiful since the advent of commercial backing to finance the huge outlay.
- Some 21 cities made initial bids for the Games in Barcelona and over 40 cities expressed interest in the 2000 Games in Sydney.
- Even Winter Olympiads now attract far more bids than previously.

Criticism of the bidding process
The bidding process has attracted growing attention and criticism in recent years:

- accusations have been made that IOC delegates have sought inducements in the form of gifts, cash and other 'favours' in return for their vote
- the involvement of businessmen and politicians has also been alleged, with the result that the IOC was forced to undertake a critical review of its procedures
- some commissioners have been removed from office, whilst others have resigned
- President Samaranch was required to give undertakings as to his own conduct.

Why cities bid for the Olympics

 **Key points**

- The honour of hosting an Olympics became a very expensive one!
- Montreal suffered serious financial difficulties following its financing of the Games of 1976.
- By 1984 a way was found to generate corporate funding that would pay for facilities.
- This was so successful that potential host cities are now plentiful; they no longer fear bankruptcy but expect to make a profit.
- TV networks now pay huge sums to secure broadcasting rights, and the resultant 'global' exposure is sought by both politicians and businessmen.
- There are high stakes to be played for in terms of infrastructure development and business and commercial benefits.
- There are clear political benefits to be gained from being associated with a successful bid.

- Potential host cities market themselves fiercely; clearly aware of the benefits of a successful bid.

The Manchester bids of 1992 and 1996

 **points**

It is now clear that both Manchester bids were lost for 'other reasons' than their intrinsic quality.

- Both bids were put together by Bob Scott, a local businessman.
- The IOC (particularly Samaranch himself) appeared to object to the nature of local politics.
- The facilities for delegates' wives were deemed inadequate (i.e. Manchester did not have London's 'boutiques').
- It became apparent that London was the only UK venue that would be acceptable to the IOC. (This point has also allegedly been made in connection with UK bids for other major sporting events.)

Atlanta not Athens – the controversy

 **points**

- This was perhaps the biggest shock of all.
- It had long been considered that Athens would be the ideal venue for the (centenary) Olympics of 1996.
- The then IOC president had declared publicly that Athens was the clear favourite.
- Atlanta was way down the list of nominations but was finally awarded the Games.
- It just happened to be the headquarters of the Coca-Cola Company!
- There were (as with the Manchester bids) suggestions that Greek politics were not to the liking of the then IOC president.

- It is perhaps not surprising that the second millennium closed with the IOC under the scrutiny of the media, the sporting world generally and with some governments questioning whether it was a fit organisation to do business in their country.

Do you know about...?

1. The Olympic bidding procedure?
2. The reasons why there is now so much competition to become an Olympic host city?
3. The issues surrounding the failed Manchester bids for the Games of 1992 and 1996?
4. The controversy associated with the abortive bid by Athens for the Centenary Games of 1996?

Exam tips

Olympic bidding linked with commercialism and politics

Growth in number of bidding countries directly linked to the growth of commercialism (and potential profit)

Governments also saw that there was economic and political advantage to be gained

7. Deviance and the Olympics

Fact:
Deviant behaviour is not attributable to sport itself but to those who seek to gain unfairly from it.

Fuller information on these themes can be found in *Advanced PE for Edexcel*, pages 85–89.

Deviance and cheating in sport

The concept of sportsmanship

Sportsmanship replaced by gamesmanship
- Reasons for different sporting philosophies

Deviant behaviour
- Institutionalised deviance

The IOC and international drug control

Deviance and cheating in sport

 **points**

- Culture and tradition play a large part in determining what is and what isn't cheating.
- Previous conceptions were challenged by the 'win-at-all-costs' attitude of American football coach Vince Lombardi in the 1950s.
- This is often cited as a turning point in the interpretation of the term 'sportsmanship'.
- The advent of European and world soccer saw many British players dismayed at the 'antics' of European and South American players.
- The Australian practice of 'sledging' in cricket has not endeared its exponents to the world's cricketing fraternity.
- Eastern bloc countries created an ideology that politicised sport and that devised ways of illegally enhancing performance.
- The globalisation of sport has brought diverse cultures into confrontation and highlighted differing attitudes to sport and sportsmanship.

The concept of sportsmanship

 **points**

- The British conception of sportsmanship was based on the philosophy of honourable performance without seeking to gain unfair advantage.
- Sportsmanship must nowadays be viewed in global terms rather than purely 'British' ones.
- Sport does not exist in a vacuum and changing social values will inevitably be reflected in sporting ones.
- The potential rewards for success may often – rightly or wrongly – cause performers/coaches/administrators to override any moral considerations.

> **Did you know?**
> The concept of sport was based on the belief that taking part was more important than winning.

Sportsmanship replaced by gamesmanship

- Sportsmanship can be defined as the intention to compete within the rules.
- Gamesmanship can be defined as the intention to compete to the limit of the rules – and beyond, if possible

Reasons for different sporting philosophies

- The adoption of sporting values was driven by nineteenth-century middle class morality.
- The value of sport was that it helped transmit desirable values through the medium of recreation.
- Viewed in that perspective, much of today's sport might be considered as entertainment rather than sport.
- The contemporary view of sport(smanship) has changed since the days of Baron de Coubertin and Avery Brundage.

Deviant behaviour

 **points**

This might be defined as behaviour intended to gain unfair advantage by means of:

- gamesmanship
- deliberate infringement of rules
- interfering with equipment
- knowingly taking banned substances with the intention of gaining unfair advantage
- being involved in an act, the intention of which is to gain unfair advantage.

Deviant behaviour is not only the province of individuals or small groups. Governments of former Eastern bloc countries supported hugely deviant programmes designed to win gold medals whatever the cost. More recently, the Republic of China has also been associated with such practices.

Deviant behaviour therefore falls into one or more of the following categories:

- institutional
- group specific
- individual

It is either:
- voluntary
- co-operative
- enforced.

Some of those guilty of 'cheating' were themselves victims of institutionalised systems. Many had little choice but to participate in the interest of their own personal well-being.

Some anger is now directed at the IOC, which, despite evidence of deviant practice, refuses to demand the return of medals.

In the former GDR, 'Plan 14.25' ordered systematic doping of athletes.

The IOC and international drug control

 **points**

- The current interpretation of drug abuse includes the deliberate and inadvertent use of substances that enhance performance.

- The IOC played a large part in establishing procedures for drug control for the summer and winter Games of 1968.
- The IOC Medical Commission is responsible for establishing all the procedures related to drug testing:
  - testing procedures have been expanded to include blood as well as urine samples since 1994
  - all international sporting bodies are now under pressure from the IOC to adopt its medical code
  - random testing means that athletes can now be tested at any time – in or out of season
  - there are now over 150 banned substances on the IOC's list.
- The IOC's anti-doping campaign is based upon three principles:
  - the protection of the health of athletes
  - respect for medical and sports ethics
  - ensuring an equal chance for everyone during competition.

Do you know about...?

1. The meaning of the terms 'deviance' and 'cheating' in connection with sport?
2. What was originally meant by the term 'sportsmanship'?
3. The difference between sportsmanship and gamesmanship?
4. The role of the IOC in the control of drugs in international sport and the principles on which it bases this role?

Exam tips

Deviance in the Olympics is also connected to politics, commercialism and (good old-fashioned) greed.

Do make sure you understand the difference between 'sportsmanship' and 'gamesmanship'

Remember that drug-taking in sport is not always a case of individual deviance.

8. Paralympics

Fact:
The Paralympics is a celebration of the sporting achievements of people with disabilities. It is *not* disabled sport!

Fuller information on these themes can be found in *Advanced PE for Edexcel*, pages 89–92.

History of the Paralympics

Impairment classifications

IOC support of the disabled movement?

Links with the Olympic movement

History of the Paralympics

 **points**

- Dr Ludwig Guttmann organised a sports competition for disabled veterans of the Second World War in 1948.
- He also ran the spinal injuries centre at Stoke Mandeville hospital.
- The first Olympic-type Games for wheelchair athletes was organised in 1960, but competition was not expanded to include other groups until 1976 in Toronto.
- Disabled athletes have shared the main Olympic venue since the Summer Games of 1988 and the Winter Games of 1992.
- The IOC made no commitment to assist the International Paralympic Committee (IPC, formed 1989) until 1988.

Impairment classifications

- The first Games to be known as the Olympic Games for the Disabled took place in Geilo, Sweden in 1980.
- The first use of the term 'Paralympics' was in Seoul in 1988.

Current impairment classifications for athletes entering the Paralympics
- Cerebral palsy (CP-ISRA)
- Spinal cord lesion, spina bifida and polio (ISMWSF)
- Blindness (IBSA)
- Les Autres or amputations (ISOD).

IOC support of the disabled movement?

- Samaranch felt that too close an association with the Paralympic movement might harm the market potential of the Games.
- He made three things clear:
  - he did not want the title 'The Olympic Games for the Disabled' used again
  - he would not allow the Olympic flag to be used for disabled events
  - there would be no inclusion of disability events in the main Olympic programme.
- As a result, the flag of the Paralympic movement has three teardrops, but Paralympic events do now take place in the main stadium.

Links with the Olympic movement

 **points**

Since 1988, the relationship between the IOC and the IPC has improved considerably. As a result of an agreement in October 2000:

- the IPC President will be co-opted as a member of the IOC
- representatives of the IPC will be included in relevant IOC Commissions
- the IOC will contribute US$300,000 towards IPC administration costs from 2001–2004
- a further US$100,000 annual subsidy will be made available for development projects
- there will be a financial contribution to assist athletes from developing countries in the Paralympic Games

- the IOC and the IPC will establish a link between their websites
- a programme of training and exchange of staff will be formulated
- agreement will be reached on the organisation of future Paralympic Games.

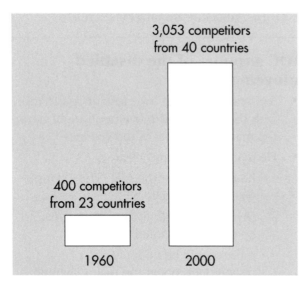

Increasing involvement of athletes in the Paralympics

Did you know?
The Paralympics represents the pinnacle of disability sport.

Do you know about...?

1. The origins and history of the Paralympic movement?
2. Why the Paralympic movement developed as a separate organisation from the IOC?
3. The development of links with the IOC in more recent times?

Exam tips

3 'key' phases:

Foundation (1948)

Crisis (Samaranch's rejection of the Paralympic movement)

Expansion and subsequent inclusion (Samaranch's 'U-turn')

Practise your exam technique

These questions require extended essay-type answers, each worth 25 marks. You will answer ONE question only in the exam.

1. What changes have occurred in the number of Olympic competitors from Africa and Asia since the mid-1960s and why has this happened?
2. The Paralympic movement is now becoming increasingly accepted as part of the Olympic movement. Briefly state the history of the movement and identify what you consider to be critical points in that history.

UNIT 3: Exercise and training

Overview

Explanatory notes

This unit is concerned with how the body performs but specifically how it performs within a sporting context.

To understand this unit you must see it as a whole picture and not as five separate headings, each with several other sections.

Assuming that we understand how the body is made up (anatomy), how it functions (physiology) and how it reacts, then we should be able to use this information to improve our performance.

This unit examines how exercise can improve our performance. The focus of the anatomical and physiological content is split into two areas:

- movement
- supply and removal of air.

Movement

This is an examination of how the skeletal and muscular systems work together. The different structures involved – such as muscles, bones and ligaments – will be identified and their specific suitability for movement will be examined.

Supply and removal of air

This is an examination of how the respiratory and circulatory systems work together.

Their individual and collective roles need to be understood within the context of providing the body with the most efficient working platform.

From a sports performer's perspective, this anatomical and physiological knowledge alone would be of little benefit unless it is accompanied with an accurate understanding of how and why the body responds to stress.

By controlling and manipulating this stress the performer is able to predetermine the efficiency of the body in a given environment.

So what does all that mean? If a sprinter is aware that:

- he/she needs to be strong to be quick
- strength is needed in both the upper and lower body
- the body responds to heavy resistance training by getting stronger,

then he/she would also be able to use this information to develop strength in both legs and shoulders, which in turn would provide greater potential for speed.

In this case, the sprinter is controlling the stress that the body experiences (heavy resistance training) in order that the body adapts in such a way that it is better able to sprint.

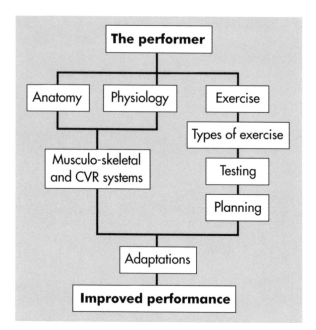

Understanding how to improve performance in a sporting context

1. Introduction to Unit 3

Unit 3 is called "Exercise and training" so it is very important not to lose sight of this and become bogged down in a study of anatomy. Obviously we need to know how relevant body parts are arranged and then how they work together.

BUT we only need this knowledge so that we can determine how these various body parts will respond to certain types of stress (in this context exercise is the primary stress) and then manipulate that stress (training) to our advantage!

The body will respond to stress in the short term and then adapt to it in the longer term.

So, when studying anatomical and physiological elements of the course try and relate them to sport in general but your sport specifically.

Keep in mind the following:

• anatomy refers to the make up of the body
• physiology refers to how the body works
• responses are temporary changes and occur immediately
• adaptations are permanent changes and they occur after prolonged exposure to a certain or consistent stress (e.g. training).

An example of the above might be based on the heart of a distance runner:

Anatomy - the arrangement of the chambers, the valves and blood vessels.

Physiology - the path of the blood, the arrival of the impulse and the conversion to an outcome i.e. heart beat.

Response - adrenaline and or presence of CO_2 leads to an increase in stimulus and an increase in heart rate.

Adaptation - After being asked to work at a specific intensity as a result of aerobic training the heart becomes bigger and stronger and so performs its job more efficiently. This leads to a drop in heart rate and a greater heart rate range for the athlete to work in future. In other words the athlete, in this case you, can work harder before their heart rate gets too high.

• Understand the anatomy as a 'map' that does not change.
• Understand that the physiology will respond to the right stress (exercise) by becoming more efficient.
• Be aware of how the principles of training, when successfully related to the appropriate methods of training, can produce the 'right stress'.

2. Immediate effects of exercise

Fact:
The body performs better at its optimum temperature. If you are too hot or too cold you will not be at your best.

Fuller information on these themes can be found in *Advanced PE for Edexcel*, pages 162–171.

Warm up
- Gross motor activity
- Stretching
- Proprioceptive neuromuscular facilitation (PNF)
- Stretch reflex
- Inverse stretch reflex
- Reciprocal innervation
- Motion and mobility
- Preventing injury
- PARQ
- Contra-indicated exercises
- 'SMARTER'
- Completing the warm up

Cool down

Immediate effects of exercise
- Aerobic (steady rate) exercise
- Performance and body temperature

Warm up

 **points**

An effective warm-up will:

- prepare the body for the forthcoming activity
- reduce the risk of injury
- improve performance.

The effects and benefits of a warm up include:

- an increase of carbon dioxide (CO_2)
- an increase in the release of adrenaline
- an increase in heart rate, cardiac output and stroke volume
- the capillaries in the working muscles and close to the skin beginning to dilate
- quickening and deepening of ventilation
- increase of localised muscle temperatures
- increased rate of metabolisation
- greater extensibility and elasticity of muscle fibres and connective tissue at joints
- quicker transmission of nerve impulses.

QUESTION: Can you identify the benefit to the performer of each of the above effects?

It is important to warm up safely and effectively. Warming up should always be specific to the performer and to the activity. So a shot putter and a trampolinist should perform very different warm-up routines. However, there are recognised principles that should be applied to all warm-up activity.

Stage 1: Initial preparation/Pulse raiser/Heart rate elevation/Gross motor skills

All warm ups should start off gradually, then increase in intensity. Large body movements would be performed such as jogging/swimming/cycling. The aim of this stage is to:

- gradually increase core temperature
- increase both ventilation and circulation rates
- prepare the body for the other stages.

Stage 2: Injury prevention

Once the localised temperature of muscles and connective tissue has been elevated, stretching can be undertaken. It is generally accepted that the initial form of stretching should be static. However, other modes should also be utilised dependent on the activity and the level of fitness of the performer. This stage will:

- help to minimise the risk of injury
- aid elasticity
- improve the range of movement
- increase of efficiency of the movement.

> **Did you know?**
> A flexible swimmer can swim more efficiently than a less flexible opponent!

Stage 3: Skill practice

This next stage of a warm up should involve a skill-related component, which works the neuro-muscular mechanisms related to the activity to follow – for example:

- practising serving in tennis
- tumble turns in swimming
- shooting baskets in basketball.

Stage 4: Sport-specific practice

Connected to the third phase is the final phase of the warm up. This phase will include the skills and exertions very similarly to situations experienced in a game situation.

Stretching

 **points**

This is the process by which the length of soft tissue (predominantly muscle but also tendons and to a lesser extent ligament tissue) is increased. There are many different approaches to stretching. The approach adopted should be appropriate to the performer and the activity to be undertaken (specificity). However, there are guidelines that should be adhered to.

- Muscles should be warm before being stretched.
- Joints should have been mobilised.
- Joints in the leg and the back should remain 'soft', which means they should not be 'locked out' or fully straightened.

Approaches to stretching include static stretching, active stretching, passive stretching and dynamic or ballistic stretching.

- Static stretching:
  - takes the muscle to a point of tension then holds it
  - is the safest method of stretching

  - stimulates the golgi tendon organs and takes advantage of the inverse stretch reflex.
- Active stretching is when static stretching is performed individually by the performer.
- Passive stretching:
  - is also called 'active assisted stretching'
  - is when a partner, or object, is used to stretch the muscle beyond its normal limit
  - is a more advanced method if stretching and care to avoid injury should be taken.
- Dynamic/ballistic stretching:
  - is quick, bouncing actions that are used to 'force' the muscle beyond its normal limit
  - can be dangerous and lead to injury or muscle soreness
  - is appropriate for explosive events such as 100 metre sprinting, *but only when the performer is experienced and has prepared the muscles for the activity*.

Proprioceptive neuromuscular facilitation/PNF

- This is an effective but advanced mode of stretching.
- It incorporates the use of the golgi tendon organs.
- The muscles are first stretched, then contracted whilst in that position.
- They then relax before the process is repeated.

Cool down

 **points**

A cool down:

- is performed after exercise
- is designed to return the body as quickly as possible to its pre-exercise state
- should involve a continuous activity that tapers in intensity.

Interspersed with flexibility exercises, an effective cool down will:

- help to prevent blood pooling
- aid the rapid elimination of waste products
- reduce the effect of post-exercise soreness (DOMS).

> **Did you know?**
> A cool down is good preparation for exercise!

> **Did you know?**
> The best time to do flexibility work is during a cool down, because the muscles are warm and injury is less likely!

Immediate effects of exercise

The body *responds* to exercise.

A temporary change is a response, but a permanent change is an adaptation. For example, if someone were to startle you, your *response* might be to 'jump'. If this became a regular occurrence, your response might become less marked. This would be an *adaptation*.

In the same way your body first of all responds and then adapts to exercise. Many of the immediate responses to exercise have already been discussed in the reasons for warming up. In summary, these responses are:

- a release of adrenaline
- a build-up of CO_2
- an increase in HR
- an increase in ventilation – quicker/deeper/heavier
- a speed up of oxygen delivery
- heat generation
- a speed up of localised muscular metabolism
- quicker production of energy glycolysis
- dilation of capillaries
- increased muscle elasticity

- greater force and speed of contraction
- greater flexibility at a joint
- increased speed of nerve impulses
- improved reaction and responses.

> **Did you know?**
> Some effects of exercise actually occur *before* exercise. These are called anticipatory effects.

Performance and body temperature

 **points**

- Our bodies perform better at certain temperatures. This is because:
  - when we are too cold, we are not very efficient and cannot work as well
  - when we are too hot, things can start to go wrong; eventually we overheat and then break down.
- As an individual performer, you could be up to 15 per cent more effective if your localised muscle temperature was 41°C compared with 37°C.
- 105°F is known as the critical threshold. At this temperature our performance will deteriorate rapidly.

> **Did you know?**
> Many élite marathon runners will try to cool down *before* a race! In doing so they try to delay the point at which they reach the critical threshold.

Flexibility: what is it?

- It is a component of physical fitness.
- It is defined as 'the ability to move a joint smoothly through its complete range of movement'.
- It is often overlooked or neglected when planning training programmes.
- However, full efficiency of movement can only be appreciated when full flexibility has been achieved.

- Flexibility can also help to prevent muscle strain and tear type injuries.
- It is dependent upon a number of factors:
  - the type of joint
  - the condition of the joint (i.e. wear and tear/damage)
  - muscle extensibility.
- Flexibility can be lost as a result of:
  - overuse
  - under use
  - ageing
  - injury.

Exam tip

If you understand why the responses to exercise are of assistance to the body, you will also understand the need for, and how to perform, an effective warm up.

3. Musculo-skeletal structures in action

Fact:
A muscle cannot return itself to its starting position. Its antagonistic muscle or gravity must do that.

Fuller information on these themes can be found in *Advanced PE for Edexcel*, pages 171–190.

Musculo-skeletal structures and function for sport and exercise – gross structures
- Connective tissue
- Muscle shapes and movement
- Muscle strength
- Characteristics of skeletal muscle tissue
- Muscle fibre types
- Cartilage types
- Posture
- The effects of exercise
- Hypo-kinetic musculo-skeletal disorders

Musculo-skeletal locations and action
- Types of muscle action
- Joints
- The knee joint
- The shoulder girdle
- The shoulder joint
- The elbow and the radio-ulnar joints
- The wrist and hand joints
- The hip joints
- The ankle joints
- The abdominal region
- Proprioception
- Joints

Musculo-skeletal structures and function for sport and exercise – gross structures

 **points**

Muscles have one primary function – to contract. In doing so, they provide:

- movement
- stability
- heat.

There are three types of muscle tissue:

- skeletal muscle
- smooth muscle
- cardiac muscle.

Muscles connect to bones via tendons and usually have at least two points of attachment. These points of attachment are called the origin and the insertion.

- The origin anchors the muscle to a bone.
- The insertion attaches the muscle to the bone(s) that move when the muscle contracts.

Connective tissue

- Most muscles consist of a 'belly' with a fibrous tendon at both ends.
- The outer protection of this belly is called the epimysium.
- The muscle belly is made up of a collection of bundles called fascicli.
- Each fasicicle has a protective sheath called the perimysium.
- The fasicicle consists of many fibres, or muscle cells, gathered together in a bunch.
- These fibres contain numerous myofibrils, which also run parallel and extend along the entire length of the muscle fibre.
- There may be hundreds of thousands of myofibrils within each single muscle fibre!
- It is the myofibrils that are the contractile element of the muscle.

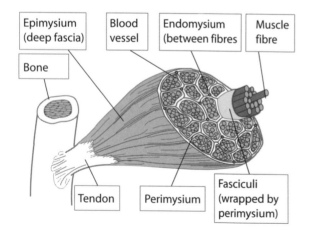

The microscopic structure of skeletal muscle

- They have characteristic dark and light bands.
- Each myofibril consists of even smaller contractile units called sarcomeres.

Muscle shapes and movement

 points

- Skeletal muscles come in a variety of shapes and sizes. They also have their fibres arranged in different ways.
- The size, shape and arrangement of fibres effects the suitability of muscles to different functions and types of movement.

Muscle fibre types

 points

- There are two types of skeletal muscle fibre:
  - slow twitch fibres (Type I)
  - fast twitch fibres (Type II).
- Fast twitch fibres can also be split into Types IIa and IIb.
- The names come from the characteristics that they have in producing and using energy.
- Athletes have varying quantities of the three fibre types.
- The muscle fibre composition of the body is largely genetic, lending weight to the assumption that élite athletes are born, not made.

Did you know?
Many top class endurance athletes may possess 95 per cent Type I muscle fibres, but some may possess as few as 50 per cent!

Types of bone

 points

The skeleton may be considered in two sections:

Characteristics	Slow Twitch (I)	Fast Oxidative Glycolytic (FOG) (IIa)	Fast Twitch Glycolytic (FTG) (IIb)
Speed of contraction	Slow	Fast	Fast
Force of contraction	Low	High	High
Size	Smaller	Large	Large
Mitochondrial density	High	Lower	Low
Myoglobin content	High	Lower	Low
Fatigability	Fatigue resistant	Less resistant	Easily fatigued
Aerobic capacity	High	Medium	Low
Capillary density	High	High	Low
Anaerobic capacity	Low	Medium	High

Skeletal muscle fibre types and its characteristics

- the axial skeleton, which is the main axis of the body
- the appendicular skeleton, which consists of the limbs and girdles.

> **Did you know?**
> Stress lines within a bone are constantly reorganised in response to the changing stress orientation, e.g. when an infant starts to walk instead of crawling.

Name	Long bones	Short bones	Flat bones	Irregular bones	Sesamoid bones
Characteristics	Cylindrical in shape found in the limbs	Small and compact in nature, often equal in length and width	Large and 'flat' in appearance	They have a complex, individual shape and are difficult to classify otherwise	Usually developed in tendons and are covered with a layer of articular cartilage
Primary function	Act as levers, and are essential in movement	Strength and weight bearing	Protection to the internal organs of the body	Providing shape	They ease joint movements
Secondary function	Production of blood cells	Intricate movement	Provide suitable sites for muscle attachment	Protection	They resist friction and compression
Examples	Femur, tibia, humerus, phalanges	Wrist (carpals), ankle (tarsals) calcaneum	The sternum, bones of the cranium, bones of the pelvis, the ribs	Vertebrae	Patella

The five categories of bone

- Bones have a basic structure that consists of:
  - diaphysis: the shaft of the bone
  - epiphyses: the ends of the bone (the exterior is compact bone whilst the interior contains spongy bone)
  - periosteum: which covers the diaphysis; it is a tough connective tissue, that enables the attachment of tendons.
- Bone is a rigid tissue. It consists mainly of collagen and calcium salts. The latter gives the tissue its non-elastic properties.
- The surface layer of all bones is formed from hard bone. Inside hard bone is spongy bone, which has spaces filled with bone marrow.
- Bone tissue can be categorised into compact/dense/hard or cancellous/spongy bone.
- Compact bone forms the surface layers of all bones and the cylindrical shaft of long bones.
- Cancellous bone lies beneath and inside the compact bone. It has a honeycomb or trabecular appearance. This is an effective way of combining strength with the minimum of weight.
- There are five categories of bone dependent upon their shape and function (see below 'The five categories of bone').

Cartilage

- Bone and cartilage differ in that bone is a rigid, non-elastic tissue and cartilage is slightly flexible/elastic.
- There are three types of cartilage, each performing different functions within the body (see below 'Types of cartilage and their functions').

Posture

 **points**

Correct posture allows the body to function optimally.

Body parts should be in alignment during both:

- static posture (sitting and standing), and
- dynamic posture (walking and lifting).

Cartilage type	Hyaline or articular cartilage	White fibro-cartilage	Yellow elastic cartilage
Characteristics	Bluish in colour Composed of a network of collagen fibres	Is a much denser tissue Is white in colour Is resistant to stretching	Is a much more pliant and flexible tissue
Primary function	Protects the bone tissue from wear and tear Reduces friction between articulating bones	Is tough Has shock absorption properties	Gives support and flexibility
Adaptations	Joint movement improves the nutrition supplied to this tissue and can encourage growth. Often thickens as a result of exercise.	Becomes compressed and looses some of its shock absorption qualities over time	Little indication that this type of cartilage is significantly effected by time
Location	Found on the articulating surfaces of bones	Found in areas of the body where high amounts of stress, e.g. knee/ intervertebral discs	External ear, the larynx and the epiglottis

Types of cartilage and their functions

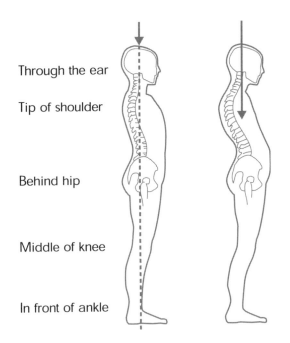

Through the ear

Tip of shoulder

Behind hip

Middle of knee

In front of ankle

Posture: correct and incorrect alignment

There are many causes of poor posture – for example:

- 'lazy' posture
- poor nutrition
- physical defects
- lack of exercise
- fatigue
- emotional factors (shyness)
- clothing
- poorly designed furniture
- certain sports.

There are also many postural deviations – for example:

- increased/decreased pelvic tilt
- kypholordosis
- poke chin
- bow legs
- flat feet.

- lordosis
- kyphosis
- round shoulders
- scoliosis
- knock knees

KYPHOSIS
...an exaggeration of posterior convexity of thoracic vertebral column (humpback).

LORDOSIS
...an exaggeration of the posterior concavity of the spine characteristic of the lumbar region. It is also called "swayback" indicating extreme anterior curvature of the lumbar spine.

SCOLIOSIS
...a condition involving lateral curve or angular deviation of one or more vertebral segments.

Typical postural defects

The effects of exercise
Adaptations that occur will depend on the nature of the training being undertaken by the athlete. Although there are many different types of training, we will look at training under two general headings: aerobic (endurance) training and anaerobic (speed) training (see below 'Aerobic and anaerobic training, and their adaptations to the muscular and skeletal systems').

Type of training	Aerobic (endurance) training	Anaerobic (speed) training
Adaptations to the muscular system	Increase the blood capillary supply to slow twitch muscles; Increase in myoglobin content and number of mitochondria in the muscles; Type IIb fibres are converted into Type IIa; Increase in muscle glycogen stores improved biochemical pathways within cells; Earlier utilisation of fat reserves as an energy source	Increase the size of fast-twitch muscle fibres (hypertrophy); Converts Type IIa fibres into Type IIb fibres; Muscle cells will store greater amounts of creatine phosphate and muscle glycogen; Improved efficiency of the energy-producing chemical reactions within cells; More powerful, faster movements.
Adaptations to the skeletal system for both aerobic and anaerobic training	Increased production of synovial fluid; greater flexibility Skeletal tissues become stronger; hyaline cartilage thickens Tendons thicken and can withstand greater muscle force Ligaments stretch slightly to enable a greater range of movement at the joint	

Aerobic and anaerobic training, and their adaptations to the muscular and skeletal systems

Hypo-kinetic musculo-skeletal disorders

 **points**

This disease occurs as a result of lack of exercise and poor lifestyle factors. There is a range of hypo-kinetic disorders:

- obesity
- lower back pain
- joint structure damage
- heart disease
- high blood pressure levels
- diabetes.

> **Did you know?**
> Exercise is thought to be a major influence in combating hypo-kinetic diseases.

Musculo-skeletal locations and action

Types of muscle action

 **points**

The main function of a muscle is to contract.

This can produce both movement and stability, which can involve three types of contraction:

- isotonic
- isometric
- isokinetic.

Isotonic contraction:

- – is when the length of the muscle changes during the exertion (either getting longer or shorter)
- – provides movement as the muscle length changes (as the muscle is attached to bone).

Isometric contraction:

- – is when, following an initial change of length, the muscle stays the same size during the rest of the exertion
- – happens when the resistance is greater than the force generated by the muscle's maximal effort and as a result the muscle cannot move the resistance. This is characterised by little or no limb movement, e.g. the initial phase of an arm wrestle or the crucifix position in gymnastics.

Isokinetic contraction:

- – is when the muscle exerts a force and

	Site	Action
The head and neck Sternocleidomastoid	Lateral neck	Lateral flexion and rotation of the neck
The back Latissimus dorsi Erector spinae group	Lower back (forms back of armpit) Lower back (medial)	Extension, internal rotation and adduction of shoulder Trunk extension
The chest Pectoralis major/minor Intercostals (external and internal)	Upper chest Between the ribs	Flexion, internal rotation and adduction of shoulder Raising and lowering the ribs
The abdomen Rectus abdominus Oblique abdominals (external and internal)	Medial abdomen Lateral abdomen	Trunk flexion and lateral flexion Trunk flexion and rotation
The hip and leg I Iliopsoas (iliacus, psoas major and psoas minor) Gluteals (maximus, medius and minimus) Adductors (brevis, longus and magnus) Quadriceps (rectus femoris, vastus lateralis, medialis and intemedius)	Lower lumbar vertebrae to upper femur Posterior hip Medial thigh Anterior thigh	Hip flexion Hip extension, external rotation and abduction Hip adduction Hip flexion, knee extension
The hip and leg II Hamstrings (biceps femoris, semimembranosus and semitendonosus) Tibialis anterior Gastrocnemius (calf) Soleus Tibialis posterior	Posterior thigh Anterior lower leg Posterior lower leg Beneath gastrocnemius Beneath soleus	Hip extension, knee flexion Dorsiflexion and inversion Plantarflexion and knee flexion Plantarflexion Plantarflexion/inversion
The arm and shoulder Deltoids Biceps brachii Brachialis	Above shoulder joint Anterior arm Beneath biceps	Shoulder flexion, extension, rotation and abduction Supination of forearm and elbow flexion True elbow flexion
Posterior arm Triceps brachii Anterior forearm Posterior forearm	Extension of elbow Flexion of wrist and fingers Extension of wrist and fingers	Wrist flexors Wrist extensors

Muscles: their location and action

works at a constant speed throughout the range of movement

- requires specialist equipment/machinery to make it occur. The resistance applied by the machine is always equal to the force applied by the muscle (e.g. when using Nautilus equipment, a cam is used to vary the load as the muscular force varies at different joint angles).

There are also two types of isotonic contraction:

- concentric contraction/positive contraction
- eccentric contraction/negative contraction.

In concentric/positive contraction, the muscle:

- actively shortens during the movement
- works in a way that is directly opposing gravity, e.g. the biceps brachii acts concentrically and shortens during a biceps curl.

In eccentric contraction/negative contraction, the muscle:

- actively lengthens during the movement
- works as a brake as it slows down the pull of gravity. (For example, during the

Muscle function	Role
Agonist	A working muscle
Antagonist	A predominantly passive muscle situated at a working joint
Prime mover	The muscle largely responsible for the movement
Fixator	Muscles that assist the movement by providing stability, primarily at the point of origin
Synergists	Muscles that assist the movement by producing stability elsewhere in the body

The role of muscles in movement

biceps curl, the biceps brachii works eccentrically when the weight is lowered. It, and not the triceps brachii, is the working muscle. The role of the biceps is to slow down the weight in the face of gravity. Without the muscle the weight would fall to the floor!)

Did you know?
There are over 600 skeletal muscles in the human body!

Joints

 **points**

- The study of joints is referred to as 'arthrology'.
- The place where two or more bones meet is known as an 'articulation', or joint.
- Joints are typically classified according to the degree of movement obtainable.

There are three types of joint, as outlined below.

- Fixed/fibrous immovable joints
  - These are very stable and allow no observable movement.
  - Bones are often joined by strong fibres called sutures, e.g. the sutures of the cranium.
- Cartilaginous or slightly movable joints
  - A cartilaginous joint allows some movement because of slight compression of the cartilage.
  - The ends of bones at the joint are separated by pads of white fibrocartilage.
  - In addition, they act as shock absorbers, e.g. the intervertebral discs.
- Synovial or freely movable joints
  - These are the most common type of joint in the body.
  - They allow a wide range of movement.

Did you know?
Fluid on the knee is caused by an inflamed synovial membrane.

– They are subdivided according to movement possibilities.
– They are characterised by the presence of a joint capsule and cavity lined with a synovial membrane.

Structure and function of a synovial joint comprises the following.

• Hyaline cartilage
  – The articular surfaces of the bones are covered with hyaline cartilage.

– This protects the bone tissue and helps to reduce friction between the bones.
• Articular capsule
  – This is a strong, fibrous tissue envelope surrounding the joint.

Anatomical Name	Location	Type of bone	Predominant function
Cranium	Skull	Flat	Protects the brain
Clavicle	Collar bone	Long	Provides leverage
Sternum	Vertical centre of chest	Flat	Protects heart and lungs
Ribs	Chest area	Flat	Protect the lungs
Scapula	Shoulder blade	Flat	Protects back of lungs
Cervical vertebrae	Upper region of the spine	Irregular	Shape and protection of the spinal cord
Thoracic vertebraev	Second region of the spine	Irregular	Shape and protection of the spinal cord
Lumbar vertebrae	Third region of the spine	Irregular	Shape and protection of the spinal cord
Sacrum vertebrae	Fourth region of the spine	Irregular	Shape and protection of the spinal cord
Coccyx vertebrae	Bottom region of the spine	Irregular	Shape and protection of the spinal cord
Humerus	Upper arm	Long	Leverage
Ilium	Upper outer part of the pelvis	Flat	Lower intestines
Ulna and radius	Lower arm	Long	Leverage
Carpals	Wrist	Short	Weight bearing
Metacarpals and phalanges	Hand and fingers	Long	Leverage
Pubis and ischium	Lower front, central part of the pelvis	Flat	Lower intestines
Femur	Upper leg	Long	Leverage
Patellav	Knee cap	Sesamoid	Protection
Tibia and fibula	Front and back of lower leg	Long	Leverage
Tarsals	Ankle	Short	Weight bearing
Metatarsals and phalanges	Foot and toes	Long	Leverage and movement

Anatomical names of bones, their location, type and functions

- The capsule adds stability to a joint and stops unwanted material from entering the joint.
  - Capsules are reinforced by ligaments.
- Synovial membrane
  - This lines the inside of the capsule.
  - Its role is to produce synovial fluid.
- Synovial fluid
  - This is a yellowish oily fluid.

Movement	Description	Example	Sporting example
Flexion	Decreasing the angle between two bones or bending a joint	Bending the trunk forwards Bending the trunk sideways is called lateral flexion Bending the arm at the elbow Moving the thigh forwards at the hip Bending the leg at the knee	
Extension	Increasing the angle between two bones or straightening a joint	Bending the trunk backwards Moving the arm or shoulder backwards Straightening the arm at the elbow Moving the thigh backwards at the hip Straightening the leg at the knee	
Abduction	Movement of a bone away from the midline of the body	Moving the arms or legs sideways away from the body Opening the fingers away from each other	
Adduction	Movement of a bone towards the midline of the body	Moving the arms or legs sideways towards the body Closing the fingers in towards each other	
Circum-duction	Bone is moved so that its end moves in a circle, and the overall movement makes the shape of a cone	Swinging the arm in a circle Drawing a circle with a finger	
Rotation	Movement of a bone around a central axis	Rotation may be internal or external – for example, the arm is able to perform both internal and external rotation	
Supination	Movement of the bones of the arm so that the palm is facing upwards	Holding out both hands with palms upwards	
Pronation	As above, but so that the palm is facing downwards	Holding out both hands with palms downwards	
Eversion	Movement of the sole of the foot outward from the ankle	Standing on the insides of the soles of the feet	
Inversion	Movement of the foot inward from the ankle	Standing on the outsides of the soles of the feet	
Dorsiflexion	Raising of the toes	'Curling' the toes upwards	
Plantar flextion	Occurs at the ankle and is the pointing of the toes	'Curling' the toes downwards	

Movement terminology I

Term	Definition	Term	Definition
Superior	Towards the head	Lateral	Towards the side
Inferior	Towards the head	Proximal	Nearer the trunk
Anterior	Front	Distal	Further from the trunk
Posterior	Back	Prone	Face down
Medial	Towards the midline	Supine	Face up

Movement terminology II

- It lubricates the articulating surfaces and forms a fluid cushion between them.
- It provides nutrients for the hyaline cartilage.
- It absorbs debris produced by minor damage between joint surfaces.
- Ligaments
  - These are strong fibrous bands.
  - They play a major role in keeping bones in place at joints.
- Articular discs (menisci)
  - These are found between the articular surfaces of the bones at the joint.
  - They are attached to the capsule.
  - Their function is to absorb shock and protect the bone surfaces.
- Pads of fat
  - These fill the gaps that surround the joint.
  - They form protective cushions for the joint structures.
- Bursae
  - These are sacs filled with synovial fluid.
  - They are located wherever friction may develop.
  - Bursitis is the inflammation of the bursae as a result of overuse and is often found in the knees, elbows and the Achilles tendon.

Exam tips

1. The general rule is that concentric contractions oppose gravity while eccentric contractions resist or slow down gravity.

2. Familiarity breeds confidence. Get used to breaking down skills that you perform, describing the movements made and the muscles working in technical terms. That way you will not feel so threatened in an examination. It will also help you to score well in your analysis of performance.

3. Adaptations occur to both muscles and bones but these adaptations differ dependent upon the nature of the exercise. This applies to aerobic and anaerobic exercise.

Do you know about...?

1. The function of a muscle?
2. The different types of muscle?
3. How muscles are attached to bones?
4. The structure of skeletal muscle?
5. The types of skeletal muscle and their suitability to different sports?
6. The different types of bones and their functions?
7. The different types of cartilage and their role in aiding movement?
8. What posture is and what can improve it and how?
9. Hypo-kinetic diseases and the best way to alleviate them?
10. How the different types of muscle adapt to aerobic and anaerobic exercise?

11. How bones and connective tissue adapt to aerobic and anaerobic exercise?
12. The different types of muscular contractions? (Can you give examples for each?)
13. The different roles that muscles take on during movement?
14. Where in the body you will find particular muscles and what movement they create?
15. Where in the body you will find particular bones and what muscles move them?
16. The different types of joints? (Can you give examples of them?)
17. How to identify all of the agonists and the movements involved within a complete skill of your choice?

4. The circulatory, vascular and respiratory (CVR) systems in action

Fact:
If fully dilated, the body's blood vessels could hold about 20 litres of blood, even though the total blood volume is only about 5 to 6 litres.

Fuller information on these themes can be found in *Advanced PE for Edexcel*, pages 190–199.

Response and regulation to exercise of the CVR systems
• Cardiac cycle
• Cardiac output
• Blood pressure
• Blood vessels
• Blood plasma volume
• Oxygen transport
• Respiration
• Gaseous exchange

Adaptation of the CVR systems
• Training effects
• Acclimatisation and altitude
• Erythropoietin (EPO)

Key points

• The heart is myogenic.
• The 'messages' sent to stimulate heart rate come from the medulla oblongata.
• The sympathetic nervous systems carries messages to speed up heart rate.
• The parasympathetic nervous system carries messages to slow down heart rate.
• The sino atrial node (pace maker), which is located in the upper right atrium, receives the message to contract.
• It sends an electric impulse out over the heart.
• The atria muscles will begin to contract, closely followed by the ventricles once the atrio ventricular node has detected the signal and sent the message out across the ventricular muscles.
• The heart rate is regulated by the autonomic nervous system.

Sensory control works in the following way.

• The medulla receives sensory information from receptors, e.g. stretch receptors and baroreceptors.
• These are located in the atria and other blood vessels.
• They detect increases in blood flow.
• As blood pressure levels increase within the vessels they need to stretch. This activates the stretch receptors, which in turn activate the baroreceptors.
• Then they bring about a reflex that slows the heart.
• Consequently, the main function of the baroreceptors is to prevent excessive blood pressure during exercise.

Hormonal control works in the following way.

- The rise in heart rate that accompanies the feeling of 'butterflies' before a sporting event is caused by nervous impulses from the brain being sent to the adrenal glands.
- These glands then secrete the hormone adrenaline.
- The effect of adrenaline is to increase the heart rate and constrict arterioles.
- This results in a rise in blood pressure.
- The effect of adrenaline is also to prepare the athlete for a rise in blood carbon dioxide concentration.

Response and regulation to exercise of the CVR systems

- The sequence of events that causes blood to be pumped through the heart is called the cardiac cycle.
- Each cycle is produced by one heartbeat.

Did you know?
The heart is capable of pumping maximally for three consecutive days!

Cardiac cycle
The cardiac cycle consists of two phases:

- a period where the heart muscle is relaxed, known as diastole
- a period of contraction, known as systole.

During these phases the following things happen.

- During diastole, there is very little pressure in the heart, so the valves remain closed.
- The atria begin to fill up from the vena cava and the pulmonary artery.
- As they begin to fill, the pressure within the heart increases.
- This forces the atrio-ventricular valves open.
- The semi-lunar valves, which prevent back flow of blood into the heart from the aorta and pulmonary artery, remain closed.
- Cardiac systole occurs, with the muscle tissue of the atria beginning to contract.

- This forces the remaining atrial blood through the atrio-ventricular valves, into the ventricles.
- The semi-lunar valves remain closed during this period of atrial systole.
- This process speeds up significantly during exercise.

Cardiac output

 **Key points**

- Cardiac output (Q) is the volume of blood ejected by the heart per minute.
- Its sum is calculated by multiplying heart rate by stroke volume.
- Q increases as a result of exercise and will continue to rise up to the point of maximal exertion.
- At this point Q will actually decrease slightly.

QUESTION: Do you know why?

Vascular shunting
- Vascular shunting occurs when the path of blood is prioritised to the parts that need it most.
- As the body has almost four times more 'storage' space than it has blood, it must regulate where the blood is sent.
- During exercise, constriction of blood vessels in the liver, the kidney and the digestive organs results in blood being diverted to the working muscles.

Did you know?
Pressure within arteries remains fairly constant.

Blood pressure

 **Key points**

- Blood pressure = Blood flow × Resistance.
- During exercise, blood flow in muscle may increase ten to fifteen times its resting value.

- This flow is not constant, but falls sharply when muscles contract and rises when they relax.
- This pattern of flow is caused by the rhythmical muscle contraction and relaxation, which alternately compresses the blood vessels to reduce blood flow, then dilates them in order to increase flow.
- If a blood vessel is made smaller (vasoconstricting), then the pressure with in that vessel will increase.
- If the vessel is made larger (vasodilating), then the pressure will be reduced.
- During exercise, blood pressure is increased. This is due to increased cardiac output and greater resistance in the contracting muscles, which constricts the walls of the arterioles.

Did you know?
Isometric exercise causes a build-up of pressure, because the muscles are not contracting and relaxing.

Did you know?
At rest only 15 to 20 per cent of cardiac output will be directed towards skeletal muscle. However, during intense exercise that figure may rise to up to 80 per cent.

Blood plasma volume

 **points**

- Approximately 55 per cent of blood consists of plasma.
- Of this, 92 per cent is water.
- If you are losing water, then some of it will be lost from plasma.
- This reduces your total blood volume but, perhaps more importantly, increases the viscosity of the blood that remains.

Did you know?
Stroke volume and cardiac output is dependent on venous return, because the heart can only pump out what it takes in.

Oxygen transport

 **points**

- The majority of oxygen diffuses into the blood in solution within the capillaries of the alveoli.
- Haemoglobin, which is carried within red blood cells, is an oxygen magnet.
- It will carry a 'reserve' of oxygen, which it also picks up in the lungs.
- Capillaries are the blood vessels that take the blood into the muscles.
- Myoglobin is a bigger oxygen magnet and is found in muscles.
- It will take oxygen from the haemoglobin.
- The myoglobin will take the oxygen to the muscle mitochondria, where respiration takes place.

This means that:

- the higher haemoglobin levels you possess, the more oxygen you can transport to the muscles
- the more capillaries you have, the more blood (and oxygen) you can get into the muscles
- the more myoglobin you have, the more oxygen you can take from the blood
- the more frequent and the greater the density of the mitochondria, the more oxygen you can process and the more aerobic energy you can generate.

Did you know?
Up to 70 per cent of the total volume of blood is contained in the veins at rest.

'Venous return' is the term used for the blood that returns to the right side of the heart via the veins. There are several mechanisms that aid the venous return process, as outlined below.

- The muscle pump
  - As exercise begins, muscular contractions compress the veins, squeezing blood towards the heart.
  - Pocket valves prevent any back flow of blood that might occur.
- The respiratory pump
  - During inspiration and expiration, pressure changes occur in the thoracic and abdominal cavities, which compress veins and assist blood returning to the heart.

Respiration

 **points**

- Ventilation/inspiration at rest
  - Stimulation of the phrenic and intercostal nerves causes the contraction of the breathing muscles.
  - During breathing at rest, inspiration is caused by the contraction of the external intercostal muscles, and the contraction of the diaphragm.
  - The overall effect of these contractions is to increase the volume of the thoracic cavity, lowering the internal pressure and thus ensuring that air is drawn into the lungs.
- Expiration at rest
  - This is largely achieved by the elastic recoil of the elastic tissues that have been stretched during inspiration, and is therefore a passive process.
  - The effect is to reduce the lung volume, thereby increasing air pressure inside the lungs, so air is forced out via the respiratory passages.
- Inspiration during exercise
  - A much larger volume of inspired air is taken in as a result of the contraction of accessory (secondary) inspiratory muscles such as the scaleni and sternocleldomastoid.
  - The trapezius and back and neck extensors also contract and increase the size of the thorax even more.
- Expiration during exercise
  - The combined contraction of the internal intercostal and abdominal muscles forces air out of the lungs, the rib cage is actively moved downwards and the abdominal muscles force the diaphragm upwards.
- Respiratory volumes

The respiratory, or lung, volumes include:

- tidal volume (TV), which is the volume breathed in and out at rest
- inspiratory reserve volume (IRV), which is the amount of air that can be inspired forcibly beyond the tidal volume
- expiratory reserve volume (ERV), which is the amount of air that can be evacuated from the lungs after a tidal expiration

Ventilation at rest	Ventilation during exercise
Largely passive	Largely active
Expiration is almost entirely passive	Expiration is more active
Breathing is shallow	Breathing is faster
Breathing is slow	Breathing is deeper
Smaller percentage of expired air is CO_2	Greater percentage of expired air is CO_2
Primary respiratory muscles only	Primary and secondary muscles used

A comparison of ventilation at rest and ventilation during exercise

– residual volumes (RV), which is the air still remaining in the lungs after any expiration.

• Respiratory capacities

The respiratory capacities include:

– inspiratory capacity (IC), which is the total amount of air that can be inspired after a tidal expiration; thus, it is the sum of the tidal volume and inspiratory reserve volumes

– functional residual capacity (FRC), which is the combined residual and expiratory reserve volumes, and represents the amount of air remaining in the lungs after a tidal expiration

– vital capacity (VC), which is the total amount of exchangeable air. It represents the sum of the tidal, inspiratory reserve, and expiratory reserve volumes.

• Total lung capacity (TLC) is the sum of all lung volumes.

Effects of asthma upon athletic performance
• Bronchiole walls constrict making breathing difficult.
• The athlete will experience a shortness of breath.
• The athlete will experience wheezing and a reduction in VO_2 max.
• The athlete may experience a lack of confidence, negative attitude, lack of motivation and so on.

Adaptation of the CVR systems

Training effects

VO_2 max is defined as the 'maximum amount of oxygen that can be taken in and used by the body'. It is recorded per minute per kilogramme of body weight. There are several factors effecting VO_2 max.

• Specific exercise – any exercise that promotes adaptation in the efficiency of the CVR system.

• Whole body movements.
• Use of training zones, heart rate values, training intensity (60 per cent to 90 per cent of maximum heart rate).
• Altitude training or similar.
• Gender.
• Age.
• Body fat.
• Blood doping (which is also illegal and dangerous!).

Did you know?
The body can always take in enough oxygen. The limiting factor is its ability to make use of it!

 **points**

Training can have the effect of making the CVR system more efficient. The effects will depend on:

• the type of training
• its intensity
• its duration.

Effects can include improved or increased ability:

• to metabolise fat
• of the blood to 'pick up' and transport oxygen from the lungs
• of the muscles to use oxygen
• to remove waste products
• to increase VO_2 max
• to work at a higher percentage of VO_2 max
• to recover, both during and after exercise
• to regulate body temperature
• to work faster/harder for longer
• to reduces risk of coronary heart disease/diabetes/health disorders.

Acclimatisation and altitude

 **points**

Altitude training is used particularly by athletes who will benefit from an improved ability to

Structural adaptations	
Improved gaseous exchange	Cardiac hypertrophy (particularly of the left ventricle) – size and strength
	Increase capillarisation (lungs/heart/muscles)
	Increased red blood cell count
	Quicker vascular response to shunting
	Increased number of muscle myoglobin
	Greater density of muscle mitochondria
	Very small increase in the surface area of the alveoli
	Improved working of the respiratory muscles

All of this points to the body making more efficient use of the oxygen which it takes in and so increasing its ability to work harder for longer during sub maximal exercise.

Structural adaptations and functional benefits of the CVR systems

take in and use oxygen. Its benefits to all such athletes are debated by exercise physiologists, but the type of athlete who certainly should train at altitude is the athlete who intends to compete at altitude.

Training takes place in an environment that is higher than sea level (1,500 metres to 6,000 metres) for 2.5 to 6 weeks. The following things occur during this training.

- Reduced oxygen levels at altitude means that haemoglobin is not saturated with oxygen in the lungs.
- This leads to an acute drop in performance.
- If training at altitude is extended, then acclimatisation will cause physiological adaptations.
- The body will create more red blood cells, and therefore more haemoglobin to compensate for the lack of oxygen saturation.
- The breathing rate will increase.
- There will be an increase in the myoglobin content in the muscles

The perception is that once the athlete returns to sea level, the physiological changes that

have taken place will allow a greater oxygen intake and transport, thus improving performance.

However, the benefits of this are not as significant as first thought, because oxygen at sea level is of a greater density than that at altitude. This can cause problems at maximal oxygen uptake level.

EPO (Erythropoietin)

- EPO is a hormone that stimulates the production of red blood cells in bone marrow.
- It is a blood protein, which is primarily produced in the kidneys during periods of hypoxia (this is a state when there is an insufficient supply of oxygen to the respiring muscles).
- Athletes who expose themselves to low oxygen saturation may increase EPO levels by six to nine times.
- rEPO is the genetically engineered form of EPO (recombinant erythropoietin).
- This gives an unfair advantage and is potentially very dangerous because it can result in:

- increased viscosity of the blood
- elevated blood pressure
- an increased risk of heart failure, stroke and thrombosis.
- Both EPO and rEPO are very hard to detect.

Blood doping: what it is, how it's done and the dangers

- Blood doping is an artificial way of increasing the number of blood cells (particularly red blood cells).
- It is done by blood transfusion – either with the athlete's own blood (taken five or six weeks earlier) or with matching blood from a donor.
- This process is contrary to the ethics of sport and is also very dangerous. It can lead to:
  - increased viscosity of the blood
  - elevated blood pressure
  - increased risk of heart failure, stroke and thrombosis
  - kidney damage
  - infection
  - overloading the circulatory system.

Exam tips

Remember that oxygen delivery and not oxygen intake is the key to aerobic performance.

Do you know about...?

1. The two nervous systems that help to determine heart rate levels?
2. How heart rate is controlled by the autonomic nervous system, by sensory control and by hormonal control?
3. The events and the order in which they occur within the cardiac cycle?
4. The terms 'cardiac output' and 'stroke volume', and how they are effected by exercise?
5. How vasodilation and vasoconstriction assist in the delivery of blood during exercise?
6. What, why and how vascular shunting takes place?
7. The role of haemoglobin and myoglobin in oxygen delivery?
8. What venous return is and the mechanisms available to aid it?
9. The mechanics of ventilation at rest and during exercise?
10. The different respiratory volumes and capacities?
11. Why asthma can affect an athlete's performance?
12. What VO_2 max is and the different factors that can effect it?
13. The difference between structural and functional adaptations?
14. Why many athletes spend time training at altitude?
15. The benefits that these athletes hope to achieve?
16. What blood doping is and the different methods used?

5. Measurement and evaluation of fitness components

Fact:
You should test fitness before you plan your training programme, at regular intervals during the programme and at its completion.

Fuller information on these themes can be found in *Advanced PE for Edexcel*, pages 199–203.

Reasons for testing

Issues in testing
- Test specificity
- Test validity
- Test objectivity
- Test reliability
- Fitness measures with age

Fitness tests
- Components of testing

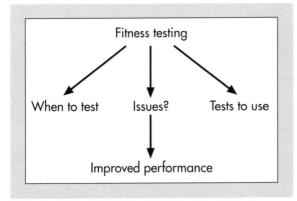

Measurement and evaluation of fitness components

Reasons for testing

 **points**

The reasons fitness testing is carried out are to:

- identify the strengths and weaknesses of the athlete
- provide baseline data for monitoring performance
- provide the basis for training principles
- assess the value of different types of training and help to modify training programmes
- predict physiological and athletic potential
- provide comparisons with previous tests and other élite performers in the same group
- enhance motivation
- form part of the educative process.

In other words, you test fitness to obtain information that is essential if the performer is to be successful.

Issues in testing

 **points**

Before undertaking a fitness test you should be fully aware of the following things.

- What you want to discover. (Are you aware of the specific areas of fitness that you wish to measure?)
- The validity of the test. (Does the test enable you to discover exactly what you want to know and is it reliable?)
- The test protocol. (Are you fully aware of how to run the test correctly and safely?)
- The condition of the athlete. (Is the athlete up to the test both mentally and physically? Has a PARQ – Physical Activity Readiness Questionnaire – been completed?)
- The need to inform the athlete. (Does the athlete understand the nature of the test and have they consented to it?)

Fitness tests

 **points**

There are many simple tests that can be performed as well as many very sophisticated ones.

Generally speaking, the more advanced and sophisticated the test, the greater its accuracy. However, such tests are often very expensive and are only usually accessible by top athletes.

Can you complete the table entitled 'Fitness tests: the test, protocol and results' below? This table identifies specific fitness tests, describes the protocol and explains exactly what has been tested for the following areas of fitness?

Do you know about...?

1. The reasons that athletes and coaches use fitness tests?
2. The relevance of the terms 'protocol' and 'validity'?
3. How to perform simple tests for all of the major components of fitness?
4. The issues that must be considered when using fitness tests?

Exam tips

1. Know why you are testing and then ask yourself if your test tells you what you want to know?
2. Is the test accurate or could you make it better. e.g. running a 100m race would not necessarily be the best test for someone wishing to test for speed.
3. Do you know why?
4. What would be a better test?

Fitness component	Fitness test	Protocol	Result/what has been measured
Cardiovascular endurance			
Localised muscular endurance			
Absolute strength			
VO_2 max			
Speed			
Acceleration			
Speed endurance			
Anaerobic capacity			
Flexibility			
Power			
Agility			
Co-ordination			
Reaction times			

Fitness tests: the test, protocol and results

6. Planning of fitness and training programmes

Fact:
Too much or insufficient exercise will have a very similar effect on your performance. It will decline. Careful planning is essential if you are to progress.

Fuller information on these themes can be found in *Advanced PE for Edexcel*, pages 204–215.

Components of fitness
- Strength
- Speed
- Power
- Localised muscular endurance
- Cardiovascular endurance
- Anaerobic endurance
- Agility
- Co-ordination
- Balance
- Reaction times
- Flexibility
- Body composition

Training principles
- Specificity
- Progression
- Overload
- Reversibility
- Thresholds
- Target training zones

Methods of training
- Continuous
- Fartlek
- Interval
- Circuits
- Sprint training
- Plyometrics

Individual differences
- Untrained versus trained
- Males versus females (all ages)

Performance-related planning
- Periodisation

Improved performance

What to think about when planning a fitness and training programme

---

You should exercise for a specific reason or outcome. That reason or outcome should be known in advance. Only then can you plan to achieve exactly what you set out to do.

Training principles

 **points**

Principles of training are quite simply training rules that should apply to all training for all sports. Below are the main principles of training.

- Sport
- Progression
- Overload
- Reversibility/regression
- Thresholds.

Target training zones

 **points**

- The concept of training zones is based on the principle of training at a specific intensity in order to obtain a specific training/physiological adaptation.
- That intensity is based on a percentage of your maximum heart rate (Karvonen).
- Karvonen identified that training at 65 per cent of your Maximum Heart Rate (MHR) would induce aerobic-enhancing adaptations.
- He used the following formula to obtain working heart rates:
  220 – your age = MHR

NB This is only a guide to your MHR

- MHR – RHR (Resting Heart Rate) = HRR (Heart Rate Reserve).
- MHR × % wanted (in this case 0 .65 per cent) – HRR = Working Heart Rate.

NB There is no definitive answer as to the exact locations of the zones in terms of percentage figures for all of the zones that could exist.

Principle of training	Definition	Applied example (for a shot putter)
Specificity	Training should be planned for the specific performer in mind	The athlete trains very intensely with heavy weights, performing compound exercises
Progression	Realistic and quantifiable targets must be set and met by the performer	The athlete ensures that progress is being made by checking his IRM every four weeks
Overload	The body will adapt to increased stress so the work load needs to increase over time	The athlete increases the intensity over a period of time by increasing the weight of the weights lifted
Reversibility	If too much time is allowed between workouts any progress will be lost and the body will revert back to its pre-exercise state	Reversibility is avoided by training regularly once sufficient recovery has been allowed
Thresholds frequency	How often you train	The athlete weight trains three times a week
Intensity	How hard you train	The athlete works in a repetition range of 3–6 at 90 per cent to 95 per cent of their one rep max
Type	The method of training used	Weight training is used
Overtraining	By training too often the body does not have time to recover and so it will regress over time	This is avoided by: careful planning; allowing sufficient rest; eating sufficient complex carbs/protein; alternating intensity levels of training

Descriptions and applications of training principles and methods

Below is a guide to the training zones and the approximate heart rate zones.

<60% = no aerobic adaptation but 50%–60% could enhance recovery

60%–70% = aerobic training

70%–85% = lactate threshold training

85%–95% = lactate tolerance and speed endurance

95%–100% = power and speed

Did you know?
Exercise is the stimulus for improvement, but the improvement only takes place during periods of rest.

Components of fitness

 **points**

- Endurance – the capacity to sustain movement or effort over a period of time.
- Local muscle endurance – the ability of the muscles to repeat movements without undue fatigue.
- Cardiovascular endurance – the ability of the cardiovascular system to transport oxygen to muscles during sustained exercise.
- Speed – the maximum rate at which a person is able to move his/her body over a specific distance.

- Flexibility – the range of movement possible at a joint. It is affected by the type of joint and muscle attachment.

- Body composition – the concept describing the relative percentage of muscle, fat and bone.

Body types may be classified according to the somatotyping technique as ectomorph, mesomorph or endomorph.

Term	Definition
Absolute strength	The maximum force that can be exerted once only
Dynamic strength	The ability to exert a force repeatedly or over a period of time
Elastic strength	Similar to explosive strength in that it involves a muscle exerting a force very quickly; the force exerted is usually maximal, e.g. long jumping
Explosive strength	Similar to absolute strength in that it refers to the ability to expand a maximum amount of energy as quickly as possible; this is usually one very quick, powerful movement but it may also include a series of movements, e.g. bounding in plyometrics
One repetition max	A measure of the maximal force that a muscle can exert 'once' without undue straining; it is important for an athlete to be aware of their 'one rep max' in order to set the intensity for future weight training sessions
Relative strength	The maximal force that can be exerted relative to muscle size or body weight; this is illustrated with the weight categories in boxing or weight lifting
Specific strength	When an athlete or muscle has a strength in a particular type of muscle action, but not for other types of action
Strength endurance	Similar to dynamic strength in that in involves the ability of a muscle to withstand fatigue when performing repeatedly
Static strength	The ability to exert a maximal force, usually against an immovable object, and then to sustain that force for up to six seconds; this would be useful in events such as scrimmaging in rugby or holding the crucifix position on the rings in gymnastics
Agility	The physical ability that enables a person rapidly to change body position and direction in a precise manner
Balance	The ability to retain the centre of mass of the body above the base of support; it is the awareness of the body's position in space and depends upon co-ordination between ears, brain, skeleton and muscles
Static balance	The ability to hold a balance in a stationary position
Dynamic balance	The ability to maintain balance under changing conditions of body movement, shape and orientation
Co-ordination	The ability to perform smooth accurate motor tasks, often with a series of correlated muscular contractions affecting a range of joints and relative limb/body positions
Power	A combination of strength and speed
Reaction time	The interval of time between the presentation of a stimulus and the initiation of the muscular response to that stimulus

Definitions of fitness

- An ectomorph has little fat or muscle and a narrow shape ('ecto' means tall).
- An endomorph is generally fat and pear-shaped ('endo' means dumpy).
- A mesomorph is muscular and wedge shaped ('mes' means muscular).

Strength is the ability of a muscle or muscle group to exert a force. It is often simplistically defined as the force exerted by muscle groups during a single maximal muscle contraction. However, as the type of force can vary so much (different intensity levels, speed of contraction, length of duration of contraction, number of similar contractions needed), then so can the different types of strength (see 'Definitions of fitness' on page 83).

Methods of training

 **points**

Methods of training refers to the categorising of types of exercise according to the use to which they are put, e.g. you can run continuously as a Fartlek session, as an interval session and so on.

Individual differences

 **points**

Pre-pubescent males and females often compete against each other, but there are differences in performance because of the following.

- Skeletal differences
  - The male skeleton is generally larger and heavier.
  - A wider female pelvis results in a slight inward tilt of the legs, resulting in a reduction in the mechanical efficiency of the running action.
  - A smaller female skeleton results in the upper body being weaker in comparison with the lower body, which is a disadvantage in events requiring

strength, e.g. javelin, discus, and all power events.

- Body fat
  - Females have a larger percentage of body fat (approximately 27 per cent) compared with males (approximately 15 per cent).
  - Consequently, females tend to have smaller maximal oxygen uptake values than males, and their greater subcutaneous fat stores tend to reduce the efficiency of the body's temperature regulatory system
- Cardiovascular differences
  - Males typically have a greater blood volume, and a greater red blood cell concentration than females, which also results in males having greater endurance capacities.
  - Males generally have a larger heart and, as a result, a larger cardiac output and lower resting heart rate.
  - Males tend to have greater endurance capacity than females due to the greater volume of oxygenated blood delivered to the body's tissues.
- Muscle mass
  - Weight-training programmes can result in roughly equal percentage strength gains in males and females, although absolute gains are greater in males than females.
  - This is a result of the initial superior male muscle mass due to higher testosterone hormone levels.
  - It is highly appropriate to dismiss the notion of a weaker sex. In fact, relative to cross-sectional area of pure muscle tissue, men and women are equal in terms of strength.
  - It is the greater fat content in females and the higher testosterone levels in men that creates the difference in the cross-sectional area of muscles and therefore strength, to the advantage of males.

Training method	Description	Advantages	Disadvantages
Continuous	A set intensity maintained for an extended duration Generally associated with aerobic activity Benefits endurance, both cardiovascular and localised muscular	Can be cheap Can be easy Can cater for large groups You set your own intensity levels	Only generally effects larger muscle groups Cannot be used to benefit other components of fitness Can be boring
Fartlek	Varying intensity levels over a specific duration.	Can cover greater total distances Can focus upon different aspects of fitness Can more realistically simulate a sporting situation	Can be hard to get the correct intensity without specific equipment, e.g. heart rate monitors
Interval	Exercise with specific work periods and specific rest periods Based around a work/rest ratio where both variables are of equal importance Can be varied to effect both anaerobic and aerobic fitness levels	Very versatile. Can be adapted to suit the needs of the individual	Requires a working knowledge of energy systems and energy replenishment to be performed effectively
Circuits	Performing different exercises at different stations	Very versatile Can be adapted to suit the needs of the individual Can provide benefits for most elements of physical and neuro-muscular fitness Can be cheap Can be easy Can cater for large groups You set your own intensity levels	
Fixed load	A set number of repetitions are performed before moving onto the next station The complete circuit is then completed as quickly as possible.		
Individual load	A specific amount of time is spent at each station with the performer attempting to perform as many repetitions as possible		
Plyometrics	Forcibly pre-stretching the muscle in the eccentric phase to produce a more powerful concentric contraction	Good method for developing power Develops supporting muscles/muscle groups	Stress on the joints Increased potential for DOMS Limited number of exercises

Training methods and definitions

Performance-related planning
Periodisation

 **points**

Periodisation refers to the breaking up of a training period (usually a season, but in the case of an Olympic athlete it might four years), into smaller parts (cycles) each of which focuses on a sub-theme of the whole programme.

- Each period has a different purpose.
- A typical example consists of four periods:
  - a preparation period
  - a pre-competition period
  - a maintenance or competition period
  - a transition or recovery period.
- The programme is designed so that athletes peak to coincide with major competitions.
- The main periods of training are called macrocycles, and the phases of training within the macrocycles are called mesocycles.
- Daily and weekly training sessions are called microcycles, and are described in terms of the type of exercise undertaken, its intensity and its duration.

Did you know?
Improvements in fitness are the result of weeks or months of exercise, not just a single session.

Do you know about...?

1. The main principles of training? (Could you apply them to your sport?)
2. Who Karvonen is, and his theory for exercise intensity?
3. The different components of fitness? (Could you identify the importance of each component within different sports?)
4. The different methods of training?
5. The methods of training and how to justify the type that should be used by an athlete from a given sport?
6. The differences between males and females both pre- and post-puberty?
7. How to relate and apply gender differences to sport?
8. Periodisation? (Do you know the difference between a macro, meso and micro cycle?)

Exam tips

1. Do not confuse principles of training with methods of training!
2. Remember, specific exercise produces a specific response.

Practise your exam technique

1. Continuous training is often associated with endurance events. Identify the main **principles** of continuous training. (3 marks)
2. Identify the **structural *and* functional adaptations** of the **cardiovascular** system that are likely to be evident in an **endurance** athlete. (6 marks)
3. An athlete's VO_2max is often a good indicator to endurance potential. **Define** the term VO_2max **and** then identify the physiological factors that can effect it. (4 marks)
4. (i) Athletes make use of a **variety** of different training methods. **Identify** a **sport** of your choice and then **list** the methods of training that you would use, **explaining** the **physiological benefits** that you would hope to get from **each method**. (8 marks)
   (ii) Identify and explain the **principles** that should be applied in order to ensure that the athlete makes progress while using these different methods of training. (4 marks)

UNIT 4: Global trends in international sport

Section A(1): World cultures: North America

Overview

1. Historical and cultural background
- Mainstream social values
- Ethics present in North American sport

2. Physical education and sport in high schools and colleges/universities
- Historical development of physical education
- Sport in high schools
- Sport in higher education
- The sports scholarship system

3. Professional (élite) sport
- The history of professional sport
- Structure of professional sport
- The status of professional sport

4. Recreational sport (mass participation)
- Sport in North American society
- Community participation
- Junior sport
- National Parks, alternative and wilderness sports

Explanatory notes

This Unit requires you to choose a particular cultural area for in-depth study, although many students also look at a second culture as 'back-up'.

The fact that each culture is broken down into four discrete study areas does mean that some comparisons may be made on a 'like-for-like'

basis and this may be useful in expanding your answer to a question on a particular culture.

The four 'study areas' in each case are:

i)   Historical and cultural background
ii) PE and sport in high schools and colleges/universities
iii) Professional (élite) sport
iv) Recreational

1. Historical and cultural background

Fact:
Sport and recreation reflect the society and culture in which they exist.

Fuller information on these themes can be found in *Advanced PE for Edexcel*, pages 221–223.

Mainstream social values

Ethics present in North American sport
- The Lombardian ethic
- The radical ethic
- The counter-culture ethic

Geographical background of North America
- North America is a huge country with a great diversity in terms of topography and climate.
- It has a large diverse population of over 260 million people.
- It was isolated from the majority of the world in terms of both geography and nineteenth-century political policy.
- It is a largely urban-based population with extensive transport and communication networks.

Mainstream social values
- The 'land of the free' and 'land of opportunity' values are mirrored in both American life and American sport.
- The USA is a meritocracy generating the American dream of rags to riches.
- The USA capitalist economy where the market dominates results in a 'win-at-all-costs' attitude.
- 'Win at all costs' is also referred to as the 'win ethic' and the 'Lombardian ethic'.

- The pioneer spirit of early American settlers is still evident in the 'frontier spirit', also linked with a need to escape the urban lifestyle.

Ethics present in North American Sport
- The win at all costs attitude is clearly evident throughout American sport.
- The frontier spirit is reflected in the philosophy that the toughest survive.
- This philosophy is also reflected in the names of American sports team names, e.g. 'the bears', 'the pioneers', 'the braves'.
- The most significant instrument of change was the newly emerging urban middle class.
- The middle class assumed responsibility for the moral/social welfare of their communities.

2. Physical Education and sport in high schools and colleges/universities

Fact:
Sport is more important than physical education in most US educational institutions.

Fuller information on these themes can be found in *Advanced PE for Edexcel*, pages 223–227.

State high schools play an important role as melting pots in such a diverse culture. Schools and colleges act as sport nurseries for professional and Olympic sports, with all such sport being funded and organised in a professional way.

Historical development of physical education

 points

- There was an early development in gymnastics, with a strong German influence, following developments in Europe.
- By 1885, public (state) school provision had begun to expand, with a growing interest in games.
- By the beginning of the twentieth century, high school and college sports stars had become established.

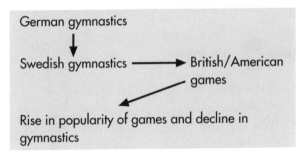

Gymnastics declined in favour of British then American games

Sport in high schools

- Sport has a greater status than physical education in terms of provision, funding and staffing.
- Many high school games take place in front of large crowds, deriving considerable revenue and kudos for their establishment.
- Both physical education and sport are controlled by the Athletic Department in each school, mirroring the decentralised nature of North American sport.
- Coaches instead of teachers are employed with the clear intention of creating winning teams.
- Coaches are required to teach a minimum number of classes in order to satisfy regulations and are also required to hold coaching qualifications, recognised by the state in which they work.

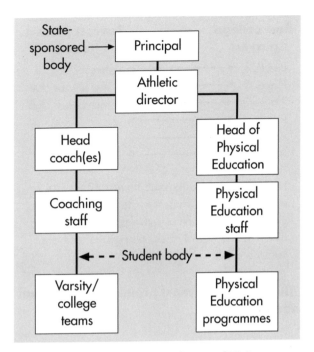

The simplified structure of sport/PE in American high schools

Sport in higher education

College sport is run in 'divisions', with the number of scholarships and players limited according to status.

- Top division colleges are allowed more scholarships than others.
- The 'bridge' between collegiate and professional sport is the 'draft system'.
- Every college game is recorded and analysed.
- The top players go into the draft (see 'The draft pick' below).
- College sport attracts large amounts of funding from both commercial and media interests.
- The most popular sports such as football and basketball also help fund other 'amateur' sports.
- The National Collegiate Athletic Association (NCAA) division one games attract audiences on a par with division one football in the UK.

Best college players	Lowest placed teams
Player 1 ◄——————►	Lowest club
Player 2 ◄——————►	Next lowest club
Player 3 ◄——————►	Next lowest club
Player 4 ◄——————►	Etc.
Player 5 ◄——————►	Etc.
Player 6 ◄——————►	Etc.

Players must go to the club to which they are drafted. However, clubs may negotiate with other clubs who have been assigned players they would like. The number of clubs/players varies from sport to sport.

'The draft pick': most prominent in football and basketball

The sports scholarship system

 **points**

- Scholarships exist in a number of academic subject areas, but those awarded to sportsmen and women attract by far the greatest attention both in the USA and abroad.

- Prior to 1990, US athletes were allowed to remain amateur but received funding and support, which allowed them to train and compete as virtually full-time athletes.

- Colleges and universities now act as the nurseries for both professional and Olympic sports.

- Every university and college has a huge sports programme and excellent facilities for élite performers.

- These would be classed as sports institutes in Europe and effectively fulfil pretty much the same function.

- the Title IX (sexual equality) amendments of 1972 laid down rights of access to sport for women and girls on an equal basis to men. A significant increase in the number of women's athletic scholarships followed almost immediately.

- The race relations legislation of the 1960s had also paved the way for fairer access to sports scholarships for athletes from racial minority groups.

3. Professional (élite) sport

Fact:
In US sport at all levels, the winner really does take all.

 Fuller information on these themes can be found in *Advanced PE for Edexcel*, pages 227–229.

 **points**

- The private sector dominates sports funding.

- The 'big four' sports – basketball, baseball, (grid-iron) football, (ice) hockey – dominate the North American sporting scene.

- Most sports are based on a conference/'Superbowl'-type structure.

- Top athletes make as much (and sometime more) money from commercial sponsorship and endorsement as they do from competition.

The history of professional sport

 **points**

- Baseball and boxing were amongst the earliest professional sports in the USA, but they never became leading 'college' sports.

- The lack of an amateur ethic and tradition meant that sport quickly assimilated the meritocratic philosophy (winning) that was already evident in North American culture.

- Both football and basketball developed from being purely college sports into modern TV sports in the 1960s.

- Technology has allowed ice hockey to spread from its original heartland in the north.

Structure of professional sport

- Sport in the USA is administered by a number of decentralised autonomous governing bodies with little interference (or support) from state or federal governments.
- The big four professional sports run on a franchise system.
- The overriding aim is profit!
- All attract considerable public support and commercial backing sport relies on the private sector – for example:
  - gate receipts
  - media fees
  - commercial sponsorship.
- Team nicknames are an important part of a team's merchandising.
- The other key player in US sport is the media. US TV companies pay huge amounts of money to buy the exclusive rights to both US and global games.

NB It should be noted that one of the few areas to receive direct federal funding is that of Olympic preparation and competition.

The status of professional sport

 **points**

- North American sports are the most technically advanced in world.

- North American sports stars are the richest in the world.
- The public is sports-mad; sport creates huge audiences.
- North America has world champions in a number of sports, although many only allow North American cities to compete and are not really 'world sports'.
- Americanisation is spreading throughout global sport.

4. Recreational sport (mass participation)

Fact:
Americans identify much more readily with 'winning' than they do with simply 'taking part'.

 Fuller information on these themes can be found in *Advanced PE for Edexcel*, pages 229–231.

Sport in North American society

 **points**

- There is a wide base to the participation pyramid, with 'little league' and school sport being very popular.
- Participation continues with intra-mural sport at high school and college.
- There is limited post-school opportunity for sports participation – a large post-school gap.
- Lifetime sports programmes offer some access to older Americans.

The role of sporting participation in North American society

- North America has not developed a sports club system like that of the UK.

- The main cultural/media focus is on professional and competitive sport.

- Private sector dominance produces little funding/opportunity for grass-roots recreational sport.

- Spectatorism (both armchair and live) has largely replaced participation.

Community participation

 **points**

- During the nineteenth century, groups such as the YMCA developed the concept that sport was a healthy, respectable activity.

- Basketball and volleyball were invented by the YMCA as a form of social control for inner city youth: this is mirrored in the 'Midnight Basketball Leagues' of more recent years.

- A recent rise in lifetime sports programmes has allowed some older Americans access to sport through Golden Olympic programmes.

- There is, however, a strong emphasis on competition, rather than recreation for health and well-being.

Did you know?

Basketball and volleyball were deliberately developed as non-contact sports.

Junior sport

 **points**

- 'Little league' sport forms the foundation of most American sports.

- Examples include:
  - 'Pop Warner football'
  - 'Biddy basketball'
  - 'Pee-wee baseball'.

- Teams are run by parents.

- Kids compete in structured competitions that mirror professional games. 'Superbowl' is the conclusion.

- These competitions attract both commercial and media attention.

- A criticism is that this approach again reinforces the win ethic.

- The counter-argument is that this reinforces in young children the 'American way of life'.

- The slogan 'Little league to Superbowl' was recently replaced with 'Little League to White House', after President Bush revealed that many of his leadership skills were developed in 'Pee-wee baseball'.

Did you know?

Parents involved in Little League sport are often accused of living out their own sporting dreams through their children.

National Parks, alternative and wilderness sports

 **points**

- The early National Parks were created on the sites of former battlefields or in areas of remote wilderness and were thus relatively easy to acquire for the nation.

- This allows urban Americans to escape into the natural environment and relive the 'frontier spirit'.

- National Parks now include a wide range of America's natural scenery, wilderness areas and historic monuments.

- National Parks are under federal control.

- State and local parks are administered separately by appropriate state or municipal authorities.

- Alternative and wilderness sports as an expression of a recreational counter-culture have enjoyed a huge surge in popularity during the last few decades.

- The wide range and ease of access to the outdoors, coupled with the tradition of the 'pioneer spirit' makes outdoor sports popular amongst all ages.
- Media coverage and a growing fashion/music cult has added to the popularity of sports such as snowboarding and surfing.

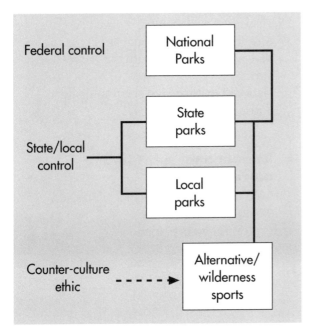

How the structure of alternative/wilderness sports developed

Section A(2): New world cultures: Australia, New Zealand and South Africa

Overview

1. Historical and cultural background

- Colonial historical development and the development of new identities and values
- State and federal policies in relation to games and sport
- Environmental factors
- Topography

2. Physical education and sport in high schools and colleges/universities

- Sport and PE in high schools including sport education
- Extra curricular sport in high schools and in higher education
- University sport

3. Professional (élite) sport

- Historical background
- Structure of professional sport
- The media and the status of professional sport
- National institutes of sport and sport academies

4. Recreational sport (mass participation)

- Role of sporting participation in New World cultures
- Community participation

1. Cultural background

Fuller information on these themes can be found in *Advanced PE for Edexcel*, pages 232–236.

Colonial historical development and the development of new identities and values
- New identities and values
- Sport as a vehicle for nation-building

State and federal policies in relation to games and sport
- Australia
- New Zealand
- South Africa

Environmental factors

Topography

Geographical background of Australia, New Zealand and South Africa
- All three countries have a great diversity of topography and climate.
- The countries have relatively small populations with space for recreation.
- The countries are all situated in the southern hemisphere, so sport is an important form of communication/link with Europe/Asia.
- The countries are largely urban-based populations with extensive transport and communication networks.

Colonial historical development and the development of new identities and values

- The historical development of these three countries is steeped in colonial values, but with the assimilation of new culture and identities.
- Colonial infrastructure included most cultural institutions – including sport and education.
- Sport was an aspect of the 'cultural power' through which the British Empire imposed itself.
- Sports were adapted to fit the new cultural image.
- Adoption of 'Kiwi' and 'Springbok' identities were seen as acceptable in the context of sporting challenge.
- Sport was a vehicle for nation-building. Playing the games of their colonial masters enabled these new communities to demonstrate both loyalty and a measure of cultural maturity.

State and federal policies in relation to games and sports

- Governments in all three countries have embraced the value of sports and games and recognised the benefits of success.
- Australia has developed its policies within a two-tier federal structure with implementation at national and state levels.
- In South Africa it is only very recently that policies have been implemented that begin to embrace the needs of its population.
- South Africa has always seen sport as an expression of its identity but until very recently this included only its white minority.

Did you know?
Apartheid was the political system in South Africa whereby the black and Asian populations were completely segregated from the white population.

Environmental factors

- All three cultures have large areas of natural beauty and wildlife.
- All have developed a national pride in the 'outback' or 'the bush'.

93

- Wilderness sports are popular due to heritage and ease of access
- Large open spaces and clean, free natural resources are a major factor in improving participation rates in Australia and New Zealand.

Topography

Australia has by far the largest landmass of the three countries, although much of it is both uninhabitable and unsuitable for most sporting and recreational purposes. In all cases, though, both terrain and climate offer a wide choice of settings for most sporting activities.

Demographical facts about Australia, New Zealand and South Africa

Country	Facts
New Zealand	• By far the smallest of the three countries, with a land area similar to that of the UK • It also has the smallest population (approximately 4 million) – making its sporting achievements in global games all the more remarkable
Australia	• Has a population of just over 18 million • Gains remarkable sporting success per head of its population
South Africa	• Has the largest population, with a little over 43 million people • Until recently, access to élite sport has until recently been restricted to a small, privileged white minority

Did you know?
Demography is the study of population structure.

2. Physical education and sport in high schools and colleges/ universities

Fuller information on these themes can be found in *Advanced PE for Edexcel*, pages 236–239.

Sport and PE in high schools including sport education
- New Zealand
- Australia
- South Africa

Extra curricular sport in high schools and in higher education
- Australian school sport
- New Zealand school sport
- South Africa

University sport

 **Key points**

- Many early schools were modelled on the same principles that were promoted in Britain's public schools.
- Many characteristics of athleticism are still present in New World schools.
- Current levels of provision in South Africa are some way behind those in Australia and New Zealand.

Sport and PE in high schools, including sport education
New Zealand
- Health and Physical Education is compulsory for all students up to the age of 15.
- The programme is centred on the Maori word 'hauora' (sense of well-being) and reflects the inclusion of the indigenous Maori culture.

- Programmes includes Sport studies, and involves topics such as sportsmanship and the place of sport in society.

Australia

- In Australia, the State of Victoria led the way with the Physical and Sport Education programme (PASE).
- This was followed by the federally-funded 'Sport Education in Physical Education Programmes' (SEPEP).
- There is a commitment to both PE and sport education as a compulsory element in school curricula and a move to develop daily PE in primary schools.

South Africa

- Early influence on development of physical education in South Africa was the work of Ernst Franz Jokl, who formed the National Advisory Council on Physical Education.
- Jokl compiled the first 'Syllabus for South African Schools' in 1940, based initially on the British system but also on Danish gymnastics.
- There is a huge discrepancy in both scope and provision between predominately white independent schools and state schools.
- Many schools in the former black 'townships' have little or no provision for physical education.

Extra curricular sport in high schools and in higher education

Australian school sport

- School sport in Australia reflects colonial influences with games afternoons and school colours.
- The Australian School Sports Council acts as federal co-ordinating body for school sport.
- Each state has a department of school sport and full-time officials administer school sport.
- There is a close association with federally run and funded programmes such as Active Australia.

New Zealand school sport

- School sport plays a significant part as an extension of physical education programmes and as preparation for sporting and recreational life after school.
- Influenced by British colonial values, sport began in the country's private education system, as in both Australia and South Africa.
- The New Zealand Secondary Schools Sports Council co-ordinates school sport.
- Its regional structure helps to promote such initiatives as 'Sportfit', with regional directors also acting in a promotional capacity, encouraging New Zealand's youngsters to become and stay active.

South Africa

- Sport in South Africa's mainstream schools is still developing since the rebirth of the Rainbow Nation.
- School sports facilities of any substance were formerly only to be found in private (white) schools.
- The United School Sports Association of South Africa (USSASA) was formed in 1994 and now co-ordinates schools sport across the country.
- There is a developing philosophy that traditional white schools should share their facilities with nearby black schools. However, even many white (state) schools have only limited facilities.
- Programmes sponsored by SANGALA (South African National Games and Leisure Activities) are now facilitating sporting opportunity in township communities.

University sport

- Universities in all three countries are affiliated to FISU (International Federation of University Sport).
- All Australia's thirty-seven universities belong to Australian University Sport, which organises over forty sports with an annual University Games.
- University sport in both South Africa and New Zealand is organised in a similar

manner with national championships and participation in major Universiades. The most recent development occurred with the formation of the South African Student Sports Union (SASSU) in 1994.

Extra mural and intercollegiate sport in Australia, New Zealand and South Africa

- This still runs on a British model, with emphasis on participation.

- However, elements of a 'win' ethic are developing due to 'global' influences.

- There is greater commitment to sport from both state and school/college authorities than in UK.

- Most competition is based around the (American) conference system, with the winner progressing to regional, then national, play-offs.

- The focus is often on a day of sport with younger/lower-grade teams playing first with a final match involving the first team.

---

3. Professional (élite) sport

Fuller information on these themes can be found in *Advanced PE for Edexcel*, pages 239–243.

Historical background

Structure of professional sport

The media and the status of professional sport

National institutes of sport and sport academies
- Australia
- State institutes of sport
- New Zealand
- The Hillary Commission
- South Africa

Key points

The British club structure of professional sport is now being replaced by an American-style commercial focus, with franchises and media control. This is mirrored in a change in Olympic sport from amateur to state-sponsored professionalism.

Historical background

- The history of professional sport in all three countries has the same colonial roots and similar patterns of development – playing 'test matches' against each other, as well as against teams from Britain. Key examples of this are in:
  - rugby (both codes)
  - cricket
  - tennis.

- Australian Rules football, centred in Victoria, is unique in that it is one of few New World sports to be fashioned out of the games of the 'colonial masters', but as a direct challenge to their control.

- Historically, there has been an earlier move towards professionalism in New World cultures – for example in sports such as:
  - cricket
  - rugby league
  - Australian Rules football.

- This is because there are fewer traditional constraints than in the UK.

- Professional sports suited the largely urban populations and entrepreneurs, especially publicans, quickly saw the commercial possibilities.

- Even amateur sports such as Rugby Union were subject to allegations of under-the-counter payments and 'boot money'. This influenced the International Rugby Board to allow open status in the mid 1990s.

- In the last decade there has been a move towards economic rationality in professional sport, and the influence of 'Americanisation' can be seen in the funding and marketing of professional sports.

- This includes a rise in importance of the media, with tycoons such as Kerry Packer and Rupert Murdoch bringing their business expertise and financial 'clout' into sport. Key examples of this are:
  - 'Super 12's' and 'Superleague' in rugby
  - the re-branding of Australian Rules football as the AFL.
- In all three countries, the professional sports star now has a status rivalling that of pop stars and movie stars. Sports people now attract huge fees for advertising and commercial ventures.

> **Did you know?**
> Open status allows both amateur and professionals to compete together, thus abolishing the difference between them.

Structure of professional sport

Professional sports tend to be administered by a system of British-style governing bodies, operating through American-style franchise agreements. Olympic sport is an exception, with increasing state input in terms of both funding and control in all three New World cultures.

In all three countries, media influences and global developments are influencing the shape of sport.

The media and the status of professional sport

- There are strong links between the media and sport in New World cultures.
- Media interests play a major role in promotion and funding of sport.
- Sport accounts for 15 per cent of TV time in Australia.
- Media coverage brings sponsorship and advertising to sport – the Sports Golden Triangle.

> **Did you know?**
> The Sports Golden Triangle is the association between sports events, sponsorship and the media.

National institutes of sport and sport academies

Australia

- Dismal performance at the 1976 Montreal Olympics led to a major review of sports structure and, following a comparative study, led to the creation of the Australian Institute of Sport (AIS).
- This was set up by the federal government in 1981 to provide the expertise and back-up necessary to produce champions.
- It was soon realised that a broader base of participation was needed at the grass-roots level and the control of sport at all levels passed into the hands of the newly formed Australian Sports Commission (ASC) in 1989.

Australian Sports Commission (ASC)
|
Australian Institute of Sport (AIS)
(Canberra)
|
Australian Coaching Council (ACC)
National sports organisations (NSOs)
Sportsearch (talent programme)

AIS satellite sites   State sport institutes

Australia: a structure for sporting excellence

State institutes of sport

- A second level of excellence provision exists at state level.
- State institutes of sport are funded by state governments and local/state sponsorship.
- This includes state lotteries (for logistical reasons 'state' and 'national' institutes often share the same sites, although each exists as an independent entity).

- Each state sports institute has a policy developed by its own administration providing programmes of excellence in activities considered to be key sports in that state.
- A key example would be the Victorian Institute of Sport (VIS).

> **Did you know?**
> The Australian Sports Commission (ASC) is the government's sporting arm. It controls policy and funding for all aspects of sport, including managing the AIS.

New Zealand

- The principal body is the New Zealand Sports Foundation (NZSF), created in 1978.
- It is a private organisation, but government funded, via the Hillary Commission.
- Its focus is 'the pursuit of excellence' and 'to assist athletes to succeed at international level and, by so doing, bring credit to themselves, their sport and New Zealand'.

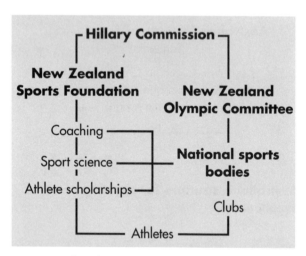

New Zealand sport: a structure for excellence

The Hillary Commission

- The Hillary Commission for Sport, Fitness and Leisure was established by an Act of Parliament (1987).
- Its role includes more than sports excellence, but, as the government's 'arm of sport', it does influence that area.

- The Commission and the NZSF perform a similar twin role as the ASC and the AIS in Australia.

South Africa

The Department of Sport and Recreation had overall responsibility for sports policy and for the provision and delivery of sport and recreation until 1988 when it and the National Sports Council were merged to form the South African Sports Commission (SASC).

The responsibilities of SASC include:

- the promotion of sport and recreation through the National Sports Council (NSC), the National Olympic Committee of South Africa (NOCSA) and the national sports federations
- funding the above-mentioned agencies
- the upgrading of facilities for national and international events.

South African sport: a structure for excellence

A special programme has been set up for the development of life skills. This programme:

- is intended to provide assistance to top athletes in dealing with success or failure
- includes media skills, financial management, interpersonal skills and mental training.

Another special high-performance sport programme focuses on:

- raising the profile of South African élite sport

- assisting in greater success for individuals and South African teams
- promoting broader representation and entering into meaningful agreements with other countries at government level.

The 'sports ambassadors' programme identifies high-profile athletes who each convey a message of nation-building to all South Africans. The Department of Sport and Recreation has also set itself the following targets, which have been assumed by the SASC:

- increasing levels of participation in sport and recreation activities
- raising sport's profile in the face of conflicting priorities
- maximising the probability of success in major events
- placing sport and recreation in the forefront of efforts to reduce crime levels.

4. Recreational sport (mass participation)

Fuller information on these themes can be found in *Advanced PE for Edexcel*, pages 243–246.

Role of sporting participation in New World cultures
- Australia
- New Zealand
- South Africa

Community participation
- Australia
- New Zealand
- South Africa
- SANREC
- National parks
- Adventure and wilderness sports

Role of sporting participation in New World cultures

- Each of the cultures under review has strong traditions of sports participation as part of a healthy outdoor life.

- In the case of South Africa, until recently opportunities have been largely limited to white minority groups.
- Post-Apartheid reforms include proposals to redress this situation.
- Policies of inclusion have traditionally been the case in New Zealand, with access for the Maori people written into the country's constitution.

Australia
- According to census data, 90 per cent of Australians participate in sport.
- Environmental and cultural factors facilitate access to recreation.
- Strong state commitment recognises the benefits of mass participation.
- Government involvement in recreational programmes is delivered through the ASC and its Active Australia programme.
- Legislation including indigenous Aborigine groups has only relatively recently been enacted – and is (unofficially) resisted in some areas.

Did you know?
Active Australia is an extension of the former Aussie Sport. Its slogan 'From Six to Sixty' is a clear message that everyone should be actively involved in recreation of some kind.

New Zealand
- The Hillary Commission is the government's recreational arm.
- Key programmes include Sportfit and Push Play.
- They are designed to maximise participation in recreation.
- Programmes such as Young People First, supported by the Hillary Commission's Community Sport Fund, offer assistance to clubs and organisations making provision for young people.
- The New Zealand fitness industry runs a Fitness New Zealand programme, designed to ensure that everyone is aware of their nearest fitness centre.

Community sport funding in New Zealand

South Africa

- The South African National Games and Leisure Activities project (SANGALA) was launched in 1996.
- It aims to involve all South Africans in healthy recreational activities.
- Provincial governments are responsible for local implementation of national sport/recreation policy.
- The SANGALA project consists of:
  - Community SANGALA – targeted at the broad community irrespective of age or status
  - Training SANGALA – specialising in the training of community recreation leaders
  - Corporate SANGALA – aimed at middle and senior management in both private and public sectors
  - Senior SANGALA – encouraging physical activity amongst senior citizens
  - Street SANGALA – a life-skills project for homeless children.
  - Movers-in-Action – aimed at developing small and large motor skills in three- to six-year olds.

Community participation
Australia
- 'Little League' sports – another indication of patterns of the 'Americanisation' of New World sport – have grown in the last two decades.
- These 'mini-sports' are based on a US format, with the emphasis on introducing children to competitive sport and sporting skills at an early age.
- Most sports played in New World countries now have a 'mini-version' – for example:
  - Mini/Walla Rugby
  - Netta Netball
  - Auskick.
- All Australia's states and territories have departments of Aboriginal affairs. These include programmes of recreational activity designed to incorporate Aboriginal culture into such activity.
- The Moneghetti Report (1993) identified low level of healthy exercise amongst young people.
- Aussie Sport and Active Australia programmes recognised a need to raise the level of activity involvement of all Australians.

New Zealand
- In New Zealand, the tradition of healthy outdoor life is allied closely with its farming culture.
- Rugby, cricket and athletics clubs form the mainstays of sporting and community life.
- Development of city life has caused alarms in terms of general levels of activity.
- Push Play, 30 minutes and Sportfit programmes have been promoted by the Hillary Commission in the same way as Active Australia is promoted by the ASC.

South Africa
- In South Africa post-Apartheid reforms have seen major infrastructure changes.
- Soccer is the sport of the masses, with a strong Township base.
- White minority groups still have better facilities and far greater representation in national teams.
- It is now likely that in time such imbalances will be redressed.
- SANREC was created in 1997, and is responsible for developing community recreational programmes, facilities and training and research.
- It has a network of nine Provincial Recreation

Committees (PRORECS), which administer its programmes within each province.

National parks/Adventure and wilderness sports: New Zealand

- There are fourteen national parks, controlled by the Department of Conservation.
- There is clear protection of Maori rights and culture within this framework.
- Recent additions to the Treaty of Waitangi ensures that these rights are not violated.

National parks/Adventure and wilderness sports: Australia

- There is a mix of both federal and state parks in Australia
- They embrace a wide range of environments and two world heritage sites (the Kakadu Rain Forest and Great Barrier Reef).
- Sites such as Ulhuru (Ayres Rock) attract large numbers of domestic and international tourists.

National parks/Adventure and wilderness sports: South Africa

- There are 53 national parks or protected areas, including the world famous Kruger National Park.
- They attract both domestic and international tourists.
- This raises issues of conservation/land use.
- Current policies centre upon conservation as opposed to recreation.

Did you know?

The range and ease of access to outdoor environments coupled with the tradition of a pioneer spirit makes outdoor sport popular amongst all age groups in New World countries.

Did you know?

Recent media coverage and the growth of an associated fashion/music cult has added to the popularity of sports such as snow/skate-boarding and surfing.

Do you know about...?

1. The mainstream social values present in New World cultures?
2. The factors in the history of new cultures that led to the development of their major sports?
3. The role sport plays in the status of indigenous population?
4. The role sport played in the development of these New World cultures in the twentieth century?
5. How and why sport has been used as a vehicle for national building?
6. How the environmental factors in New World cultures can affect participation in sport?
7. The concept of the Bush ethos and how it is evident in New World cultures?
8. How the education system reflects the history of New World cultures?
9. Why extra-curricular sport is so important to New World high schools?
10. The sports institute system and its role in Olympic preparation?
11. Historical, geographical and other factors that contributed to the growth of outdoor recreation?
12. The role of the media in New World sport?
13. How the concept of Little League is reproduced in New World cultures?
14. Why participation in sport and recreation is so high in New World cultures?

Exam tips

Make sure the you fully understand:

- the compromise between centralised and decentralised systems
- the compromise between traditional British sports system and new model of Americanisation
- the importance of global success through sport
- the role of the state in funding and organising sport.

Section A(3): Developing cultures: with reference to Argentina and Kenya

Overview

1. Historical and cultural background
- Argentina
- Kenya
- Native indigenous population
- Culture and sport
- State policies in relation to games and sports
- Sport as foreign policy
- Nation building
- Environmental and topographical factors

2. Physical education and sport in high schools and colleges/universities
- Historical development of physical education
- School sport
- Physical education in high schools
- University sport

3. Professional (élite) sport
- History of professional sport
- The structure of professional sport
- The commercial nature of professional sport
- Role of armed forces as sports nurseries
- Disproportionate selectivity in sports played
- Move to West of players and coaches

4. Recreational sport (mass participation)
- Sporting participation in developing cultures

1. Historical and cultural background

Fuller information on these themes can be found in *Advanced PE for Edexcel*, pages 247–252.

Argentina

Kenya

Native indigenous population
* Argentina
* Kenya

Culture and sport
* Argentina
* Kenya

State policies in relation to games and sports
* Argentina
* Kenya

Sport as foreign policy

Nation building

Environmental and topographical factors
* National parks: Argentina
* National parks: Kenya

Geographical background of Argentina and Kenya
* Argentina and Kenya are both large countries with a great diversity of topography and climate.
* They have relatively small populations with space for recreation.
* Colonial links introduced sport to both cultures, though selectivity has occurred.
* There is a mix of urban and rural-based populations with developing transport and communication networks.

Argentina
* Europeans first occupied Argentina in the early sixteenth century and the Spanish established a permanent colony on the site of the present Buenos Aires.
* Formal declaration of independence from Spain was made in 1816 after periods of civil strife.
* Argentina established limited national unity and adopted a constitution in 1853.
* There has been a high degree of military influence in both day-to-day and long-term politics – including sport.

Kenya
* Britain and France became interested in East Africa in the second half of the nineteenth century when they were attempting to control the trade routes to India and Asia.
* The development of trade with the major European powers and the opening of trade routes meant most of major towns grew up along the developing railway built to transport goods.
* British (and European) influences were instrumental in the shaping of many areas of life, including that of education and sport.
* Missionary schools formed the backbone of early education eagerly adopting the British public school philosophies of 'muscular' Christianity and athleticism.
* 'British' culture became the norm in influential circles until the Mao-Mao terrorist unrest.
* The subsequent Lancaster Agreement brought colonial life to and end in the mid-1960s.

Native indigenous population
Argentina
About 85 percent of Argentina's population is of European origin and the country has relatively few mestizos (indigenous Indian population) – unlike most other Latin/American countries (see 'Culture and sport' on page 110).

> **Did you know?**
> Argentina's population has a native minority. The opposite applies in Kenya.

> **Did you know?**
> Soccer was introduced to Argentina by William Watson Hutton, a Scotsman.

Kenya

- The indigenous population of Kenya has been broadened over centuries but is still influenced by tribal groups and cultures, such as:
  - hunter/gatherers (the oldest population group)
  - Cushites
  - Nilotes
  - Bantus
  - Kalenjin.
- The only large population centres are Nairobi (1.4 million) and Mombassa (1 million).
- Only around 25 per cent of the country's population live in an urban environment.

Culture and sport

 **points**

Argentina

- English or British influence in the development of sport in Argentina may well have begun in the early 1800s.
- Early games of cricket and football were also played, largely by British expatriate teams.
- Hockey became popular amongst Argentines in the early years of the twentieth century with the first team coming from San Martín Athletic Club in 1905.
- British influence was again evident in the establishment of that most 'Argentinian' of sports – polo.
- Rugby union was another colonial legacy. The first known game was played in 1873 between 'Banks' and 'City', suggesting a distinct middle class connection. It has now gained world recognition.

Kenya

- Although running has the limelight, a range of other sports are played in Kenya.
- Kenya's cricketers now compete in that sport's world cup tournament.
- The national football team successfully qualified for the second round of the 1998 World Cup, and soccer is by far the most popular sport both in terms of attendance and participation levels.
- Rugby is growing in popularity and the annual Safari and Paris–Dakar rally motoring events draw both enthusiasts and tourists to Kenya each year.
- Basketball is probably Kenya's fastest growing sport.
- The seeds of the country's sports were sown by the early colonists and many of them date from just after the beginning of the twentieth century.
- The emergence of a host of middle- and long-distance runners in the 1970s is a more recent and key sporting development.

State policies in relation to games and sports

 **points**

Argentina

- The Peronist administration developed and supported sport in Argentina as a means of re-building national pride.
- More recent policies recognise that social and economic benefits can be gained in the promotion and provision of sport at all levels.
- Although centralised infrastructure is now in place, severe economic difficulties inhibit effective implementation.

Did you know?
Argentina and Kenya are among the world's poorest economies.

Kenya

- Until the 1960s, Kenya's sporting policies reflected the needs of its colonial masters rather than its indigenous population.
- Independence coincided with the emergence of élite distance runners and limited investment in infrastructure.
- The Ministry of Home Affairs, Heritage and Sports oversees the control of sport, but this is only part of its huge area of responsibility.
- Kenya's lack of economic resources inhibits the support of a more sophisticated infrastructure.
- The Kenyan National Olympic Committee (NOCK) is an entirely independent organisation that promotes Olympism as well as the broader concept of amateur sport.

Sport as foreign policy/Nation building

Both countries have the following in common.

- Sport is an important aspect of foreign policy.
- Sport is also seen as an important element of nation-building.
- Sporting success is important as a political/economic shop window.

Key examples for Argentina include:

- football
- polo
- rugby union.

Key examples for Kenya include:

- middle-/long-distance running
- increasingly, soccer, basketball and cricket.

Did you know?
The term 'shop window' refers to sport being used to show off a country.

In each case:

- success brings in foreign currency, attracts multi-national investment and brings global exposure
- élite athletes in both countries act as important role models
- sport can also be used as an important tool of social integration and health promotion.

Environmental and topographical factors

Country	Land area (sq km)	Population
Argentina	2.8 million	36.3 million
Kenya	0.6 million	28.1 million

Land area/population of Argentina and Kenya

(See also Argentina and Kenya: Comparative topography and demography on page 112).

Did you know?
Demography is the study of a society's population structure.

National parks: Argentina

- Argentina has eleven major areas designated as national parks offering a wide range of outdoor activities in a variety of environments.
- Because the majority of the population live in an urban environment, only the more affluent can afford to visit these areas.

National parks: Kenya

- Kenya has forty-three national parks including the world famous Masai Mara National Park, amounting to a considerable proportion of the country's land area.
- Kenya's national parks are both wildlife and botanical sanctuaries, and have been set aside for the purposes of conservation, education and recreational.

Country	Topography	Demography
Argentina	• Varied topography, including mountains, plains, rivers and a sea coast • Is larger than Kenya	• The fact that more than one-third of the population live in or around Buenos Aires is a significant factor • 85 per cent of the population live in other urban areas • This means that team games prosper in heavily-populated communities • It also means that those limited sports facilities that do exist are accessible to a higher proportion of the population than is the case in Kenya
Kenya	• Has diverse physical features including arid and semi-arid lands, a coastal belt, and a basin around Lake Victoria • The Great Rift Valley splits the country in two and Kenya has the second highest snow-capped mountain (Mount Kenya – 5,199 metres) in Africa • The country has both 'short' and 'long' rainy seasons, which have implication for both agriculture and lifestyle	• Unlike Argentina, less than 1 per cent of Kenya's population are of non-indigenous extraction • The vast majority of people (85 per cent) live in rural surroundings (isolated villages) • There are implications here for access to sport and recreation facilities – particularly in a desperately poor economy lacking a sophisticated communications network

Argentina and Kenya: comparative topography and demography

2. Physical education and sport in high schools and colleges/ universities

Fact:
State provision for physical education and sport is limited because of economic hardship.

Fuller information on these themes can be found in *Advanced PE for Edexcel*, pages 252–256.

Historical development of physical education
• Argentina
• Kenya

School sport
• Argentina
• Kenya

Physical education in high schools
• Argentina
• Kenya

University sport

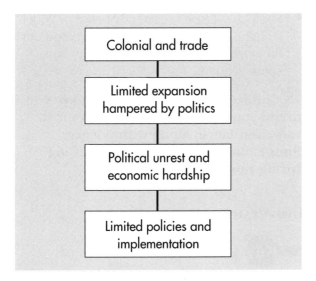

Historical influences of physical education in Argentina and Kenya

Historical development of physical education

Argentina

- Early forms of physical education developed within the private sector, funded by 'European' commercial interests.
- Although Argentina was never a British colony, the pattern of development was effectively the same – with industry and commerce acting as the 'colonising influences'.
- There was an emphasis on 'English' models of games, drill and 'PT'.
- National provision for physical education is very recent (1995).

Kenya

- Formal education in Kenya has much in common with other former colonies, this being the result of nineteenth-century missionary/colonial influences.
- Physical education was based on the English model of muscular Christian philosophy.
- Private/colonial schools offer superior resources, including playing fields and sometimes gymnasia.

School sport

Argentina

- In private schools, organisations such as Asociación Deportiva Estudjantil (ADE) organise sport.
- There is less provision in state schools, other than in the province of Buenos Aires.
- Children play in junior teams organised by local sports clubs.

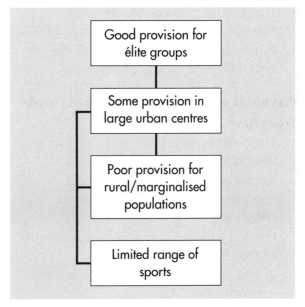

School sport in emergent cultures

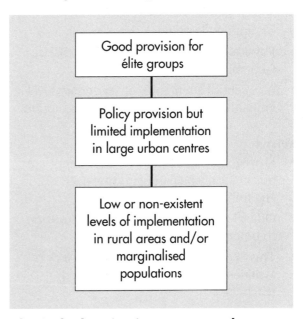

Physical education in emergent cultures

Kenya

- School sport is administered through the 55 school regions.
- There are district and national championships in sports such as:
    - athletics
    - soccer
    - cricket
    - netball.
- The National Schools Athletic Championships was inaugurated in 1967.
- Participation is limited because of the extremely high rural population.

Physical education in high schools

Argentina

- The National Institute of Physical Education was created in 1985.
- Its task was to co-ordinate physical education courses and train physical educators.
- Physical education programmes are centred around four learning blocks:
    - the body and its movements utilising gymnastics
    - bodily health and well-being
    - motor games and the use of 'play'
    - applied learning.
- Physical education is part of EGB (Basic General Education).
- Low school attendance at secondary level limits the effectiveness of this programme.

Kenya

- Provision of sports and PE equipment are borne locally by parents (known as Harambee).
- Official policy requires physical education to be taught in state schools.
- This is not widely adopted due to lack of facilities and/or adequately qualified teachers.

- Some assistance is currently being provided by the Commonwealth Sport Development Program in the training of teachers and sports leaders.

NB Children in Kenya still have to pay to attend state schools – a major factor in non-attendance, along with poverty, famine and the difficulty of travelling during rainy seasons.

University sport

 **points**

- Both countries are affiliated to FISA, the world student sport organisation:
    - Argentina through the Conito Tecnico del Deporte Universitario Argentino
    - Kenya through the Kenya University Sports Association.
- In both countries, university sport is nothing like as sophisticated and commercialised as in the USA.
- Many Kenyan students take part in university sport in South Africa and the USA – largely because of basketball or athletic scholarships.
- Argentine students also take up athletic scholarships in the USA – predominantly in basketball and soccer.

3. Professional (élite) sport

Fact:
Professional sport has been established for far longer in Argentina than it has in Kenya.

Fuller information on these themes can be found in *Advanced PE for Edexcel*, pages 256–258.

History of professional sport

The structure of professional sport
- Argentina
- Kenya

The commercial nature of professional sport

Role of armed forces as sports nurseries

Disproportionate selectivity in sports played

Move to West of players and coaches

History of professional sport

 **points**

- The Basque game of pelota was one of the first sports to acquire professional status in Argentina.
- Football became Argentina's leading sport: a Scotsman, Alexander Watson Hutton, is credited with the real expansion of the game.
- Professional sport arrived in Kenya following independence in 1963 and currently includes:
  - athletics
  - basketball
  - cricket
  - rugby
  - soccer.
- Before independence, 'colonial' amateur sporting principles controlled sport in Kenya.

The structure of professional sport

Argentina
- Comite Olimpico Argentino (CAO) and Confederación Atletica de Deportes (CAD) amalgamated during the Peron administration (1945–55) to form the CADCOA, which combined the two aspects of high performance sport.
- In 1989 the Secretaria de Deportes de la Nación (National Secretariat of Sport) was created.
- This organisation co-ordinates community, educational, high performance (including professional) and Olympic sport.
- It also awards scholarships to gifted athletes and organises Olympic preparation and selection.

Kenya
- The Ministry of Home Affairs, Heritage and Sports has overall responsibility for sport.
- Governing bodies of individual sports rely on income from limited commercial involvement.
- Sport at national level is organised by the Kenya National Sports Council (KNSC), which supervises more than 30 individual sporting associations.
- Government sports officers work in all provinces and districts developing sports programmes.
- The Kenya National Sports Institute is situated in Kasarani (Nairobi).

The commercial nature of professional sport

In both cultures the commercial appeal of professional sport and sports people is broadening rapidly. Key examples are:

- distance running, soccer and basketball in Kenya
- Argentina's soccer stars, polo players and rugby players
- the removal of colonial constraint in Kenya and military dictatorship in Argentina, which have allowed professionalism to grow.

Both countries have benefited from increased sporting and non-sporting commercial activity. The media is also important in providing a platform for commercial activity and creating role models.

Commercialisation of sport in Argentina and Kenya

Role of armed forces as sports nurseries

Both countries utilise military organisations as part of a limited sports infrastructure. Military service is often used to enable athletes to pursue virtually full-time training.

Argentina

- Argentina has a tradition of almost complete military control of sport.
- It is able to provide favourable conditions for training and competition.
- Selection favoured élitist officer-class and excluded most other social groups.
- Recent political changes have seen a decline in military control.

Kenya

- In Kenya, military or police service is still considered to be advantageous for sportsmen and women.
- Conscription means that the military acts as an important filter of sporting talent.
- In a desperately poor economy, military establishments can provide scarce sporting facilities.

- Kenya is a member of the International Military Sports Council (CISM) and hosted the First African Military Games in April 2002.

NB CISM has 172 member countries including the UK.

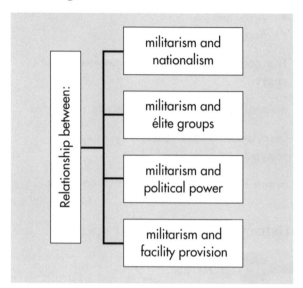

Military influence in sport in Argentina and Kenya

Disproportionate selectivity in sports played

- Both countries face problems of limited resources and infrastructure.
- Limited resources can be maximised by restricting the number of élite sports to be funded.
- This is slightly less of a problem in Argentina, where much longer established professional sports clubs provide some infrastructure for training/coaching young sports people in a number of sports.
- In Kenya, those sports requiring the least capital investment and which utilise natural resources and talent are given priority.

Move to West of players and coaches

Players and coaches from both countries have moved to Europe to further their careers and maximise their earning potential. Key examples include:

- Kenyan athletes, who attend European Grand Prix meetings from which appearance and prize money can be earned
- Kenyan basketball players, who go to the USA on 'Athletic' scholarships, with some now playing professional basketball in Europe and South Africa
- Argentine footballers and coaches, who join teams in European leagues
- Argentine polo players, who are much sought after and attract lucrative fees all around the world.

4. Recreational sport (mass participation)

Fact:

Provision for grass-roots sport is hampered in both Argentina and Kenya by economic hardship.

Fuller information on these themes can be found in *Advanced PE for Edexcel*, pages 258–259.

Sporting participation in developing cultures
- Argentina
- Kenya

Sporting participation in developing cultures

Argentina
- 'Plazas Programme' involves community sports leaders working in the centre of urban communities ('plazas' or civic squares).
- A largely urban population allows reasonable access to the limited facilities available.
- The potential benefits of mass recreation (health, social integration and national defence) are now generally considered to be worthwhile.
- Although the Secretaria de Deportes de la Nación is responsible for Sport for All

Concentration of limited facilities in urban areas

Lack of funding inhibits provision in rural/remote regions

Utilisation of military facilities to augment poor provision

Adoption of recreation for health, defence and nation-building

Common features of sporting participation in developing cultures

policies, there are severe restrictions on levels of implementation due to severe economic hardship.

Kenya
- A largely (85 per cent) rural population makes any meaningful provision even more difficult to achieve.
- Government-funded district sports officers do work in all areas with the brief of developing mass sports programmes, but the main focus appears to be discovering talent.
- Commonwealth Sport Development program offers some assistance in the form of student placements and sports leadership appointments in rural/remote areas.
- Inter-tribal hostility/rivalry inhibits the effectiveness of limited provision.

Do you know about...?
1. How sport fits in with the mainstream social values of developing cultures?
2. How colonial history shaped the emergence of sport in developing cultures?
3. How the governments of developing cultures promote sport and recreation?

Do you know about...?

4. How sport is used by developing cultures as a form of foreign policy?

5. How sport is used in developing cultures as a form of nation building?

6. How environmental and topographical factors can affect access to sport in developing cultures?

7. How the education system reflects the history of developing cultures?

8. The problems developing cultures face in developing school sport programmes?

9. What is meant by the term 'disproportionate selectivity' in relation to sport in developing cultures?

10. The role played by the armed services in promoting sports excellence in developing cultures?

11. Why multi-national companies are so keen to support élite athletes from developing cultures?

12. Why so many élite athletes from developing cultures go West to further their sports careers?

13. The benefits global success can bring to a developing culture?

14. What socio-cultural factors in developing cultures hinder Sport for All programmes?

15. The role sport can play in the promotion of health and defence in developing cultures?

Exam tips

Make sure that you understand about:

- colonial history as a key factor in sports development
- how environmental and topographical factors hinder access to sport for many
- how an emergent culture tends to select a small number of sports that suit environment and tradition
- why global sports success is an important 'shop window' for developing cultures.

Section A(4): Asian cultures

Overview

1. Historical and cultural background
○ Societal values and sport
○ State and federal policies in relation to games and sports
○ Sport as a foreign policy
○ Political factors

2. Physical education and sport in high schools and colleges/universities
○ Development of physical education
○ Sport in high schools including extra-curricular sport
○ Sport in higher education

3. Professional (élite) sport
○ The commercial nature of professional sport
○ The role of company teams
○ The role of the media and the status of professional sport
○ Role of armed forces as sports nurseries
○ The Asian Games

4. Recreational sport (mass participation)
○ Mass participation, social control, integration, health and defence
○ Religious constraints: women and Islamic states

1. Historical and cultural background

 Fuller information on these themes can be found in *Advanced PE for Edexcel*, pages 260–264.

Societal values and sport
- Cricket and the British Empire
- The Christian message

State and federal policies in relation to games and sports

Sport as a foreign policy

Political factors

Geographical background of Asian cultures
- In most Asian countries there is a cultural mix of eastern and western philosophies.
- British and European colonial and trading practices have played a large part in development of sport and recreation.
- There is a large range of topographical and climatic zones.
- There is a mix of urban and rural-based populations with developing transport

---

Societal values and sport
- Asian cultures have a cultural mix of eastern and western philosophies.
- British and European colonial and trading practices have played a significant part in shaping values.

- Much of the indigenous culture is still present in religion, music and the arts.
- Administrative, infrastructure and education systems are based on British models.
- Sport is a little more complex, but again there is a mix of British and indigenous culture.

Cricket and the British Empire
The historical association of the British Empire and much of the Asian sub-continent meant that cricket became a central plank in the development of recreation and sport.

The Christian message
Along with British trade came Christianity in the form of missionary and 'British' schools and organisations such as the YMCA and YWCA.

These Christian organisations played an important role in developing sport in Asian cultures. Key examples include:

- the first ever western-style 'sports meeting' (track and field athletics), which was held at St John's College, Shanghai in 1890
- the North China Games, which were held between 1913 and 1934 with the YMCA playing a major organising role.

Even where colonisation did not occur, the 'colonial model' was applied wherever British interests gained a trading or business foothold.

Did you know?
By 1900, there were over 6,000 'British' clubs, churches and other institutions influencing life (and sport) in China.

Native indigenous populations

- India has many ancient sports, some of which are still practised in the regions in which they originated, e.g. Kabbadi.

- The 'caste system' in India has severely restricted access to some sub-cultural groups – just as the social class system did in the UK.

- China had its own ancient culture, including various forms of physical improvement such as martial arts, games and yangsheng (the art of keeping fit).

- Japan also had its ancient and class-associated recreations and sports. The Samurai warrior class and the Sumo wrestler are two examples of this.

Did you know?

Tai Chi is a Chinese martial art that uses soft, slow movements often linked to meditation.

State and federal policies in relation to games and sports

 **points**

- Most Asian cultures have a centralised system of sports administration.

- Some of these are limited in terms of extent and funding.

- Sport in China is very much under the centralised control of the state.

- This is a very similar model to the former Soviet and Eastern bloc systems.

Did you know?

'Centralisation' means that power and decision-making have a single source – usually the government.

- In Pakistan, the Pakistan Sports Board (PSB) is under direct control of the Ministry of Sport, Culture and Tourism. Its purpose is to promote sport and develop standards of competition in Pakistan sport to international level, and to regulate and control those sports.

- In India, the Sports Authority of India (SAI) has central control of all sport and recreation, but its effectiveness is limited by lack of funding.

Sport as foreign policy

 **points**

- Sport is part of the foreign policy in all Asian cultures.

- Sporting successes provide a positive 'shop window' for these cultures.

- Success brings in foreign currency.

- Success attracts multi-national investment and puts countries in the global media.

- Élite athletes act as important role models.

- Sport is also used as an important tool of integration and health promotion.

Political factors

 **points**

- In the case of China, it is almost impossible to separate politics and sport, e.g. slogan 'Promote physical culture and build up the people's health'.

- The State Physical Culture and Sports Commission develops programmes in schools, factories and rural communes.

- Religious traditions and constraints do raise issues of equal access to sport especially in terms of gender in Muslim cultures.

2. Physical education and sport in high schools and colleges/universities

Fact:
Physical education in many Asian cultures still reflects some of the ancient traditions and values.

 Fuller information on these themes can be found in *Advanced PE for Edexcel*, pages 264–266.

Development of physical education
- The Chinese model
- Other activities
- India and Pakistan

Sport in high schools including extra-curricular sport
- India
- China

Sport in higher education

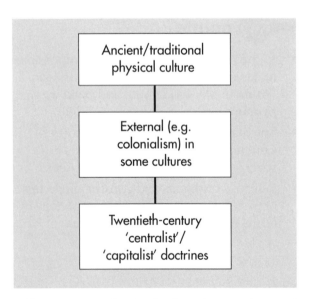

Influences on physical education and sport in Asian cultures

Development of physical education

 **Key points**

The history of physical education in Asian cultures has been influenced by four dynamics:

- indigenous historical influences
- external historical influences
- more recent 'political' and 'global' influences
- economic constraint.

The Chinese model
- Physical education in China is mandatory for all pupils in state schools.
- The curriculum is highly structured, and includes an emphasis on formal gymnastics and western-style games.
- Curriculum activity is supported by spare-time activities, and (in line with custom outside of the school) morning exercises and exercises during class breaks, followed by further exercise after school.

Other activities
- In Japan, physical education in schools is administered by a division of the Physical Education Bureau.
- Although existing within a capitalist culture, physical education is run strictly on 'centralist' principles.

India and Pakistan
- In both India and Pakistan, high levels of population and poor economies have conspired to prevent full implementation of an education system for all.
- This also has clear implications for the funding and implementation of programmes of physical education.

Sport in high schools including extra-curricular sport

- School sport in India is run by the Department of Youth Affairs and Sport. It is highly selective in terms of the range of activities offered.

- State championships take the form of inter-state tournaments,. which are organised by the School Games Federation of India.
- In China, school sport takes place in secondary sports schools and schools of sport and physical culture.
- These schools are part of mainstream education, but attendance is reserved for gifted performers.
- Students may be sent to national team squads from the age of fifteen.
- Those not sent to national squads are trained as teachers of physical education.

Sport in higher education

- The majority of Asian countries have some level of international contact and FISU.
- University sport, along with military and worker sport, is highly organised; championships at local, regional and national level are highly coveted.
- In India, hockey is by far the most popular sport with over 120 universities participating in the national championships each year.

3. Professional (élite) sport

Fact:
The development of global media technology has been a major influence in the growth of professional sport in Asian cultures.

 Fuller information on these themes can be found in *Advanced PE for Edexcel*, pages 267–269.

The commercial nature of professional sport

The role of company teams

The role of the media and the status of professional sport

Role of armed forces as sports nurseries

The Asian Games

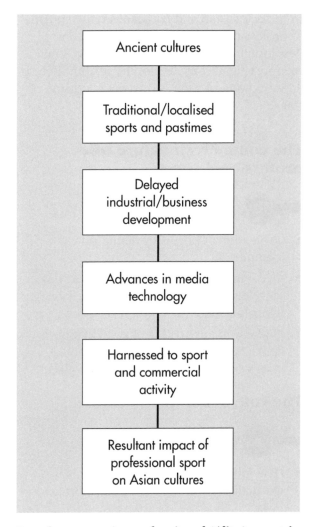

Developments in professional (élite) sport in Asian cultures

Professional sport in Asian cultures has a relatively short history, with few exceptions such as Sumo wrestling in Japan and the emergence of professional baseball there in the 1930s.

Baseball is now the most popular sport in Japan; it is rivalled only by volleyball and the rapidly developing interest in football (through global/media influence).

China has had limited development of professional sport due to political and ideological constraints. There has been recent growth of professional baseball league sponsored by an American marketing company keen to exploit the huge market.

In India, Pakistan and Bangladesh, the spread of professional cricket and a more recent development of interest in soccer have been the most significant developments, but there is little tradition of professional sport outside of this.

The commercial nature of professional sport

 **Key points**

- Professional sport is by definition commercial.
- In Asian cultures, professional sport has developed in line with the relatively recent global upsurge in commercial sport.
- Success in the hosting of two Olympiads and a World Cup has further enhanced Asia's potential as a global market-place.

The role of company teams

 **Key points**

- The involvement of company teams is a particular feature of high level sport across Asia.
- The large industrial/commercial/ technological conglomerates that are still part of the Asian economy therefore find that they are also part of the sporting as well as industrial infrastructure.

> **Did you know?**
> Many professional clubs in the UK began as company teams.

The role of the media and the status of professional sport

 **Key points**

- In India, *Sportstar* magazine is in its 23rd year of publication. The newspapers *Tribune India* and *Bangalore Age* cover sport and feature advertising related to sport.
- Asian TV companies increasingly cover sport. Also, the availability of satellite television has heightened the awareness of professional sport in terms of popularity and marketing potential.
- The Indian national TV network (Doordarshan) is one of the largest such organisations in the world and operates 21 channels, many covering sport.

Role of armed forces as sports nurseries

 **Key points**

- All Asian cultures have a history of military involvement in sport.
- Conscription also means that the military acts as an important filter of sporting talent, especially in light of low attendance at schools.
- There are army/military championships in many Olympic activities with military personnel being included in full national squads.

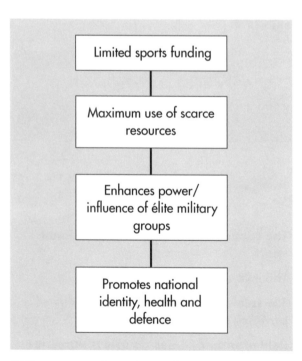

Military sport in Asian culture

- In poor economies, the utilisation of military facilities is a substitute for inadequate levels of funding for sport.
- Military involvement in sport often reflects the political power held by such institutions.

The Asian Games

The Asian Games are important both as an expression of cultural identity and a platform for Asian athletes to graduate on to the wider international stage.

- The first Games was held in 1951 in New Delhi with then newly-independent countries such as Korea, India, the Philippines and Indonesia finding an early sporting outlet as an expression of their new freedom.
- The Games are also part of an agreement between Asian leaders to work towards harmony and unity amongst Asians.

4. Recreational sport (mass participation)

Fact:
In Asian cultures, sport and exercise have been valued since ancient times as part of a healthy lifestyle.

Fuller information on these themes can be found in *Advanced PE for Edexcel*, pages 269–271.

Mass participation, social control, integration, health and defence

Religious constraints: women and Islamic states

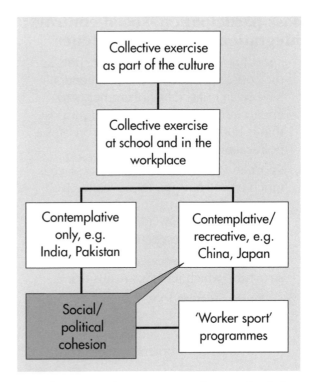

Developments in recreational sport in Asian cultures

 **points**

- Collective exercise including Tai Chi has been part of pastoral and spiritual life for as long as history has been recorded.
- Workplace sport and physical exercise form part of the daily routine of countless workers, for whom such activity is as much part of their culture as the philosophies on which they are based.
- Mass sport in Japan has a definite 'Olympic' flavour. The Japanese National Olympic Committee and the Japanese Amateur Sports Association (JASA) organise a whole range of activities for all sections of the community – including a National Sports Festival.
- In Korea also, enthusiasm for sport is fostered amongst the very young, with intramural sporting competition being a major feature of early school life. Success at this level brings entry to the Children's Games each spring and, possibly, the National Games each August.

Mass participation, social control, integration, health and defence

- Sport-for-All policies, workplace sport and the concept of mass recreation generally have been utilised by governments to impart a sense of belonging and purpose that is both health-giving and promotes a political message.

- Sport and/or exercise in the workplace is much more common in the 'collective' cultures of China, Japan and Korea. Its traditional roots have played a major part in its continued acceptance.

- China has a sophisticated workplace sports structure, which includes teams from:
  - trade organisations
  - railways
  - water and power industries
  - government workers' associations.

> **Did you know?**
>
> In China it is compulsory for workers to take part in mass recreation before, during and sometimes after work.

Religious constraints: women and Islamic states

- Some Islamic societies forbid men and women to mix socially and/or recreationally.

- Some other Asian cultures still frown upon women openly 'displaying' themselves.

- In such cases, the sporting environment is simply one aspect of a much larger area of contention (issue) which involves the relationships between politics, religion and gender (i.e. discrimination).

- Many women from Asian or Islamic countries face great hurdles before the freedom to compete openly is accorded them by their own cultures.

Do you know about...?

1. How sport fits in with the mainstream social values of Asian cultures?
2. How colonial history shaped the emergence of sport in Asian cultures?
3. How the governments of Asian cultures promote sport and recreation?
4. How sport is used by Asian cultures as a form of foreign policy?
5. How sport is used in Asian cultures as a form of nation building?
6. How environmental and topographical factors can affect access to sport in Asian cultures?
7. How the education system reflects the history of Asian cultures?
8. The problems developing cultures face in developing school sport programmes?
9. The roles companies play in the provision of professional sport in Asian cultures?
10. The role the armed services play in the development of sports excellence in Asian cultures?
11. The importance of the Asian Games in élite sports development in Asian cultures?
12. Why so many élite athletes from developing cultures go West to further their sports careers?
13. The benefits that global success can bring to a Asian culture?
14. The popularity of daily exercise in Asian cultures and how it reflects the philosophy of these cultures?
15. The role that sport can play in the promotion of health and defence in Asian cultures?

Exam tips

Make sure that you understand:

- that Asian Sport is a mix of western and eastern philosophies
- that daily exercise is part of Asian culture
- that the recent upsurge in professional sport is due to commercial/global factors
- that global sports success is an important shop window for Asian cultures.

Practise your exam technique

(a) Many of the early programmes of physical training in the UK were based on military drill and placed little importance on pupil enjoyment. Why was this? (3 marks)

1. Explain how high school sport and professional sport in the USA are closely linked (4 marks)

2. Explain the draft system present in US sport and explain how its reflects the ideals prevalent in the US (4 marks)

3. How are elements of 'Frontier Spirit' reflected in the North American sports scene? (3 marks)

4. How did the historical and cultural background of America shape the sports now played? (4 marks)

5. How did the historical and cultural background shape the sports now played in New World cultures? (4 marks)

6. Explain why both outdoor education and outdoor recreation are popular concepts in New World Cultures. (4 marks)

7. How have New World cultures used comparative study to develop élite sports programmes results, from poor performance in the 1976 Olympics in Australia, later for other New World Cultures?

  (4 marks)

8. Why has the structure of élite sports in developing cultures been different to that which has occurred in many of the more wealthy nations? (4 marks)

9. How have European/global cultures influenced the development of sport and recreation in Asian countries:
    i)   historically? (2 marks)
    ii) currently? (2 marks)

Unit 4 Section B: A synoptic analysis of trends in international sport through global Games

Overview

1. Sport as a show of national identity
- The benefits of sporting success
- Sport used as a shop window
- Government influence and policy in sport
- Motivation and pride
- Systematic approach to preparation for political/national success
- Use of global games for protest
- Power of the boycott
- Apartheid and the old South Africa
- 'Ping-pong' diplomacy
- International sport as a focus for nationality

2. The pursuit of global excellence
- Systems of nurturing sports talent
- Similarities and differences between countries and the factors that affect this
- How the East German model has been copied in many countries
- The use of academies and sports schools
- Funding of élite athletes
- The appliance of sports science through different training regimes
- The role of drugs and medicine in global sport
- Geographical and cultural differences

3. Deviance and cheating in global Games
- Reasons and methods
- The increasing commercialisation of global sport and its effect on deviance
- Sporting ethics – their rise and fall
- Drug abuse, bias and violence
- Role of international sports bodies in combating cheating

4. Commercialisation and media in global sport
- Amateurs and professionals – the development of 'open sports'
- Role of TV and the 'Americanisation' of global games
- Sponsorship and sports as commodities
- The rise of the sports star: the agent and the promoter
- The 'win ethic' versus the recreational ethic
- The relationship between international competition and friendship on an individual basis and group basis

5. Opportunity in global Games
- Individual differences
- The influence of race, gender, and religion
- Olympic and other ideals
- Sport as a vehicle to break discrimination
- Ethnic games and counter-cultures
- Issues of stacking, centrality and myths

SECTION B: A Synoptic analysis of trends in International sport through global Games

1. Sport as a show of national identity

The benefits of sporting success

 **points**

These benefits may be:

- internal and/or external
- economic and social

Benefits may take the form of:

- increased levels of tourism
- increased attendance at major fixtures
- increased levels of commercial activity and employment
- improved health of population

Sport used as a shop window

The sporting 'shop window' is a market place in which a nation displays it's sporting talent and in doing so gains publicity for its cultural, economic and political infrastructure.

 **points**

- the transformation of formerly amateur sports into professional ones has stimulated governments into embracing sport as a tool of national promotion
- many governments now adopt a more proactive attitude to developing sporting infrastructures
- this is due to the increased globalisation of sport and the huge commercial rewards available
- Hitler using the 1936 Olympic Games for propaganda
- Eastern Bloc countries using success in global games to show power of their political ideology

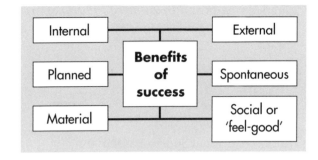

- Korea using hosting of 1988 Olympics to show advanced economic and social development
- Australia's success at hosting and winning medals at the 2000 Sydney Olympics

Government influence and policy in sport

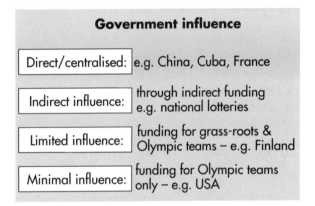

Governments offered limited financial assistance assistance to sport at times of major events.

- now, the drive for global sports success has resulted in increasing government input
- achieving excellence at a global level requires athletes to concentrate full time on their sports and receive full sports science support
- Increasingly, this is provided by state-funded bodies

 **points**

- Australia – Australian Institute of sport managed by the *Australian Sports Commission*

- France – *National Institute of PE and Sport* (INSEP) managed by Ministry of Youth and Sport
- United Kingdom – *UK Sports Institutes* managed by UK Sport
- United Sates – Olympic Training Centres funded by federal government
- India – Regional Sports Academies managed by *Sports Authority of India*
- Argentina – *Secretaria de Deportes de la Nacion* awards scholarships to gifted athletes

Motivation and pride

Individual – the motivation to compete and the pride in any achievement is a purely personal thing. Sports psychologists tend to refer to such motivation as being derived from internal or external sources.

The motivation for those who support minority causes can be both personal and group-orientated. Their actions may have a wider impact on processes of **access** and **integration**.

Government motivation

Based on the rewards that success might bring:

- not merely for those involved as competitors but for the nation as a whole.
- governments will make what political 'mileage' they can out of any success: both in terms of domestic well being, enhanced international image and opportunities for trade/business

Systematic approach to preparation for political/national success

The means by which nations now prepare their young people for international sporting success are far more highly structured and sophisticated than has previously been the case.

- this reflects the changing of sporting philosophy, from amateur to professional and from the recreational ethic towards the win ethic

> **Did you know?**
> The Recreational ethic is based on the philosophy that sport is about taking part rather than winning.

Key example:

The Eastern European model of Sports Excellence
Between 1950 and 1990, the Eastern Bloc countries led the world in sport as a direct result of their centrally funded systems of excellence. These were based on both sound scientific research and the use of sports academies.

Use of global games for protest

 **points**

- global Games receive coverage in the global media, often live
- creates a world stage
- global Games have been used for *protest* – both systematic and non-systematic – on several occasions
- individuals, groups and governments have also used global Games as a platform for propaganda

Examples include:

- 'black power salute' at the Mexico Olympics in 1968
- Arab terrorists at the Olympic Games of 1972
- USA led boycott of Moscow Olympic 1980
- USSR "tit for tat" boycott of LA Olympics in 1984
- terrorist bomb at the Atlanta games of 1996

> **Did you know?**
> Systematic protest means planned/premeditated protest.
>
> Non-systematic protest means non-planned/spur of the moment protest.

Power of the boycott

- boycotts are forms of systematic protest – often government initiated
- Sport is used as a political tool since it has little or no economic impact on government budgets

Apartheid and the old South Africa

 **points**

- South Africa's policy of apartheid split the sporting world for almost thirty years
- In the old South Africa, privilege was the backbone of sports selection; excluding all non-whites
- the Olympic community took a lead role in excluding South Africa
- the Gleneagles Agreement excluded South Africa from a wider range of global games
- in a number of professional sports – rebel tours sought to gain commercial advantage
- political and social change in South Africa in 1996 saw the birth of the '*rainbow nation*'
- South Africa's new leaders recognised the importance of sport
- the image of Nelson Mandella and Francois Pinear sharing the stage after South Africa's victory in the Rugby World cup was a powerful one

> **Did you know?**
> Apartheid was the South African policy that based privileges on racial origin.

'Ping-pong' diplomacy

This term is used where sporting contact clears a path for politicians and underlines the power of sport, both on and off the field.

Examples of this include:

- America and China staging a table-tennis tournament prior to the Olympic Games of 1976
- England playing Argentina at football after the Falklands conflict

- a United Nations team playing an Afghanistan team at football

International sport as a focus for nationality

Success of teams and individuals on the sports field has become part of an expression of nationality.

For smaller nations and those with little other global impact, success in international sport is a very important vehicle of 'self-promotion'. e.g. : –

- Scotland, Wales and Northern Ireland – football
- New Zealand – rugby (both codes)

2. The pursuit of global excellence

> **Fact:**
> The level of sporting excellence attainable in any culture is governed by nature of provision and the degree to which discrimination is absent.

Systems of nurturing sports talent

The means by which nations prepare their young people for International sporting success.

 **points**

These systems often reflect the political philosophies of their country of origin.

There are two main models:

- **centralised** and controlled system – as in China
- **de-centralised** and devolved 'free-market' system – as in the USA.

In order to compete at the global level athletes must now train full time. **Scholarships** cover the cost of training, coaching and equipment as well as the cost of residence.

	Purpose	Funding
National Sports Institute	Residential – an extended period Short/occasional courses for specific purpose	Direct or indirect state-funding Privately funded, sponsorship or funded by 'small' bursary
Regional Sports Institute	Usually non-residential – for an extended period Short/occasional courses for specific purpose	Direct or indirect state-funding Privately funded, sponsorship or 'small' bursary
State-run sports school	Residential for extended period – often involving young children	Funding nominally 'shared' but effectively state-funded
Sports school run in normal state schools	Usually non-residential with exception of some private schools	Fees if residential, state or parentally funded if day schools
Communist countries	Sports schools: Physical culture institutes: National squads: Often residential – all ages – extended period	Almost always totally state-funded
USA	No specific Sports academies or sports schools	'athletic' scholarship, or privately funded place

- United Kingdom – World Class Performance grants through National Lottery
- Australia – scholarships through A.I.S.
- France – scholarships through INSEP
- India – through SAI approved centres and Boys' Company Sport Units attached to Army units

The 'nurturing' of talent implies a caring environment and clearly, this is not always the case.

Some sports, particularly ice-skating, gymnastics and swimming, have traditionally required their future stars to train hard when very young, often to the detriment of their physical and psychological well-being in both the short and longer term.

Similarities and differences between countries and the factors that affect this

It is impossible to have a 'level playing-field', where all countries possess the same resources and potential or cultural orientation towards élite sport. The degree to which certain factors are present – or otherwise – contribute significantly to sporting outcomes both nationally and globally.

Some of these variables include:

 **points**

- wealth
- population levels/types/distribution
- political philosophy/dogma
- centralised/de-centralised administration
- historical/cultural association with sport

- land area/physical topography
- global/political relationships with other countries

How the East German model has been copied in many countries

The former **East German** model of 'early talent identification', sports schools, high level coaching and advanced scientific support is now being widely copied throughout the world.

Key points

- former East German coaches have been employed in many of the national sports academies now being set up
- this model – along with others of former eastern bloc countries were entirely centralised and state-funded
- political necessity required the adoption of 'questionable practices' in many of these sports schools, where the ends justified the means!

Did you know?

That East German female swimmers were forced to become pregnant in order to enhance vitamin levels and subsequently to have an abortion.

The use of academies and sports schools

- *'Sports academy'* is a generic term applied to establishments with the primary aim of developing performance to the highest level – largely with promising and/or established athletes
- the term *sports school* tends to be associated with young people (often as young as seven or eight years old) being sent away to a residential facility which also provides a full time education.

Funding of élite athletes

The funding of élite performers varies, as do the types of sponsorship that fund them. Funding includes both centralised to decentralised models.

Funding:		
College athletic scholarships	Lottery schemes	State-funded systems
United States	UK, Australia	China, Cuba

← - →

De-centralised   Centralised

Scholarships

Two main forms:

- *academic* – at a university, funded on the basis of sporting ability, in return for which commitment to the university athletic programme is expected
- *State* – money awarded to a promising athlete, for approved use, such as training expenses

Types of funding

- *lottery funding* – United Kingdom: money from proceeds of publicly supported lotteries
- *government funding* – India: money from central government collected from taxes
- *voluntary funding* – Australia: sports schools attached to state schools, funded by parents and local businesses
- *private sector funding* – US high schools receive income from huge attendance at inter-scholastic sports competitions, which fund both athletic programmes and often much of the rest of the school.

The appliance of sports science through different training regimes

In order to compete at global level athletes now need to incorporate sports science in their preparation.

The following elements of sports science are used by most élite athletes:

- biomechanics
- nutrition
- sports physiology

- sports psychology
- physiotherapy and rehabilitation

Some athletes may live in communities where there are severe economic constraints. As science plays a more influential role in sporting performance then athletes from richer nations will have an advantage.

The role of drugs and medicine in global sport

 **points**

- supplements are legal additives with performance-enhancing properties that athletes use in their preparation. These might include ingredients such as *creatine monohydrate* and *amino acids*
- drugs are illegal performance-enhancing substances and those that have been identified by sporting authorities have been banned because they produce artificially enhanced performances
- they may also produce harmful long-term side effects, although some athletes ignore this in order to try and win!

The list of such substances includes:

- diuretics
- beta blockers
- growth hormones
- steroids
- amphetamines
- narcotic analgesics

Geographical and cultural differences

 **points**

- geographical factors influence recreational and sporting patterns, particularly in extreme instances
- winter sports and water sports are unlikely to be fully developed in countries with unsuitable environments

Sport, recreation & culture	
Primitive cultures	simple, naturally available activities
Emergent cultures	as above but with some targeted investment and technology
Advanced cultures	full range of naturally occurring and technologically enhanced activities

- a *primitive* or *emergent* culture is far more likely to resort to patterns of recreation that both tradition and topography can support
- land area, communications, transport systems and demographic spread can also make the implementation of recreational policies easier or more difficult to implement, irrespective of political or cultural influences

Culture

Cultural influences on sport and recreational patterns are reflected in the nature of activities normally found within a particular society.

Factors include:

- Traditions and philosophy regarding physical contact – India not adopting the colonial game of rugby
- Traditions and philosophy regarding Gender – limited access for women in many Asian cultures

3. Deviance and cheating in global Games

Fact:
The reason why anyone cheats is to gain unfair advantage.

Reasons and methods

 **points**

- **cultural values** vary, so that what is perceived as cheating in one part of the world may not be regarded quite so harshly in another
- some athletes may have little choice but be part of a **deviant regime** against which they have little or no redress
- cheating is sometimes associated with the perceived benefits that a particular (usually political) culture may derive from international sporting success

Cheating occurs at three levels:

- individual – without reference to others
- group – collusion between (e.g.) coach, doctor and athlete
- institutional – in order to promote a particular philosophy or doctrine

The increasing commercialisation of global sport and its effect on deviance

Two issues here:

- the upsurge of commercial interest and involvement in sport
- how the growth of commercial interest has influenced deviant behaviour

Sport: the growing business

 **points**

- increasing commercial interest in global sport
- multi-national companies utilise a relationship with sport in order to give themselves a more acceptable image, broaden their appeal to consumers and maximise their profit margins
- sponsorship and advertising as well as the personal endorsement of goods and services by leading sports stars are the major means used by commercial interests

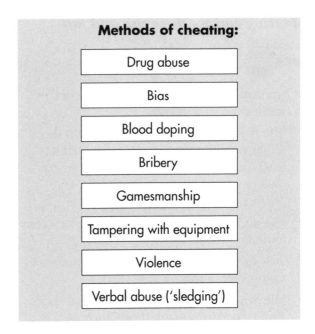

Methods of cheating:

| Drug abuse |
| Bias |
| Blood doping |
| Bribery |
| Gamesmanship |
| Tampering with equipment |
| Violence |
| Verbal abuse ('sledging') |

to market their wares in an ever growing global market place

- rapid growth of a **communications technology** capable of taking these messages around the world has also had a major influence in both market growth and levels of commercial involvement

Growing business – growing deviance?

- sport is now business and the drive is to make maximum profit: both for corporations and for sports performers
- the maxim, 'the end justifies the means' is now used in connection with sporting endeavours
- this is done without regard for the ethics/morals that traditionally applied in the theatre of sport
- there have been allegations of bribery in football and of match fixing in cricket
- some of the above included the alleged possibility of **personal gain** on the part of individuals – but all suggested rather larger 'business interests' behind the scenes
- if sport is now part of the global market-place then it also becomes susceptible to the deviant practices and behaviours that are to be found there

Sporting ethics – their rise and fall

 **points**

- sporting ethics are a reflection of current values within a culture
- the recreational ethic was created in the English public schools and gave birth to such terms as: 'fair play', 'sportsmanship', 'winning' and 'losing honourably', and 'respect for one's opponent'
- the above reflects a now outdated Victorian morality
- however, many sports still frame their rules using such terms
- the Win ethic now dominates global sport and is associated with terms such as 'win at all costs', 'gamesmanship' and *'nice guys finish last'!*

Ethics:

> **Victorian ethic:** participation more important than winning

> **Post-Victorian ethic:** winning – but within the rules

> **Lombardian ethic:** win-at-all-costs

> **Post-Lombardian ethic:** win-at-a-profit-at-all-costs

Drug abuse, bias and violence

The use of illegal substances, the biased behaviour of some officials and violent behaviour both on and off the field of play can all be seen as products of an increased emphasis on winning rather than simply 'taking part'.

 **points**

In the context of sport, drugs are illegal performance-enhancing substances.

Additionally, many are known to have harmful side effects, which some athletes ignore in their quest for medals and money.

Performance-enhancing substances include:

- diuretics
- beta-blockers
- growth hormones
- steroids
- amphetamines
- narcotic analgesics

Did you know?
That the first death of an athlete caused by drugs in modern Olympic sport was a Danish cyclist in the 1960 Games in Rome.

Bias

- biased behaviour on the part of sports fans is (within reasonable limits) an acceptable part of supporting one's team or individual sports star.
- the biased behaviour of **officials** is unacceptable but we must be careful to differentiate between behaviour that is intentionally biased and that which is perhaps the result of genuine error, or simply a differing point of view.
- **inconsistencies** in the decisions of football referees or cricket umpires have long been the subject of allegations of biased behaviour but very difficult to prove
- this has led to the use of television/video replays and extra officials – e.g. the 'third umpire' in cricket.

Violence

- violence on the field of play can either be pre-meditated or spontaneous
- it is likely that both intent and response are heightened by:
  i) the *pressure* of the situation
  ii) the *rewards* on offer for success
- violence off the field of play can be a reflection of:

i)   bias and/or violence displayed by performers or officials

ii) social disorder which manifests itself in the sporting arena

- in the currently prevailing circumstances, the excuse that physical assaults are part of 'the rough and tumble of the game' is no longer considered to be an acceptable defence for violence on the field of play

Role of international sports bodies in combating cheating

Problems:

- consensus as to what is and what isn't cheating is more difficult to achieve across a range of cultures

- effective monitoring and implementation on a global scale is far more difficult than at 'national' level

- in global Games a further layer of administration often complicates matters

- there is also an increased level of commercial pressure

Solutions:

- there is a need to develop a 'global culture' of fair play and what is and what isn't cheating

---

Retroactive punishments:

Banning of athletes/teams/nations

Fining of athletes/teams/nations

Withdrawing points

Proactive intervention:

Educating athletes about 'hollow victory'

Rewarding fair play: awards/entry to competitions

Involving all in agreed standards of behaviour

- identified standards should be applied – and be seen to be applied – in a global context

- actions need to include a proactive approach as well as the traditional retroactive punishments (see opposite)

4. Commercialisation and media in global sport

Amateurs and professionals – the development of 'open sports'

The clear distinction that once existed between amateur and professional sport has now almost disappeared – certainly at the élite level of performance.

 **points**

Main Reasons

- Requirement for full time training to compete at global level

- Sport now a career for most global athletes

- Commercial interests have created a 'sports-related' market place

- Increasing problems over 'shamateurism' during 1980's and early 1990's led to most sports adopting "Open" rules

- now means that professional sport dominates all sporting activity

Examples of 'shamateurism':

- athletic scholarships funded by colleges and private companies in USA

- state sponsorship or state jobs: as in former communist countries

- trust funds in the United Kingdom

- so-called 'amateurs' who are in fact receiving 'under-the-counter payments'

Did you know?

That open competition is where amateurs and professionals compete together

---

Role of TV and the 'Americanisation' of global Games

 **points**

- American sporting practice and culture now dominates the world
- American-inspired win ethic now dominates professional sport
- American concept of the sporting triangle also dominates the funding of elite sport globally
- a key theme is the increasing relationship between sport and television, in both terrestrial and satellite formats
- television has been particularly influential as a marketing agency for sport and associated commercial enterprise

Sponsorship and sports as commodities

Sponsorship brings much needed finance to events, competitions, leagues, development programmes.

In return, the sponsor receives agreed advertising priority, assistance with marketing promotions and a degree of influence over the way an event is staged and/or its timing.

Sponsorship or control?

The degree of **influence** a sponsor is allowed to exert will clearly reflect the level of financial support injected or the ability of the sport/event to survive without such investment.

In this respect alone, sport at an élite level has clearly become a **commodity** which in many cases can attract huge television audiences far in excess of the capacity of any single stadium.

 **points**

Examples of sponsors influence:

- changing times and dates of events to suit sponsor and /or TV prime time
- changing rules to make game more attractive to TV
- changing playing kits to make more attractive to TV
- putting sponsors logo on playing surface/around stadium/ in name of competition

The rise of the sports star: the agent and the promoter

 **points**

Sports stars

- today's sports stars can earn *vast fortunes* – very quickly – and quite often from many sources
- sources of income include: playing contract, win reward bonuses, product endorsements, media fees

The key to huge earning potential is in an athlete becoming a household name. They can then command 'appearance money' or lucrative wage contracts and may be asked to endorse products and appear in TV commercials.

> **Did you know?**
> Endorsement is where a well-known sports star allows his or her name to appear on a product.

Agents

- the earning potential of sports stars is now maximised by **agents** acting on their behalf

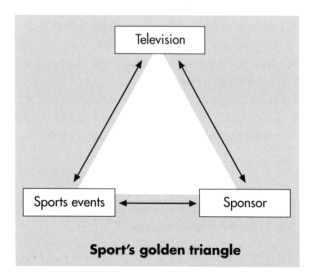

Sport's golden triangle

- these agents are also aware that their own income is governed by their bargaining ability
- there is a body of opinion that their role has contributed to spiralling wage demands in many sports – but particularly in football

The promoter

In boxing and athletics particularly, it is the **promoter** who has enabled the stars of these sports to amass considerable personal wealth.

The role of the promoter:

- boxing – to arrange contests and match contestants. This has led to a huge increase in the number of World Championships and so-called 'world boxing authorities'
- athletics – offering appearance money and prize-money incentives in conjunction with sponsors, although this does not apply in major Games/championships

The 'win ethic' versus the recreational ethic

 **points**

- the '**win ethic**' is very much a reflection of American cultural and business values transposed into sporting values
- the diffusion of American sporting values into the global arena has meant that the 'win ethic' has become part of a global sporting philosophy
- the 'recreational ethic' was born of British and European educational philosophies of the 19th and early 20th centuries
- this ethic is perhaps best typified in the sporting values of the British public schools of that time
- paradoxically, the influence of 'American values' on global sport and the resultant commercial pressures has forced a re-evaluation of the recreational ethic at élite levels
- It is even more ironic that the counter-culture ethic, born out of a rejection of commercial and political 'interference' in

sport, has itself become a target for the very influences it was created to oppose. In élite or global sport, financial reward can only be achieved by winning. It is therefore entirely logical that the joy of participation on its own is insufficient to ensure success – financial or otherwise.

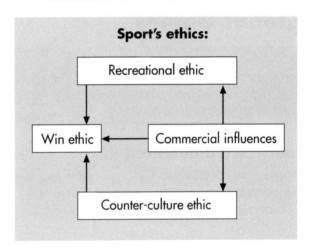

Sport's ethics:

The relationship between international competition and friendship

 **points**

An individual basis
- friendship between individuals – even the closest rivals – is invaluable in breaking down **cultural barriers**
- in some sports (e.g. cricket and football) it is quite common for groups/individuals to spend extended periods in other countries

- this facilitates **cultural exchange** and the development of greater understanding and tolerance

A group basis

- both individuals and groups can facilitate exchanges of views and experiences in both the sporting and non-sporting sense
- increased involvement of governments in sport facilitates an increased level of semi-official ministerial contact

5. Opportunity in global Games

> **Fact:**
> Opportunity should be constrained only by lack of personal ambition – not by others

Individual differences

Opportunity is influenced by constraint and in the context of sport. This means that several factors must be considered.

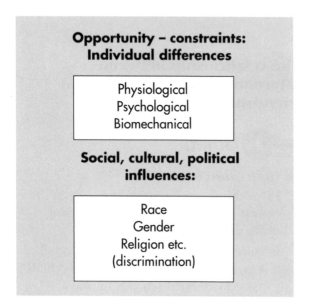

Opportunity – constraints: Individual differences

Physiological
Psychological
Biomechanical

Social, cultural, political influences:

Race
Gender
Religion etc.
(discrimination)

In terms of 'athletic capability', opportunity presents itself to those whose **physiological**, **psychological** and/or **biomechanical** make-up best lends itself to the nature of the activity.

The influence of race, gender and religion

Opportunity can also be constrained by other than purely physical/biological limitations. Issues centred upon **race**, **gender** and/or **religion** are amongst the most prominent in terms of the restriction of access and **opportunity** in sport at all levels.

Race

Race is influential in the sense that some minority groups are discriminated against:

- this clearly restricts opportunity both at local and global levels
- racial groups may also be linked to certain body-types and there may be a positive or negative impact upon opportunity as a result of this

Gender

The increase in the number of women participants in most sports may lead one to believe that gender issues no longer rank amongst the leading areas of contention.

However:

- in some cultures it is still not accepted that women should compete in sports events for a range of reasons.
- there are issues surrounding women who wish to box, play rugby or participate in any sport thought to be 'inappropriate': usually by men but sometimes by other women.

Religion

- in the western world, performance on the 'Sabbath' is held in very low esteem by certain religions.
- in some Islamic countries, women are not only forbidden to take part in sport publicly but also from attending any outside activity where both sexes are involved.

Olympic and other ideals

Baron de Coubertin's aims for the Olympic movement: -

The aims of the Olympic Movement are to promote the development of those fine physical and moral qualities which are the basis of amateur sport and to bring together the athletes of the world in a great quadrennial festival of sports; thereby creating international respect and goodwill and thus helping to construct a better and more peaceful world.

This philosophy has been formalised through the Olympic Charter and most other global sports have used it as the basis of their own rules and regulations.

The arrival of sporting professionals into the Olympic arena has been justified with an agreement on the part of competitors to respect the **spirit of Olympic competition**.

The 'ideal' of 'sportsmanship'

The term **sportsmanship** now has a much broader application than a purely 'Olympic' context.

- the traditional interpretation of sporting philosophy embodied such qualities as chivalry, honour and **integrity** and a sporting demeanour that was as honest in its intention as in its application.
- now replaced by '**gamesmanship**', where winning becomes the primary aim – linked to financial reward.
- sport reflects society and as the level of deviance in society has increased, there has also been a similar change in attitude within sport.

Sport as a vehicle to break discrimination

Sport is one of the tools used by governments and sporting organisations to encourage nations to change policy (e.g. sporting sanctions against South Africa in the latter part of the twentieth century.)

Sport, especially global sport, is big news in most cultures and therefore any use that can be made of its popularity is particularly advantageous.

Ethnic games and counter cultures

The increasing globalisation of sport and the growing level of professionalisation has in turn created a greater exposure of some **ethnic games** and activities along with the development of a number of '**counter cultures**'.

 **points**

- televising of Kabbadi.
- beach volleyball becoming an Olympic Sport?
- the development of Scottish Highland Games and other traditional sports into global "strongest man" competitions

Many alternative cultures, founded on an ethic 'recreational enjoyment', have created sports such as skateboarding and mountain-biking, as well as diverse forms of ski-ing and other extreme sports. Many of these sports have become 'professional' and are creating their own heroes and sporting icons.

> **Did you know?**
> Counter cultures are activities or groups whose philosophy is different from a mainstream culture.

Issues of stacking centrality and myths

A series of sport-related theories often linked to race and ethnic background, appear to have impact on both access to sport and progression up the sports pyramid.

- **centrality** – where the dominant group in society takes up the dominant role in sports culture to ensure that opportunity is granted to its 'own kind' rather than 'outsiders' – e.g. white quarterbacks in US football
- **stacking** – where certain racial groups are channelled into specific sports or positions

135

within a sport – e.g. black fast bowlers in cricket

- **myths** – where stereotypes become so prevalent that generalised statements enter into common usage – e.g. 'black men can't swim' / 'white men can't jump'
- the term '**white flight**' refers to developments such as the disappearance of white sprinters from the global sporting stage

Do you know about...?

1. The 'benefits of sporting success', other than those which quite clearly accrue to successful performers?

2. What is meant by the term 'shop window' as it applies to sport, and how has this changed since the demise of the soviet bloc countries and the growth of professional sport?

3. How has the nature of government involvement in sport changed in the last twenty years and what are the reasons for this?

4. How does the funding of élite sport differ in a communist country such as China to that in a 'free-market' country such as the USA?

5. Why so many countries appear to have adopted an academy system as the best means of developing élite athletes?

6. What pressures may have led to the reported increase in deviance at global games?

7. How individual differences can affect an individual access to sport on a global level?

8. How geographical and economic factors can affects a nation's impact on sport at a global level?

Practise your exam technique

Sample essay titles:

1. Discuss why groups and individuals have used global games for protest
2. Global games can both enhance and inhibit the promotion of sport amongst minority and disadvantaged groups
3. The drive to win in global games has eroded any sporting ethics - Discuss
4. Why have most global games altered their rules regarding amateur and professional performers?

UNIT 6: Scientific principles of exercise and performance

Section A: Exercise and energy systems

Overview

1. Introduction to basic chemistry for sports science
- Chemical reactions

2. Energy concepts for exercise physiology
- Energy concepts
- Measurement of energy

3. Molecular muscle cell structures
- Motor units and motor neural firing patterns
- Structures of the motor unit
- Propagation of a nerve impulse
- Neuromuscular junctions
- Muscle cell (fibre) structure
- Sliding filament theory

4. Energy systems and the energy continuum
- ATP in energy production
- Energy systems
- Mode of energy regeneration
- Fatigue
- Recovery process
- Nutrition

5. Physiological responses and adaptations of the energy systems
- Responses to high intensity exercise
- Adaptations to high intensity exercise
- Responses to aerobic exercise
- Adaptations to aerobic exercise

Explanatory notes

A knowledge of chemistry will help with an understanding of the chemical processes going on in the body. It provides a useful background to the content of the unit.

Revising for exams is much easier if you understand key concepts. It is not possible to see all the different chemical reactions taking place without very specialised equipment. It is therefore helpful if you can create a visual image of the key processes.

Brief history

- Exercise physiology is relatively new in the history of the development of science.
- In 1921, Archibald Vivian Hill was awarded the Nobel Prize for his findings on energy metabolism.
- Many of the terms we use today stem from his research, e.g. oxygen debt, VO_2 max.
- Initial research focused on whole body responses, but developments such as muscle biopsies came in the mid-1960s.
- A clear understanding of muscle physiology and energy systems provides the basis for principles of training and fitness.

Key terms and definitions

Although this section is not examined it will help you to learn about energy systems. Take a look at the key terms and definitions below, which will help.

- **Matter**: all matter is composed of elements.
- **Elements**: 26 elements occur in the human body. Carbon, oxygen, hydrogen and nitrogen make up 96 per cent of its mass. Each element is made up of atoms.
- **Atoms**: these consist of neutrons, protons [p+] (the nucleus) and electrons [e-] (orbiting the nucleus). An atom is electrically neutral because the number of protons and electrons are equal.
- **Molecules**: these are formed when two or more atoms share electrons after a chemical reaction.

- **Compound**: contains atoms of two or more different elements. Organic compounds contain carbon; inorganic compounds lack carbon.
- **Bonding**: isolated atoms look to fill their outer shell and chemically react or bond with others to achieve this.
- **Ion**: when an atom loses/gains an electron, its electrical neutrality is lost. A particle with a negative or positive charge is an ion, e.g. Hydrogen ion = H+.
- **Electrolyte**: this is a compound that splits into positive and negative ions in solution.
- **Acids**: these are substances that release H + and a base accepts H+. The more hydrogen ions contained in a solution, the more acidic it is.
- **pH**: the concentration of H+ is measured in pH units. The pH scale runs from 0 to 14, with 7 being neutral. A solution with a pH below 7 is acidic and above 7 alkaline.
- **Buffers**: our body uses these to control its levels of H+.

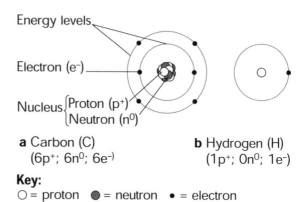

a Carbon (C)
(6p+; 6n⁰; 6e⁻)

b Hydrogen (H)
(1p+; 0n⁰; 1e⁻)

Key:
○ = proton ● = neutron • = electron

The structure of a carbon atom and a hydrogen atom

> **Did you know?**
> Electron interactions are the basis of all chemical reactions.

1. Introduction to basic chemistry for sports science

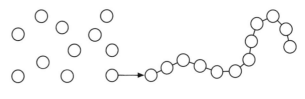

Amino acids   Protein molecule

 Fuller information on these themes can be found in *Advanced PE for Edexcel*, pages 369–371.

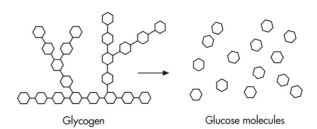

Glycogen   Glucose molecules

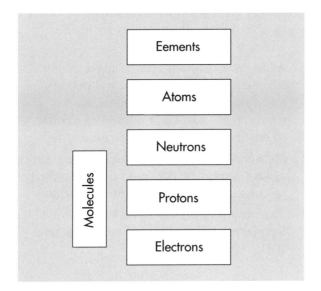

Understanding matter

Examples of synthesis and decomposition reactions

Did you know?
Enzymes are catalysts that increase the rate of reactions. The names usually end in 'ase', e.g. Creatine Kinase, ATPase, phosphofructokinase.

Chemical reactions

* Exothermic reactions release energy.
* Endothermic reactions require energy.
* Synthesis reactions – anabolic – A + B → AB.
* Decomposition reactions – catabolic – AB → A + B.
* Oxidation is the loss of electrons.
* Reduction is the gain of electrons.

2. Energy concepts for exercise physiology

Fact:
Energy may be defined as the capacity to perform work or put mass into motion.

Fuller information on these themes can be found in *Advanced PE for Edexcel*, pages 371–373.

Energy concepts

Measurement of energy
- Metabolic rate
- Work

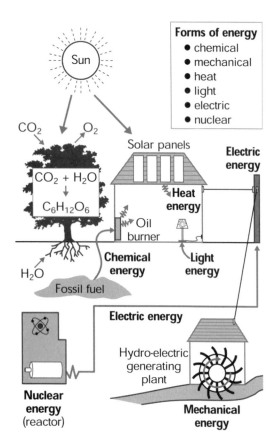

The relationship between different forms of energy

Energy concepts
- All energy on earth comes from the sun.
- Plants use this light energy to form carbohydrates, fats and proteins.
- Animals (including humans) eat plants and other animals.
- The muscle fibres convert the chemical energy from these sources into the kinetic (mechanical) energy necessary to perform movement – or store it as potential energy.

Measurement of energy

Measurement of energy expenditure, work and power has many applications in sports science.

- A coach may require knowledge of the energy requirements of an activity in order to plan dietary programmes for his/her athletes.
- A fitness consultant prescribing a weight loss programme for a client will need to know the energy requirements of exercising at particular intensities in order to ensure success of an exercise regime.
- Measurement of energy expenditure against energy intake (food diary) can help calculate and maintain an energy balance.
- Calculation of energy requirements for living over 24 hours (basal metabolic rate – BMR).

Metabolic rate
- BMR is the energy required for essential physiological functioning after 8 hours sleep and 12 hours fasting.
- This may vary between 1200 to 2400 kcal/day.
- It decreases approximately 2 per cent and 3 per cent per decade in men and women respectively.
- Women have a smaller BMR due to their lower fat-free mass.
- To calculate total metabolic rate we must add together the energy requirements of physical activity.

NB The estimated BMR for males is that 1kg of body weight burns 1 kcal per hour. For females, 1kg of body weight burns 0.9 kcal per hour.

QUESTION: Can you calculate your own BMR? (e.g. a 70kg male = 70 × 1kcal × 24hr = 1680 kcal)

Typical metabolic rate
- The average total metabolic rate of an individual engaged in normal daily activities is between 1800 and 3000 kcals.
- An active sportsman/woman who is training hard may need between 5000 and 7000 kcal.

Work

- work is measured in Newtons.
- work = force × distance

It can be measured in calories or joules.

- force = mass × acceleration (gravity 9.81m/s)
- power is the rate at which work is being performed.
- $\text{power} = \dfrac{\text{work}}{\text{time}} = \dfrac{\text{joules}}{\text{seconds}} = \text{Watts}$

A 70kg man steps up and down on a 50cm bench for ten minutes at rate of thirty steps per minute. The amount of work performed during this task can be computed as follows.

Force = 70 kg × 9.81 = 686.7 N

Distance = 0.5m step × 30 steps/min × 10 min = 150m

Work = 686.7N × 150 m = 103 000 joules

Power = $\dfrac{103\ 000 \text{ joules}}{600 \text{ seconds}}$ = 171.7 Watts

---

Did you know?
An easy way of calculating force is to simply multiply mass (in kgs) by 10.

---

work = force × distance

force = mass × acceleration (due to gravity – 9.81m/s) – measured in Newtons (e.g. lift a 5kg weight through a vertical distance of 2m)

work – 5kg × 2m = 10 kilogram-metres (kgm) × 9.81 = 98.1 joules

---

Units of measurement

An ongoing problem in sports science is the failure to standardise the units of measurements.

- Energy is measured in calories (1000 = 1 kilocalorie) or joules (1000 = 1 kilojoule).
- A calorie is the amount of heat energy needed to raise the temperature of 1g water through 1°C.
- Food labels give energy content in both forms and we can calculate from the label below that 1kcal = 4.186kJ.

NUTRITIONAL INFORMATION		
TYPICAL VALUES	**Per 100ml**	**Per tablespoon (15ml)**
Energy	1205kJ/288kcal	181kJ/43kcal
Protein	1.7g	0.25g
Carbohydrate	9.0g	1.35g
Fat	27.0g	4.05g

Example of a food label showing kilocalories and kilojoules

Do you know about...?

See page 144, which gives a checklist of questions you should be able to answer about this section.

Exam tips

It is essential to practise the calculations needed to work out BMR, work and power. Use different subjects of different weights to check that your calculations are correct.

3. Molecular muscle cell structures

> **Fact:**
> For muscles to contract, they must first receive an electrical impulse.

Fuller information on these themes can be found in *Advanced PE for Edexcel*, pages 373–379.

Motor units and motor neural firing patterns

Structures of the motor unit

Propagation of a nerve impulse

Neuromuscular junctions
- Controlling strength

Muscle cell (fibre) structure

Sliding filament theory
- Stage I
- Stage II
- Stage III
- Stage IV
- Stage V

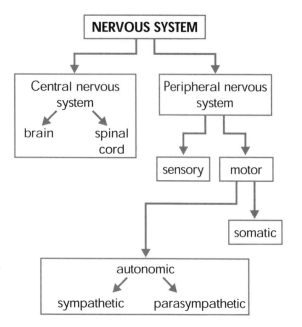

Anatomical divisions of the nervous system

Motor units and motor neural firing patterns

- The nervous system provides the body with its own internal wiring system along which electrical impulses can be sent and received.
- The system that carries these impulses is divided into:
    - the central nervous system (CNS)
    - the peripheral nervous system (PNS).
- The PNS can be further divided into:
    - the sensory portion, which contains afferent fibres that transmit impulses *to* the CNS
    - the motor portion, which conducts nerve impulses along efferent fibres *away from* the CNS.

Structure of the motor unit

- The motor unit comprises a motor neurone plus the muscle fibres attached to it.
- The motor neurone is a cell body containing the nucleus, the centre of operation for the neurone.
- The dendrites conducts electrical impulses *towards* the cell body.
- The axon carries electrical impulses *away from* the cell body.
- The myelin sheath is an insulating layer of Schwann cells that contain myelin.
- The nodes of Ranvier are gaps that appear in the myelin sheath along the axon.
- Saltatory conduction is when nerve impulses jump from node to node to enable rapid conduction.

Propagation of a nerve impulse

- Neurones are considered excitable tissue because of their ability to conduct an electrical signal.
- This signal is initiated via a stimulus that causes a change in the resting electrical charge on either side of the nerve cell membrane.
- Neurones have a negative charge on the inside of the cell compared with the outside.
- The neurone is polarised.

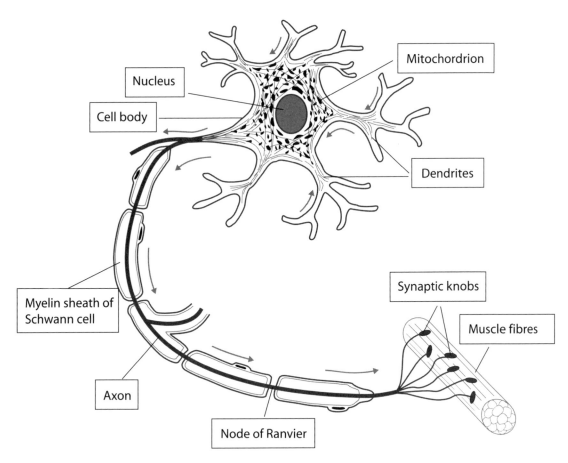

Nucleus

Cell body

Mitochordrion

Dendrites

Myelin sheath of
Schwann cell

Axon

Node of Ranvier

Synaptic knobs

Muscle fibres

Did you know?
The velocity of a nerve impulse can reach 120 metres per second.

For an impulse to start travelling along the neurone this resting potential has to be changed (= depolarisation).

- This is caused by Na^+ flowing in.
- If this depolarisation reaches a threshold (from –70mV to –55–50mV) then an action potential is reached and the impulse will travel down the neurone.
- There must be a minimum depolarisation of 15–20mV to initiate the action potential (impulse).
- If this is not reached, then no impulse will be propagated. This is referred to as the 'all or none' law.
- Before another impulse can be initiated the resting potential must be returned through repolarisation. This is accomplished by K^+ flowing out.

Motor unit = motor neruone plus muscle fibres

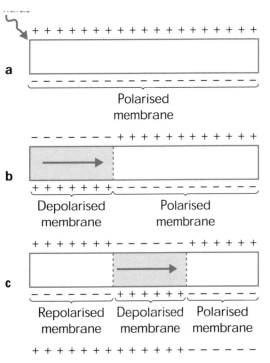

a — Polarised membrane

b — Depolarised membrane / Polarised membrane

c — Repolarised membrane / Depolarised membrane / Polarised membrane

Propagation of a nerve impulse

Neuromuscular junctions

- Neurones communicate at junctions called synapses (sites of impulse transmission).
- Impulses are carried across a small gap (20–30 nanometers) by a neurotransmitter called acetylcholine, which allows depolarisation of the motor end-plate portion of the sarcolemma of the muscle cell.

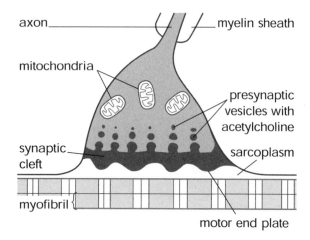

Neuromuscular junction

Controlling strength

Controlling strength and duration of contraction requires the following.

- Recruitment of more motor units.
- Increased frequency of impulses to allow no time for muscle to relax (wave summation).
- Recruitment of motor units in a rotation system to allow certain units to relax when others are contracting (spatial summation).

Muscle cell (fibre) structure

Muscles are made up of:

- connective tissue layers (epimysium, perimysium, endomysium)
- the sarcolemma (muscle cell membrane)
- the sarcoplasm (muscle cell cytoplasm)
- the mitochondria (the 'powerhouse' of the cell and major site of ATP resynthesis)

- the sarcoplasmic recticulum (membranous channels storing calcium ions)
- transverse tubules (small tubes that carry the impulse to the myofibrils)
- myofibrils (rod like structures that run the entire length of the muscle cell)
- sarcomeres (myofibril sections, containing actin, myosin, troponin and tropomyosin).

See 'The structure of skeletal muscle' on page 145.

Sliding filament theory

This theory can be broken in to five stages.

Stage I

- Impulse arrives at and crosses the neuro-muscular junction.
- Depolarisation is transmitted down the transverse tubules into the muscle fibres causing calcium ions (Ca^+) to be released from the sarcoplasmic recticulum.

Stage II

- The Ca+ bind to the troponin (tropomyosin complex).
- This reveals the active binding sites and enables the myosin heads to attach to the actin to form a cross bridge.

Stage III

- The myosin cross-bridge is energised by the breakdown of adenosine triphosphate (ATP).
- The energy given to the myosin enables it to pull the actin inwards and thus contract the muscle.
- The pulling of the action by the myosin is known as the power stroke.

Stage IV

- The myosin detaches from the actin when an ATP molecule binds to its head. Then ATP is broken down again and Stage III can be repeated.
- The contraction cycle can be repeated as long as Ca^+ are available.

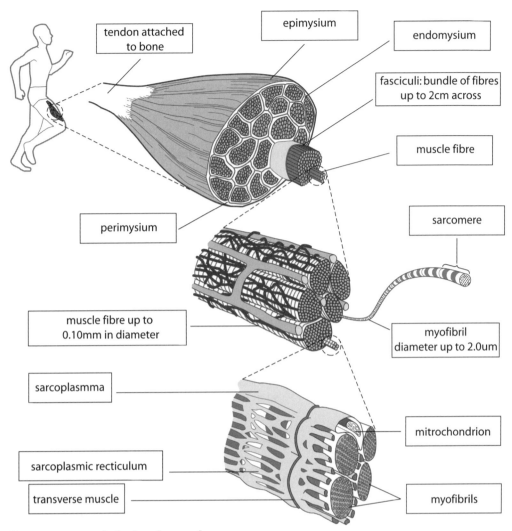

epimysium

endomysium

tendon attached to bone

fasciculi: bundle of fibres up to 2cm across

muscle fibre

sarcomere

perimysium

muscle fibre up to 0.10mm in diameter

myofibril diameter up to 2.0um

sarcoplasmma

mitrochondrion

sarcoplasmic recticulum

transverse muscle

myofibrils

The structure of skeletal muscle

Stage V

When the impulse stops the contraction cycle is broken and the Ca+ are pumped back into the sarcoplasmic recticulum.

NB Ratchet mechanism = alternate use of myosin cross bridge.

Do you know about...?

See page 144, which gives a checklist of questions you should be able to answer about this section.

Exam tips

There are lots of new terms to learn.

1. In your revision, try to restrict the terms to four or five per night and spread the load over a few weeks.

2. Always test yourself to check your learning.

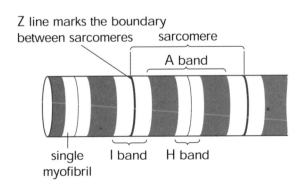

Z line marks the boundary between sarcomeres

sarcomere

A band

single myofibril

I band   H band

Microscopic view of a myofibril

4. Energy systems and the energy continuum

Fuller information on these themes can be found in *Advanced PE for Edexcel*, pages 379–391.

ATP in energy production

Energy systems
- ATP-PC (phosphocreatine) system/alatic anaerobic system
- Lactic acid system/anaerobic glycolysis
- Aerobic system

Mode of energy regeneration
- Continuum

Fatigue

Recovery process
- Oxygen debt
- Lactic acid and recover
- Glycogen and recovery

Nutrition

ATP in energy production

Adenosine Triphosphate (ATP) is the only substance we can use. It often referred to as 'energy currency', beause it powers all forms of biological work.

$$ATP \xrightarrow{\text{ATPase}} ADP + P_1 + \text{energy}$$

ATP breakdown is catalysed by the enzyme ATPase.

Energy systems

There are three energy systems that produce energy to resynthesise ATP:

- ATP–PC
- lactic acid
- aerobic.

All energy systems operate at once. It is the duration and intensity of exercise that influences which one predominates.

NB It is important that you remember the concept of concurrent activity. You will learn about each system in turn, but remember that they all operate at once.

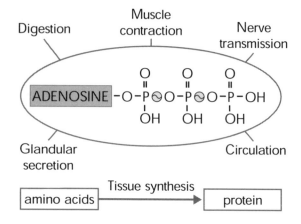

Universal energy currency

ATP–PC (phosphocreatine) system/alactic anaerobic system

- Energy substrate (fuel) = phosphocreatine (a high-energy bonded molecule).
- Enzyme action = creatine kinase (amount = 120g of creatine in our body, 95 per cent of which is found in muscle).
- Duration = 8–10 seconds before the PC is depleted.

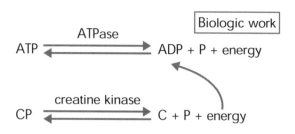

Energy from phosphocreatine breakdown

- Intensity = PC gives immediate source of energy to resynthesise ATP at a high rate.
- By-products = free phosphate (Pi).
- Sporting example = 100 metres/short sprints in a game.

Lactic acid system/anaerobic glycolysis
(2 ATP resynthesised)

- Energy substrate (fuel) = carbohydrate.
- Enzyme action = phosphofruktokinase (PFK), lactate dehydrogenase (LDH) (amount = 440g in the form of glycogen – stored in muscle and liver– and glucose).
- Duration = 30 seconds to 3 minutes.
- Intensity = medium.
- By-products = lactic acid and associated H^+
- Sporting example = 400 metres, repeated runs in football/rugby/hockey.

Aerobic system
(38 ATP resynthesised)

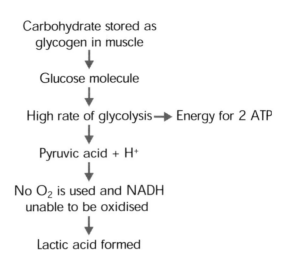

Lactic acid system/anaerobic glycosis

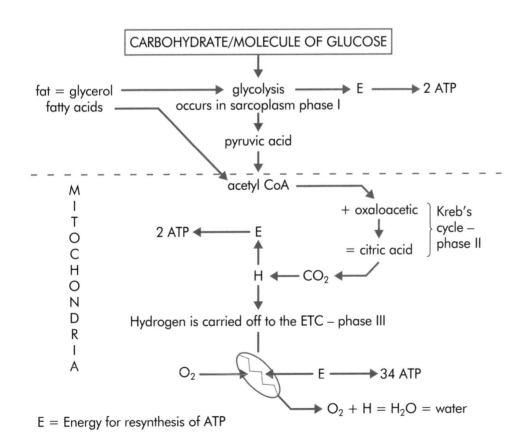

Aerobic system

- There are three sections:
  - Glycolysis (2 ATP)
  - Kreb's Cycle (2 ATP)
  - The Electron Transport Chain (34 ATP).
- Energy substrate (fuel) = carbohydrate, fat, protein.
- Enzyme action = phosphofruktokinase (PFK) and pyruvate dehydrogenase (PDH) (amount = 440g of CHO and 10.5kg of fat – 70kg man with 15 per cent body fat).
- Duration = hours.
- Intensity = low.
- By-products = CO_2, H_2O.
- Sporting example = 10,000 metres, mountain hike, jogging.

Mode of energy regeneration

Although we have considered the three energy systems as distinct entities, this is not actually the case.

- Providing energy for the resynthesis of ATP involves all the systems operating at once.
- When we begin exercise, the demands for energy can increase by as much as *120 times*, e.g. in all-out sprinting.
- Anaerobic sources can supply energy at four times the rate of aerobic sources.

Thus it is the duration and intensity of the exercise that governs which of the energy systems can resynthesise ATP at the required rate.

Did you know?

It is hydrogen ions (H+) that cause acidity.

Continuum

We may view the energy systems as a continuum with the PC system providing the majority of energy for high intensity exercise lasting 8–10 seconds.

- As duration increases, intensity of supply decreases and we use the lactic acid system.

- When the duration of exercise exceeds 3 minutes, the majority of energy comes from the aerobic system.
- However, as the intensity increases, lactic acid begins to accumulate.

Distance	Time (h:m:s)	% Anaerobic	% Aerobic
100m	9.79	90	10
400m	43.18	70	30
800m	1:41.11	40	60
1500m	3:26.0	20	80
5000m	12:39.36	5	95
10000m	26:22.75	3	97
42.2km	2:05:42	1	99

Approximate contribution of anaerobic and aerobic energy sources to total energy production in different athletic events

Fatigue

- Fatigue may be viewed as a simple imbalance between ATP requirements of a muscle and its ability to resynthesise ATP.
- This depletion of PC reduces the intensity of ATP resynthesis and thus the muscle reduces the power output.
- It has also been shown that rises in Pi following PC and ATP breakdown interferes with the cross-bridge formation in muscle cells.
- Lactic acid dissociates into lactate and H^+ and it is H^+ that causes an increase in acidity in the cell.
- The build up of H^+ is thought to interfere with Ca^+ binding to the troponin-tropomyosin and thus interferes with cross-bridge formation in muscle. This results in reduced power.
- The increase in acidity (pH reduced to 6.9) also interferes with enzyme action. PFK is particularly affected. This slows down glycolysis and therefore reduces ATP resynthesis, resulting in fatigue.
- The decrease in pH also affects the free nerve endings and produces pain (burning sensation).

Onset of Blood Lactate Accumulation (OBLA)

- The point at which lactic acid builds up so the H^+ interfere with muscle functioning occurs between 30 seconds and 3 minutes, depending on the intensity of exercise and the fitness of the athlete.

- This point has received much research attention and is often measured as the lactic acid threshold, the anaerobic threshold or the onset of blood lactate accumulation (OBLA = 4 mmol/litre).

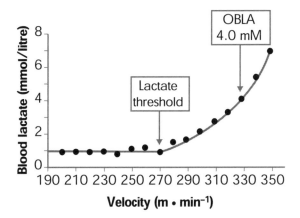

Blood lactate levels rise as a result of high intensity exercise

Recovery process

Oxygen debt

- Historically, the term oxygen debt has been used to refer to the excess oxygen uptake above rest after exercise.

- Excess post-exercise oxygen consumption (EPOC) is now also used for several functions during recovery.

- It is important that a coach/athlete should know about recovery after different types of exercise in order to help planning of rest interval durations during training.

- ATP and PC stores are replenished quickly.
  - 50 per cent of PC is restored within 30 seconds of recovery.
  - 75 per cent restoration takes about 60 seconds.
  - Full replenishment takes three minutes.

Lactic acid and recovery

- 70 per cent of lactic acid is oxidised during exercise.

- 20 per cent is converted to glucose (Cori cycle in the liver).

- 10 per cent is converted to protein during recovery.

- It takes approximately one hour to remove our lactic acid if we cool down with some gentle exercise. This can be doubled if no exercise is taken.

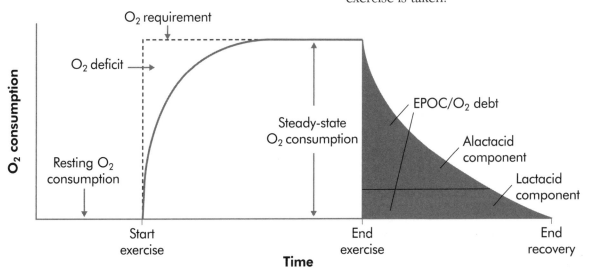

Oxygen need during exercise and recovery

Glycogen and recovery

- Eating/drinking carbohydrates especially in the first hour after exercise will restore glycogen.
- Conversion of lactic acid.

Nutrition

- High performance in physical activity is achieved with a careful dietary balance.
- The six essential nutrients are:
  - carbohydrates
  - fat
  - protein
  - vitamins
  - minerals
  - water.
- A well-balanced diet should consist of:
  - 60 per cent carbohydrate (CHO)
  - 30 per cent fat
  - 10 per cent protein.

Extra nutrition advice for sportsmen/women

- CHO: 7–10 grams per kilogram of body weight per day (g/kg/day).
- Carbo-loading: up to 70 per cent of diet from CHO at least three days before competition with reduced training load.
- Protein:
  - 0.8g/kg/day for ordinary people
  - 1.2–1.4g/kg/day for endurance athletes
  - 1.2–1.7g/kg/day for strength athletes.
- Fat: 20–25 per cent of diet from fat with less than 10 per cent saturated, e.g. visible animal fat.
- Vitamins: supplementation is unnecessary for athletes who have a balanced diet.
- Water: at least 2 litres should be consumed per day to remain hydrated. In exercise lasting more than an hour, 600–1000ml of fluid (containing 4–8 per cent CHO) is recommended.

Ergogenic aids

Ergogenic aids are work-producing substances or phenomena believed to increase performance. These include nutrients, drugs, hypnosis, blood doping, oxygen breathing, warm-up and biomechanical aids. See table on page 151.

Do you know about...?

See page 144, which gives a checklist of questions you should be able to answer about this section.

Exam tips

1. This is the most complex section of the syllabus. It requires that you have patience and utilise a variety of learning methods in order to grasp a full understanding of the importance of energy systems.
2. Once you have absorbed this knowledge you should apply it to your Personal Exercise Plan.
3. Try to learn one system at a time, but never forget that they *all work at once* (energy continuum).
4. Most exam questions refer to duration and intensity of exercise to show that you can apply the predominant energy system to the requirements of the exercise.

Ergogenic aid	Benefits (action)	Dangers
Creatine	• Shown to increase work output during repeated sprints in some subjects with low creatine levels • Lowers recovery time	• No recorded dangers as long as correct dose is taken ($4 \times 5g$/day for five days) • Weight gain and water retention reported in some athletes
Anabolic steroids	Stimulates protein synthesis and tissue growth – increase in training-related strength	• Genital abnormalities • Liver disease • Aggressive behaviour ('road rage') • Heart disease
Human growth hormone (HGH)	Stimulates protein synthesis and tissue growth	Excess HGH has been associated with diabetes, heart and bone disease
Amphetamines	• Stimulates the central nervous system • Increases arousal • Decreases reaction time • Decreases sense of fatigue • Enhanced fat utilisation	• Very dangerous and addictive • Elevated HR • Increased blood pressure • Irregular heart beat • Insomnia • Aggressive behaviour • Reports of deaths of athletes who have pushed themselves too far
Caffeine	• Stimulates the central nervous system • Increases arousal • Decreases reaction time • Enhanced fat utilisation	• Addictive • Produces nervousness, insomnia and tremors
Bicarbonate	• Helps buffer build up of H^+ • Shown to improve performance in high intensity exercise lasting 1–10 seconds	• Diarrhoea • Vomiting • Cramps
Erythropoietin (EPO)	Stimulates red blood cell production and thus oxygen carrying	• Increased blood viscosity • Large increase in blood pressure • Risk of coronary event and death

Ergogenic aids, their benefits and dangers

5. Physiological responses and adaptations of the energy systems

Fact:
Appropriate responses are much more likely to occur where effective adaptation has been achieved.

Sportsmen and women want to know that their training is beneficial. To obtain this information they need to have knowledge of training principles, energy systems and fitness tests.

Fuller information on these themes can be found in *Advanced PE for Edexcel*, pages 392–393.

Responses to high intensity exercise

Adaptations to high intensity exercise

Responses to aerobic exercise

Adaptations to aerobic exercise

Responses to high intensity exercise	Adaptations to high intensity exercise	Exercise to encourage adaptation
ATP stores depleted after 2 seconds	Muscle hypertrophy	Strength training – high resistance, low reps
ADP levels rise and stimulate PC breakdown	Increase in glycolytic enzymes	Speed and strength training
PC stores depleted after 8–10 seconds	Increase in PC stores	• Speed/strength training • Shuttle runs that will test time in system and recovery
Lactic acid (plus H⁺) produced as anaerobic glycolysis dominates after 10 seconds	Increase in glycogen content	Speed and strength training
Lactic acid inhibits enzyme action, interferes with cross-bridge formation and affects the free nerve endings = pain and fatigue	• Increase in buffering capacity (stopping the build up of H⁺) • Athletes can tolerate higher levels of lactic acid	8 weeks of anaerobic training has increased buffering capacity by 12–15 per cent
Onset of blood lactate accumulation (OBLA) at 4 mmol/l blood	Improve time to OBLA	• Training at a high intensity above your lactate threshold • Speed or HR may measure intensity.
• DOMS – delayed onset muscle soreness occurs 48 hours after high intensity training, especially eccentric muscle contraction • Micro-damage to the muscle cells which causes inflammatory response • **Not linked** to lactic acid		

Responses and adaptations to high intensity exercise

A level students can do this by monitoring their training programmes and test results and recording this information in their IPP.

Armed with a knowledge of the physiological responses and adaptations that have occurred, they can set out specific plans and goals for future training.

Responses/adaptations to high intensity exercise

- Responses are immediate changes to the energy systems during exercise.

- Adaptations are long-term changes to the energy systems resulting from training.

Responses/adaptations to aerobic exercise

- Responses are immediate changes to the energy systems during exercise.
- Adaptations are long-term changes to the energy systems resulting from training.

Responses to aerobic exercise	Adaptations to aerobic exercise	Exercise to encourage adaptation
Anaerobic systems provide energy in first few minutes of exercise	Increase in capillary density in muscle	Continuous training – long, slow distance, Fartlek training
Aerobic system then metabolises CHO and fat	Increase in number and size of mitochondria	Interval training – sessions that include intensities above the lactate threshold have been shown to improve aerobic capacity
Intensity and duration determine the source of fuel used – higher intensity CHO predominantly used	Increase in the number of oxidative enzymes	
Prolonged exercise – gradual shift from CHO to fat as source	Increase in stores of glycogen and myoglobin	Refer to target training zones in Unit 3 to help with designing exercise that will encourage adaptation
As duration and intensity increase then muscle glycogen becomes depleted and liver glycogen plays an important role	Fall in lactic acid production for a given intensity of exercise	
As CHO stores are depleted there is a greater reliance on fat.	Increase in ability to metabolise fat as a fuel	
'Fat burns in a carbohydrate flame' so glycogen depletion will affect fat metabolism and lead to fatigue.	Increase in the ability to work at a higher % of VO_2 max without reaching the lactate threshold Increase in stroke volume, blood volume and cardiac output Increase in oxygen transport and utilisation by muscle and thus the arterio-venous oxygen difference is greater	

Responses and adaptations to aerobic exercise

Do you know about...?

1. The different forms of energy?
2. The units of measurement used to measure energy?
3. How to measure your BMR?
4. How to calculate work and power?
5. Experiments that involve you in calculating work and power (e.g. Margaria Step Test)?
6. All the components of a motor unit?
7. How a nerve impulse is propagated? (Can you explain this?)
8. How to increase the strength and duration of a muscle contraction?
9. The five stages of sliding filament theory?
10. How ATP provides energy and how is it resynthesised?
11. The three energy systems in detail?
12. The notion of the energy continuum?
13. What causes the onset of blood lactate (OBLA) and how this contributes to fatigue?
14. Why we have excess post-exercise oxygen consumption (EPOC) after exercise?
15. How long it takes to restore phosphocreatine stores, remove lactic acid and restore glycogen?
16. What makes up a balanced diet?
17. What extra nutritional advice you could offer to a sportsman/woman?
18. The benefits/actions and dangers of a number of different ergogenic aids?

Exam tips

Make sure that you understand the difference between (short-term) responses and (long-term) adaptations.

Practise your exam technique

1. If all muscle contractions are maximal how can the forces exerted by the same muscle vary so much? (4 marks)
2. Explain how a motor unit transfers a neural impulse into a muscular contraction. (9 marks)
3. Using a sporting example explain the concept of the energy continuum. (6 marks)
4. Explain why performance deteriorates with a build up of lactic acid. (3 marks)

Section B: Option A: Sports mechanics

Overview

1. Fundamental qualities of motion
- Matter, time and space
- Motion

2. Analysis of linear speed, velocity and acceleration
- Linear motion

3. Force
- Impulse
- Internal force

4. Planes and axes of rotation

5. Gravity
- Newton's laws of motion

6. Principles related to the stability of the body
- Centre of gravity
- Equilibrium
- Friction
- Influence of external forces

7. Momentum

8. Air resistance and fluid friction
- Magnus effect

9. Angular motion
- Moment of inertia
- Angular velocity
- Point of release

Explanatory notes

This unit is about understanding the biomechanical functions of the body. It builds on the work already covered in Units 2, 3 and 5 of *Advanced PE for Edexcel* as well as that in Section A of Unit 6.

In combination with these other units, the learner should be able to understand how to improve performance and, like all the other units, this section should not be viewed as a standalone section of the specification, but as one part of a larger approach to developing ways of enhancing performance.

A knowledge of sports mechanics should allow the learner to understand:

* how a body initiates/stops movement
* the similarity between the concepts of linear motion and angular motion
* the effects of internal and external forces on that motion.

Armed with this knowledge, the performer should be better able to analyse performance and find ways of enhancing that performance.

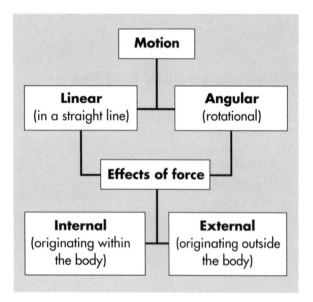

1: Fundamental qualities of motion

Fuller information on these themes can be found in *Advanced PE for Edexcel*, pages 396–397.

Matter, time and space

Motion

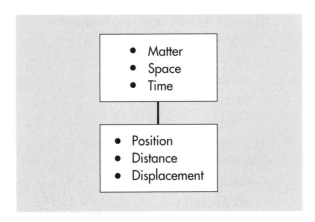

- Matter
- Space
- Time

- Position
- Distance
- Displacement

Qualities of motion

Matter, time and space

 **points**

- Matter is anything with mass. It is measured in kilograms (kg).
- Time is the measurement used to describe how long an event takes. It is measured in seconds (s).
- Space is the room/area/volume taken up by an object.

- It is measured in m² (two-dimensional) or m³ (three-dimensional).
- Linear space is measured in metres (m).

Motion (change in position)

- Position is a description of the exact point in space an object occupies, usually with reference to a fixed point.
- Distance is the measurement of actual ground covered, the total pathway. It is a scalar quantity (size only) and the measurement is the metre (m).
- Displacement is the measurement of how far an object has moved from its starting point, regardless of the route taken.
  - It is a vector quantity having size and direction.
  - The measurement is the metre (m) and a sense of direction, e.g. north-west, 20° from the horizontal.

Did you know?
Force is used to change an object's motion. Force is related to direction as well as speed, which is why it is necessary to understand the concept of displacement.

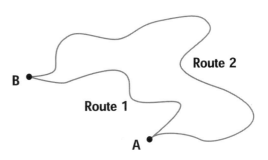

Two routes: different distances, same displacement

In the example entitled 'Two routes' (see above), Route 1 and Route 2 will have the same displacement, but Route 2 will cover a far greater distance.

Do you know about...?

1. The definitions of matter, space and time?
2. The units of measurement for each?
3. The definitions for position, distance and displacement?
4. The sporting examples that show the difference between distance and displacement?

Exam tips

Make sure that you can define/differentiate between distance and displacement. It is important that you are able to give practical sporting examples to support your answers.

2. Analysis of linear speed, velocity and acceleration

Fact:

Linear motion describes the movement of a body along a straight or curved line.

Fuller information on these themes can be found in *Advanced PE for Edexcel*, pages 398–400.

Linear motion
- Speed
- Velocity
- Acceleration

Scalar and vector quantities

Graphic descriptions of linear motion quantities

Distance/time, velocity/time and acceleration/time graphs

Linear speed, velocity and acceleration

Linear motion
- Linear motion refers to a change in position of an object in a straight line (backwards or forwards).

Scalar and vector quantities
- Scalar quantities have size/magnitude only, for example:
  - distance
  - speed
  - mass
  - volume.
- Vector quantities have size and direction, for example:
  - force
  - acceleration
  - velocity
  - displacement.
- Vectors are represented by a line with an arrowhead.
  - The length of the line represents the size of the force.
  - The angle of the line from the horizontal represents the direction (as does the arrowhead).

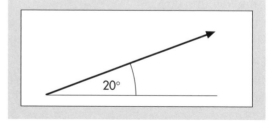

$$\text{Speed} = \frac{\text{distance}}{\text{time}}$$

Unit of measurement = ms^{-1}

Speed is a scalar quantity (size only)

$$\text{Velocity} = \frac{\text{displacement}}{\text{time}}$$

Unit of measurement = ms^{-1}

Velocity is a vector quantity (size and direction)

$$\text{Acceleration} = \frac{\text{change in velocity}}{\text{time taken to change}}$$

$$= a = \frac{v - u}{t}$$

Unit of measurement = ms^{-2}

Acceleration is a vector quantity (speed and direction)

Formulae for measuring linear motion

- In order to be able to measure this motion, we need to know the formulae (see 'Formulae for measuring linear motion', page 150) and definition (see right).

- Distance = the ground covered in moving from A to B.

- Displacement = the shortest possible route from A to B.

Did you know?
Acceleration is measured in ms^{-2} because the formula involves velocity (ms^{-1}) being divided by time (s). Therefore you get metres per second … per second!

- Speed = the rate of change of position.
- Velocity = speed in a given direction.
- Acceleration = rate of change in velocity.

Below are some graphic descriptions of linear motion qualities.

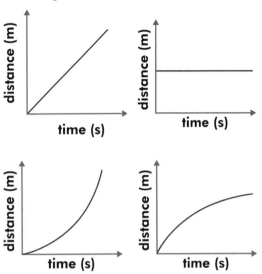

Changes of motion shown on a graph of distance against time

- You can describe the motion of an object by looking at a *distance v time* graph in the following ways:
  - a diagonal line represents steady speed
  - a horizontal line represents stationary
  - a curved line represents acceleration (or deceleration).

- You can describe the acceleration of an object by looking at a *velocity v time* graph in the following ways:

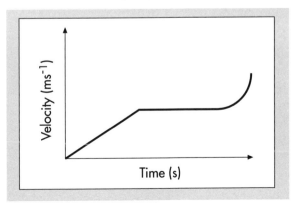

A velocity v time graph

- – a diagonal line represents acceleration or deceleration
- – a horizontal line represents steady speed
- – a curved line represents increasing/decreasing acceleration.
- The gradient of the line can be used in various calculations:
    - – gradient $= \dfrac{\text{the change in the 'y' value}}{\text{the change in the 'x' value}}$
    - – distance v time graph; the gradient represents speed
    - – displacement v time graph; the gradient represents velocity
    - – speed v time graph; the gradient represents the size of acceleration
    - – velocity v time graph; the gradient represents the size and direction of the acceleration.

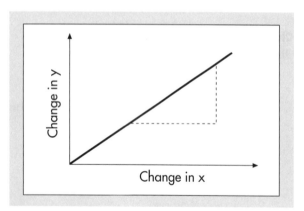

Using the gradient of a line in various calculations

Did you know?
Graphic descriptions of linear motion qualities is one area where students easily get confused because of the similarity. The graphs may look the same, but they represent totally different motions. Make sure you know the difference!

Do you know about...?
1. The difference between scalar and vector quantities?
2. How to represent a force in diagrams?
3. Linear motion quantities – speed, velocity and acceleration?
4. The formulae used to calculate these quantities?
5. The correct units of measurement for speed, velocity and acceleration?
6. Being able to tell the motion of an object by just looking at a distance v time graph?
7. Being able to tell the motion of an object by just looking at a velocity v time graph?
8. Calculating speed velocity and acceleration using the gradient of the various graphs?

Exam tips
1. Make sure you can accurately read, draw and sketch graphs for linear motion.
2. Always give the correct units in any calculations.
3. Take a ruler into the exam to help take accurate graph readings.

3. Force

Fact:
Force is the pushing or pulling effect of an action exerted on an object, usually altering its state of motion.

Fuller information on these themes can be found in *Advanced PE for Edexcel*, pages 400–407.

Impulse

Internal force
- First class of lever
- Second class of lever
- Third class of lever

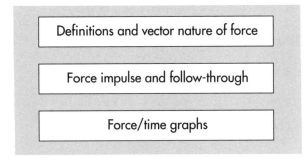

Definitions and vector nature of force
Force impulse and follow-through
Force/time graphs

Force: topics

 **points**

Force can have a number of effects on a body:

- if applied to a stationary object, it will move
- if applied in the same direction as a moving object, the object will accelerate
- if applied in the opposite direction to a moving object, the object will decelerate
- if applied in a different direction to the moving object, the object will change direction.
- When a number of forces act at the same time, the overall effect is known as the net or resultant force.
- Even a small resultant force will produce acceleration (or deceleration).
- When two forces act together, the parallelogram rule is used to calculate the resultant force.
- When two forces act at 90° to each other, Pythagoras' theorem is used to calculate the resultant force.
- When more than two forces act at the same time, the resultant force can be calculated by repeatedly using the parallelogram rule.

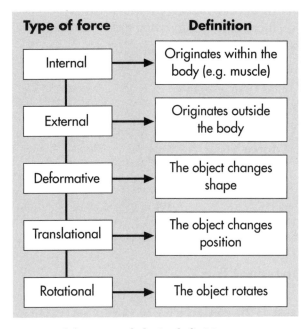

Type of force	Definition
Internal	Originates within the body (e.g. muscle)
External	Originates outside the body
Deformative	The object changes shape
Translational	The object changes position
Rotational	The object rotates

Types of force and their definitions

- If enough dimensions are known, any missing dimensions can be calculated using:

$$\text{sine} = \frac{\text{opposite}}{\text{hypotenuse}} \qquad \text{cosine} = \frac{\text{adjacent}}{\text{hypotenuse}}$$

$$\tan = \frac{\text{opposite}}{\text{adjacent}}$$

Impulse

 **points**

- Impulse is the change in momentum of an object.
- Impulse = (change in) momentum = force × time.
- Impulse is measured in kilogram metres per second ($kgms^{-1}$).
- Impulse is often represented graphically, with the shaded area under the graph representing impulse.
- Impulse is a vector quantity.
- Examples of impulse include:
  - kicking a ball
  - a vertical jump
  - hitting a golf ball.

- In 'striking' actions, impulse can be increased by improving follow-through.
- Impulse can also be applied to impact actions, e.g. catching a fast rounders ball.

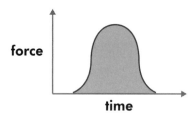

Force against time = impulse

Internal force

 **Key points**

- Internal force is produced by muscle contraction.
- The muscles work with the skeletal system to form levers.
- The order of lever is dependent on how the lever works.
- The most common type of lever used is the third class lever.
- All levers consist of:
  - a fulcrum (pivot point/joint),
  - load (resistance/object)
  - effort (force/muscle).

Measuring the moment of force
- The moment of force = force × distance to the fulcrum.
- The distance from the fulcrum must be measured at right angles to the force.
- Clockwise moment = anticlockwise moment.

First class lever

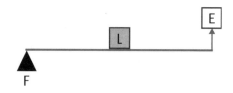

Second class lever

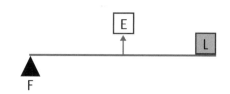

Third class lever

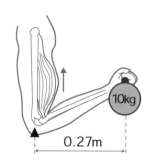

Calculating the moment of force

Do you know about...?

1. The different effects force can have on a body?
2. The different types of force?
3. The resultant effect of a number of forces acting at the same time?
4. The Parallelogram Rule?
5. Pythagoras' theorem?
6. SOH CAH TOA?
7. The definition of impulse?
8. Calculating impulse?
9. The effect of follow-through?
10. The effect of impulse on impact actions?
11. How the body produces internal force?
12. How the skeletal system works with the muscular system to produce levers?
13. Calculating the moment of force required to move an object?

4. Planes and axes of rotation

Fact:
Almost all human movement involves rotation of a body part around an imaginary axis of rotation.

Fuller information on these themes can be found in *Advanced PE for Edexcel*, pages 407–408.

Longitudinal axis

Lateral axis

Dorso-ventral axis

 **points**

- Actions involving rotation occur around at least one of three axes of rotation.
- The longitudinal axis might be imagined as a vertical pole running through your head to your feet.
- The lateral axis is like a pole running through your middle from left to right.
- The dorso-ventral axis is like a pole running through your middle from front to back.
- All three axes pass through the body's centre of mass.

5. Gravity

Fact:
All objects (bodies) are attracted towards the earth's centre with an acceleration of $9.81\,\text{ms}^{-2}$.

Fuller information on these themes can be found in *Advanced PE for Edexcel*, pages 408–410.

 points

- Gravity 'pulls' everything towards the centre of the earth.

- The force due to gravity is proportional to an object's mass.
- Gravitational field strength of earth is 9.81 Newtons per kilogram of mass (usually rounded up to 10N per kg).

Principles associated with Newton's laws of motion

Sporting examples of the application of Newton's laws

Reaction forces

Gravity, its principles and sporting examples

Newton's laws of motion

Newton's First Law

Newton's First Law states that if the resultant force is zero, the object will either continue to be stationary or move at a constant speed, i.e. if the forces are balanced there will be no change in velocity.

Newton's Second Law

Newton's Second Law states that if the resultant force is greater than zero, acceleration will occur. This acceleration will be proportional to the size of the resultant force.

$$F = m \times a$$

and

$$a = \frac{F}{m}$$

Newton's Third Law

Newton's Third Law states that for every action there is an equal and opposite reaction. This means that when object A exerts a force on object B, object B exerts an equal but opposite force on object A.

Did you know?

A 4 kilogram shot will always have a mass of 4 kilograms. However, although that same shot will have a weight of 40N on Earth, it could be weightless in space, due to zero gravity!

Do you know about...?

1. The effect of gravity?
2. The gravitational field strength of earth?
3. The principles associated with Newton's laws?
4. Sporting examples of Newton's laws in action?

Exam tips

Make sure you learn Newton's laws!

6. Principles related to the stability of the body

Fact:
A body can only be balanced if its centre of gravity lies within the perimeter of its base.

Fuller information on these themes can be found in *Advanced PE for Edexcel*, pages 410–411.

Centre of gravity

Equilibrium

Friction

Influence of external forces

Centre of gravity

 **points**

- The centre of gravity represents the point at which weight is acting upon an object.
- The centre of mass represents the point around which the mass is balanced in all directions, i.e. the balance point.
- Centre of gravity and centre of mass refer to the same point. As all objects on earth are subject to the force of gravity, centre of gravity is actually the more correct terminology.
- A we are only concerned with objects on earth, either definition can be used.
- In objects that continually change shape, such as the human body, the centre of gravity will also continually change.
- In uniform objects, the centre of mass/gravity will remain constant.

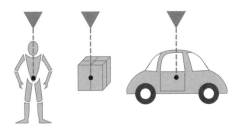

A balancing act

> **Line of gravity**
> - an object suspended from its centre of gravity (CoG) will hang in a balanced position.
> - An object suspended by any other point, will hang in such a way that its CoG will lie directly below the point from which it is suspended.

Equilibrium

- In order to be stable, the CoG must lie within the perimeter of the base of support.
- The larger the area of the base, the more stable an object will be.

- If the CoG moves outside the base of support, the object will topple.
- The further away from the base of support the CoG moves, the less stable it becomes, i.e. tall, thin objects are less stable than short ones.
- The weight of an object will also influence its stability.

Difficult to knock over

> **Did you know?**
> Some sprinters deliberately move their CoG outside the base of support in order to get a good start to a race.

> **Did you know?**
> Some athletes change their body shape to alter the CoG to their advantage, e.g. high jumpers and basketball players.

Friction

 **points**

- Friction is not always a bad thing. Without it we couldn't walk, run or jump!
- Friction is a force that opposes movement.
- Friction can occur in three ways:
  - between two solid surfaces that are trying to grip, e.g. a bike tyre and road
  - between two solid surfaces that are trying to slide, e.g. a skater on ice
  - between a solid object and the air/fluid

it is trying to pass through, e.g. a swimmer.

- Friction will slow an object down unless there is a driving force to counteract the friction.

- Friction can be increased/decreased by footwear, floor surface, or wearing gloves.

- Friction increases as speed increases.

- When a layer of fluid is placed between the two contact surfaces, friction is greatly reduced, e.g. tyres have poor grip on a wet road, speed skaters go faster on a thin liquid layer on the ice.

Did you know?
Synovial fluid is found in some joints and reduces friction between the bones. Without it, there would be much more wear and tear on the bones.

Influence of external forces

- External forces will have different effects on an object, dependent on whether the resultant force passes through the CoG or not.

- If the resultant force passes through the CoG, the object will move in the direction of the resultant force.

- If the resultant force does not pass through the CoG, the object will rotate.

- Athletes can counteract this rotation by changing body shape.

- The pathway of the CoG of an object in flight will always follow a parabola, even though the body may continually change shape.

- The Fosbury flop technique in high jump is an excellent example of an athlete changing body shape to alter his/her CoG.

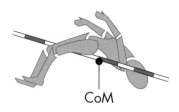

CoM

Arching back to change the CoM

Did you know?
In the high jump, the performer's CoG passes under the bar, whilst he or she passes over the bar.

Do you know about...?

1. The definition of the centre of gravity (CoG)?

2. How suspended objects are affected by the line of gravity?

3. How the position of the CoG affects stability?

4. The good and bad effects of friction?

5. Actions to take to decrease/increase friction?

6. The effect of the resultant force passing through the CoG (or not)?

7. How athletes use knowledge of external forces to their advantage?

Exam tips

Use practical examples in answers where they are asked for in the question.

7. Momentum

Fact:
In most sporting situations, friction and/or air resistance will act to reduce momentum.

Fuller information on these themes can be found in *Advanced PE for Edexcel*, pages 414–416.

Key points

- Momentum describes the degree or amount of motion possessed by an object, i.e. how difficult it is to stop the object moving.

- Momentum is a vector quantity (size and direction).
- linear momentum = mass × velocity
- The unit of measurement is kgm^{-1}
- In a sporting context, mass tends to remain constant. Therefore to increase momentum, we need to increase velocity.

Conservation of momentum
- When no external forces act on a collision, momentum will not change.
- Momentum before collision = momentum after collision.
- Examples of conservation of momentum include
  - collision of bowls
  - collision of snooker balls
  - collision of cars.
- Momentum is conserved only when no other outside force acts upon an object.

Do you know about...?

1. The definition of momentum?
2. The formulae used to calculate momentum?
3. How to increase momentum with sporting examples?
4. Conservation of momentum in collisions?

Exam tips

There's no short cut … learn the maths! And don't forget to use the correct units in answers.

8. Air resistance and fluid friction

Fact:
Air resistance and fluid friction are caused by objects trying to push the air/fluid out of the way to pass through it.

 Fuller information on these themes can be found in *Advanced PE for Edexcel*, pages 416–418.

 Key points

- Fluid friction and air resistance act in the opposite direction to the movement of an object.
- Both forces slow objects down.
- Resistance increases proportionately with the square of a body's velocity.
- The greater the speed of an object, the more resistance it will encounter.
- The shape and size of the object will affect the amount of resistance encountered.
- Resistance can be decreased by streamlining the object.

Concept of fluid friction
Opposing forces of lift and drag
Bernoulli effect and its application to spinning balls and thrown missiles

Air resistance and fluid friction

Drag and lift forces behave in the following ways.

- Drag occurs when air is not allowed to pass smoothly over or around an object.

- Drag can be reduced by the effects of streamlining.
- Lift occurs when the pressure difference of air passing below and above an object causes the object to move from high pressure to low pressure. (This can be lift up or lift down!)
- The greater the speed of the object, the greater the pressure difference and the greater the lift. This is known as the Bernoulli effect.
- When applied to spinning balls and objects in flight, the same effect becomes known as the Magnus effect.

Did you know?

RAF pilots spend far more time studying the Bernoulli effect than you do. It's the same principle that keeps their aeroplanes in the sky!

Magnus effect

 **points**

- A ball with no spin will allow airflow to pass smoothly over top and bottom and resistance will be low.
- By applying spin, airflow will be affected, as will pressure difference, and the flight path of the ball will be changed.
- Racquet players apply spin to the ball to deceive their opponents.

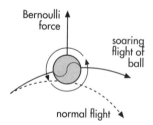

Backspin

Do you know about...?

1. The effects of air resistance and fluid friction?
2. How this relates to Newton's laws?
3. How to reduce the effects of air resistance and fluid friction?
4. How drag and lift occur?
5. The Bernoulli effect and the Magnus effect?

Exam tips

Be able to sketch explanations of the Bernoulli effect.

9. Angular motion

Fact:
The more closely mass is distributed to the axis of rotation, the easier it is to begin or halt rotation.

 Fuller information on these themes can be found in *Advanced PE for Edexcel*, pages 418–422.

Moment of inertia

Angular velocity

Point of release

Definitions of moment of inertia

Effects on rotation of lengthening and shortening of radius of gyration

Effect of release point

Angular motion: topics

Moment of inertia/Angular velocity

- Angular motion contains similar elements to linear motion.
- Angular momentum refers to the amount of angular motion.
- Angular velocity is the rate of spinning.
-
$$\text{angular velocity} = \frac{\text{angle turned (radians)}}{\text{time taken to turn}}$$

- angular momentum = moment of inertia × angular velocity
- Moment of inertia is the moment of force required to start (or stop) an object rotating.
- moment of inertia = mass (for all body parts) × rotational radius^2

$$MI = \sum (m \times r^2)$$

- The unit of measurement is kgm^2
- Around the longitudinal axis, MI can be increased by moving body parts away from the axis of rotation.
- Around the longitudinal axis, MI can be decreased by moving body parts closer to axis of rotation.
- Around the lateral axis, MI can be decreased by 'piking' or tucking.
- Around the lateral axis, MI can be increased by straightening the body.

Point of release

- In rotational actions such as the hammer throw or discus, the point of release will determine where the object lands.
- Release too early, the object will fly into the cage.
- Release too late, the object will fly into the cage or land outside the landing area.
- The angle of release will also affect distance.
- The object must be thrown at the optimum angle to gain lift and stay in the air longer.
- Release too high and gravity will pull it down to earth quicker.
- Release too low it will land too quickly.

Do you know about...?

1. The formulae used in calculations of angular motion?
2. How MI can be increased and decreased?
3. The effects of the point of release of a thrown object?

Exam tips

1. Learn the maths!
2. Use the correct units in answers.

Practise your exam technique

1. Use a sporting example to explain the difference between distance and displacement. (2 marks)
   You must use a sporting example or you will only score a maximum of 1 mark.

2. Give an example of a vector and scalar quantity, identifying the characteristics of each quantity. (2 marks)
   Again, you must give examples.

3. Describe the motion of the object in each of the following graphs.

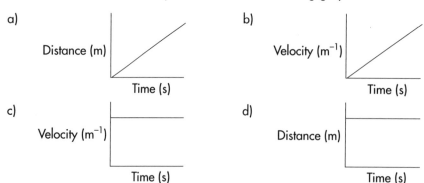

   a) Distance (m) / Time (s)

   b) Velocity (m^{-1}) / Time (s)

   c) Velocity (m^{-1}) / Time (s)

   d) Distance (m) / Time (s)

   There will often be questions about analysing graphs. You ought to be able to recognise the motion for each type of graph.

4. A croquet mallet has a mass of 700g. The ball has a mass of 75g. The mallet has a velocity of 5 ms^{-1} at impact and slows to 2 ms^{-1} after the "collision".
   Calculate the velocity of the ball after the collision. Show all you calculations. (5 marks)

   You need to know the formula and make sure you use the correct units of measurement i.e convert g into kg.

5. A sprinter in a 100m race reaches 12 ms^{-1} within 4s of the start of the race. If the athlete's mass is 60 kg, calculate the force exerted to reach this speed. (4 marks)
   Make sure you show your workings. Just the correct answer will not achieve maximum marks.

6. Explain how footballers like Beckham, are able to swerve the ball round the defence when taking direct free kicks. (3 marks)
   Make sure you make 3 different points to gain the marks.

7. *Using sporting examples*, explain how an athlete can speed up or slow down the rate of spinning. (3 marks)
   You must use a sporting example **and** make 3 different points.

Section B: Option B: Sports psychology

Overview

Explanatory note

The sports psychology module builds on some of the themes covered in Unit 2 Section A: Acquiring Skill in *Advanced PE for Edexcel*. Knowledge and understanding of individual differences are built on, and the impact of the sporting environment on the individual and the team are investigated. Students should be aware of the impact of psychological concepts on performance and measures that can be put in place to ensure that their impact is positive rather than detrimental to performance.

The keys to utilising sports psychology are the concepts of:

- concentration – focusing on the task in hand and not being distracted by the situation or those around you
- confidence – believing in your own ability, which can become a self-fulfilling prophecy; if you believe you will win you are likely to

- coping – all performers must learn how to deal with the stresses and strains of competition and to optimise their performances.

These important psychological concerns are vital in all areas of sport, in all activities and at all levels. Psychology is another weapon in the armoury of the coach and the performer, and can be the final piece in the performance puzzle.

The key to performing well in exam questions in this area (as in others) is the application of theory to practice. You must learn and understand the theory and be able to apply it to a range of sporting examples. No theory should be seen in isolation and the relationship between the individual topics in this section should be considered, as should their link with all other aspects relating to the sporting performance.

1. Introduction to Option B

Fact:
The increase in the use of psychologists in sport has enabled the field to develop into a separate field of sports science.

Fuller information on these themes can be found in *Advanced PE for Edexcel*, page 423.

Key points

- Sports psychology has developed from its roots in traditional psychology into a discipline in its own right.
- The function of the psychologist is to obtain the optimum performance and to minimise the negative impact of pressure.
- Many psychological theories can be and are applied to the sporting arena.
- Sports psychologists may work with individual performers and/or the whole team or group.
- The role of the sports psychologist is to:
  - prepare the performer mentally for performance
  - help performers concentrate and focus on the task
  - help performers to develop self-belief and develop confidence
  - develop coping strategies for dealing with the variety of situations experienced in the sporting arena
  - develop team cohesion in order to maximise the team's potential.

Performance

Physical attributes
- Skill levels
- Physical fitness
- Strength

Psychological preparation
- Focus/concentration
- Confidence/self-belief
- Dealing with pressure
- Avoiding stress

Associationist perspectives

Thorndike's law

Law of exercise
- Repetition of a response strengthens the link to the stimulus

Law of effect
- A satisfier strengthens the link whilst an annoyer weakens it

Law of readiness
- The learner needs to be physically and mentally prepared to learn

Classical conditioning
Through his experiments with dogs, Pavlov found that a response that is unrelated to the stimulus can be conditioned to follow the stimulus:
- Food → Salivation
- Bell + Food → Salivation
- Bell → Salivation

Operant conditioning
The bond between a stimulus and a response can be influenced by the outcome:
+ve reinforcement → Strengthen
-ve reinforcement → Weaken
Punishment → Weaken

Performance and the psychology of performance

2. Learning theories

Fact:
Learning is a key element in optimising performance. The learning process is developmental and continuous.

Fuller information on these themes can be found in *Advanced PE for Edexcel*, pages 423–427.

Associationist perspectives

Cognitive perspectives
- The Gestalt school
- Harlow and Gagné

 **points**

As we learn we move through three distinct phases:

- cognitive – the forming of a mental picture
- associative – attempting and practising
- autonomous – the skill is performed with little/no conscious thought.

There are two different schools of thought relating to learning:

- associationists
- cognitivists.

The key difference between the two is that:

- associationists believe that we develop a link between a specific stimulus and a particular response
- whereas cognitivists believe that learning is a case of developing an understanding.

Did you know?
Learning through doing is often the best way to learn.

Associationist perspectives

- Pavlov (1870), Thorndike (1932), Skinner (1938) and Hull (1943) identified learning as a sequence of linking situations with responses.
- Thorndike identified three laws that are still accepted today:
  - law of exercise
  - law of effect
  - law of readiness.
- Hull saw learning as drives, needs and incentives in his drive theory.
- Pavlov developed the concept of classical conditioning relating to instinct responses – the linking of unrelated responses to stimuli.
- Skinner developed the concept of operant conditioning – the moulding of behaviour through the rewards/punishment of a particular response.

Cognitivist perspectives

- Cognitive theories of learning differ to the associationist/connectionist viewpoint in that they see earning as a holistic function.
- They suggest that we learn by gaining an understanding of the situation and selecting an appropriate response as opposed to learning a specific response to a specific stimulus.

The Gestalt school

The Gestalt school of thought (Koffka, Koehler and Lewin) saw learning as an initial trial and error process.

- The learner experiments until a solution is reached.
- This 'insight' is gained as a result of 'cognitive' thought processes.

This form of learning requires an awareness and understanding of the 'whole' rather than a 'parts' approach. We need all of the information in order to make an informed learning choice

Harlow and Gagné

Cognitivists and associationists are the two extremes of a continuum of theoretical perspectives. Theorists have attempted to link the two.

Harlow (1949) and Gagné (1970) suggest that simple learning can involve linking a stimulus with a response, whilst more complex learning requires understanding and thought to solve a problem.

Do you know about...?

1. Learning as a continuous/lifelong process?
2. The fact that theorists have different views on how we learn?
3. How the theories differ?
4. How we can make use of knowledge of learning theories to help optimise sporting performance?
5. How the Gestalt approach links with whole approaches to teaching?
6. Why teachers should use positive reinforcement rather than punishment?
7. Why reflex saves by a goalkeeper are not necessarily pure instinct?
8. Why repeated practice will make us learn better?
9. How teaching athletes to go on the B of the 'Bang' is linked to Pavlov's dogs?
10. How learning and understanding may differ?

Exam tips

When discussing theories of learning, always give examples and explain how there are contrasting viewpoints.

3. Personality

Fact:
- Our personality is what makes us unique. It is the sum of the individual's characteristics.
- The continuing debate revolves around nature or nurture. Are we born with a particular personality or does it develop with our experiences?

Fuller information on these themes can be found in *Advanced PE for Edexcel*, pages 427–430.

Psychoanalytic perspectives

Interactionalist perspectives

Humanist perspectives

Trait theories of personality

 **Key points**

- Researchers and theorists have strived for nearly a century with little success to identify ' a sporting personality'.
- All personality types appear to succeed in sport as in life.
- Individuals of completely different personalities can do an equally good job in any role.
- Different theories view the formation and the changeability of our personalities very differently. The different schools of thought include:
  - psychoanalytical
  - interactionalist
  - humanistic
  - trait.

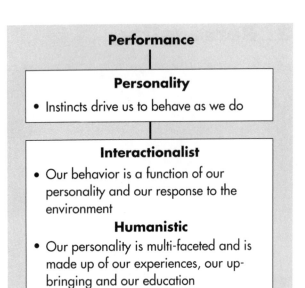

Performance and personality

Psychoanalytic perspectives

This school of thought was championed by Sigmund Freud, who saw personality as an innate function inherited from our parents. The psychoanalytic perspective suggests that we are driven by instincts that lead us to behave in particular ways.

We may be driven by:

- death instincts
- destructive and dangerous drives, such as aggression
- life instincts
- positive and creative drives, such as empathy.

Freud suggested that our mind is made up of three components:

- id – biological drive
- ego – self-preservation drive
- superego – our drive to achieve our ideal self.

Did you know?
Sigmund Freud (1865–1939) revolutionised the study of dreams with his work *The Interpretation Of Dreams.*

Interactionalist perspectives

This school of thought suggests that we behave in a manner governed by our core personality, although the specific situation/environment in which we are operating also influences this behaviour.

Our behaviour in different situations can therefore be explained by the impact of the environment and its interaction with our core personality.

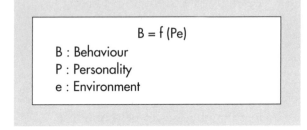

$B = f(Pe)$ (where f = function)

Humanist perspectives

The humanistic perspective views personality in a slightly different way and suggests that we are made up of many parts, all of which combine to influence our behaviour.

Rogers (1957) and other humanists see the key to personality being the self. The self is a multi-

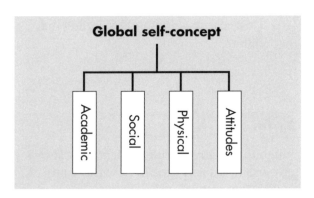

Rogers' global self-concept

dimensional concept all of which combine to form our global self.

Trait theories of personality

- Trait psychologists suggest that personality is an innate predisposition to behave in a particular way in a particular situation.
- It is suggested that personality is set at birth and remains relatively stable throughout our lives.
- Trait theorists talk in terms of extroversion and introversion, neurotic and stable etc., viewing individuals in terms of a continuum of personality traits ranging between two extremes.
- Psychologists such as Eysenck and Cattell have supported these approaches.

Do you know about...?

1. The fact that psychologists have differing views of personality?
2. Psychoanalytical perspectives?
3. Interactionalist perspectives?
4. Humanistic perspectives?
5. Trait perspectives?
6. The nature versus nurture debate?
7. The different personalities in sport? (Do you know how they perform?)
8. The different personalities in sport. (Do you know what sports they may play?)
9. The impact of personality on performance in different situations?
10. Why we behave differently in different situations?

Exam tips

Always apply theoretical concepts to sporting examples, e.g. trait theorists would suggest that a personality such as Paul Gascoine behaves as he does because of the personality traits he was born with.

4. The performer in action: Theories and applications

Fact:

- The use of psychologists in sport has been common in North America for several decades.
- They are now as common as fitness coaches in most professional sports.
- The sports psychologist's role is to optimise performance.
- Without the mind, the body is useless.

 Fuller information on these themes can be found in *Advanced PE for Edexcel*, pages 430–439.

Achievement motivation

Attribution theory
- Performance satisfaction
- Performance expectancy
- Learned helplessness

Uses of attribution
- Confidence
- Effort
- Pressure reduction
- Motivation

Self-efficacy

Self-motivation

Observational learning

There are many psychological theories that may be applied to the sporting arena. Many of them are theories with their roots in traditional psychology, and which have been adapted and updated to suit the sporting arena.

Achievement motivation

 **points**

- Whenever we take part in sport, the decisions we make are often influenced by our personality.
- If you put two different individuals in the same situation, they are likely to respond differently depending on their achievement orientation, e.g. one player may decide to shoot whilst another may decide to pass.

$$nAch = (Ms - Maf) \times (Ps \times (1 - Ps))$$

- nAch: Need to Achieve
- Ms: Motive for Success
- Maf: Motive to avoid Failure
- Ps: Probability of Success
- 1-Ps: Incentive value of success

Achievement motivation

Atkinson (1974) recognised that individuals can be placed on a continuum of achievement orientation:

- Need to Achieve (nAch) – the need to be challenged
  - Individuals with a high nAch will select the difficult option to push themselves as far as they can.
  - They are not worried about failing, e.g. someone with a high need to achieve will choose to shoot at goal rather than to give an easy pass to someone else.
- Need to avoid failure (naF) – fear of failure or making mistakes.
  - Individuals with a high naF will select the easy option in order to avoid failure.
  - They are more concerned with avoiding failure than maximising their level of achievement, e.g. someone with a high need to avoid failure will pass to

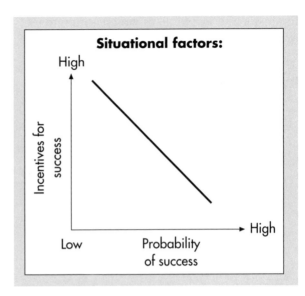

Situational factors

someone else rather than risk shooting at goal themselves.
- A high nAch individual will take risks. This can be useful if the performer is involved in an activity where risks bring rewards and failure has little consequence, e.g. an attacking player in hockey or a goal shooter in netball.
- A high nAf individual will not take risks. This is suitable where the performer is required to perform a task in which a mistake can be costly, e.g. a defender in football needs to clear the ball rather than attempting to dribble the ball and lose possession.
- Roberts (1974) suggested decisions are not only based on the likelihood of success, but also the rewards that might result from success. He suggested that high achievers would still choose the difficult option, but only where there is some chance of success – and subsequent rewards.
- It is important that a coach knows what motivates a performer and uses this in setting targets for development.
- Covington (1984) recognised the importance of goal orientation and categorised them in terms of:
  - mastery goals – incremental targets where the targets are challenging but achievable

- failure avoidance goals – incremental targets that are easily achieved.
- Those who prefer failure avoidance goals are those who work in 'the comfort zone'. They may never be challenged, take risks and may not fail, but are unlikely to improve.

Attribution theory

Weiner (1979) developed a system of analysing reasons for a result or performance. Attribution theory is used to identify causal factors in poor performance and allow them to be eradicated. Conversely, any factors leading to success can be maintained or improved.

- Attribution theory highlights differences between high and low achievers.
- Weiner identified the range of factors 'blamed' for a result and grouped them into four general categories:
  - ability
  - effort
  - task difficulty/quality of opponent
  - luck.

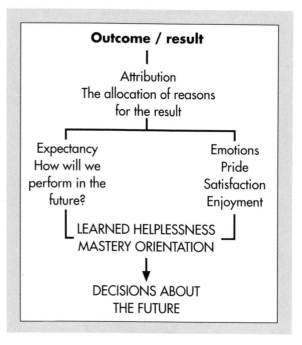

Locus of causality

		Internal	External
Stability	Stable	Ability	Task difficulty
	Unstable	Effort	Luck

Weiner's attribution model

- These four factors are placed within two dimensions:
  - stability – does this happen regularly?
  - causality/control – is this due to the performer or an outside agency?
- Attribution is both an analysis of what happened and a predictor of performance (performance expectancy).

Outcome / result

Attribution
The allocation of reasons for the result

Expectancy
How will we perform in the future?

Emotions
Pride
Satisfaction
Enjoyment

LEARNED HELPLESSNESS
MASTERY ORIENTATION

DECISIONS ABOUT THE FUTURE

Attribution theory

- It is important that performers are encouraged to use positive thinking rather than attributing failure to internal/stable factors.
- Focusing on failure will lead to learned helplessness, i.e. expecting to fail.
- This modifying of focus and renegotiation of blame is known as attributional retraining.

Uses of attribution

The importance of this approach is that it allows us to identify factors influencing performance and to work on specific areas of improvement – for example:

- confidence – a performer who attributes winning to internal and stable factors can be helped to improve confidence, because these factors will be reinforced and repeated
- effort – a performer who recognises a lack of effort as being responsible for his/her failure can be made to realise that greater effort (in training and/or performance) will lead to a better performance
- pressure reduction – prior attribution or attributional retraining helps to reduce

pressure before a competition, e.g. by playing down your chances of winning you get a bigger boost in confidence

- motivation – correct attribution can help the performer realise what needs improving and this can help focus attention on 'problem areas'. This often helps in overcoming a plateau in performance.

The confidence spiral

- The impact of confidence on performance has been a key area of psychological research. If we recognise the positive impact of self-confidence then we can build the confidence of the performer.
- Weinberg (1995) suggested that the confident performer will:
  - remain calm under pressure
  - concentrate more
  - set challenging goals and persevere with them
  - be more motivated
  - take risks in order to achieve.
- The positive benefits of high self-confidence must be controlled, as over-confidence can be detrimental to performance. It can lead to:
  - excessive risk taking
  - lack of effort (complacency)
  - lack of concentration.
- Bandura (1975) developed a self-efficacy model, identifying the factors influencing confidence. He saw four key elements as being important in the development of confidence and ultimately, good performance:
  - performance accomplishments – previous success or failure

Self-efficacy

 **points**

Did you know?
Self-efficacy is defined as 'the level of confidence in the likelihood of achieving a goal' (Coolican, 1996), or 'self-confidence in any given situation' (Bandura, 1977).

- Self-confidence is a vital component of the successful performer. Many top performers have been described as ' arrogant'.
- This confidence can become a self-fulfilling prophecy; if we expect to win we often will.

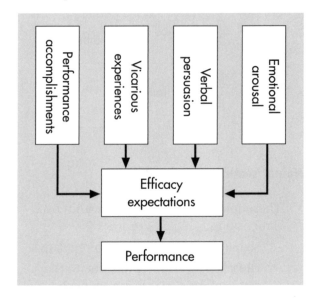

Self-efficacy model: Bandura

– vicarious experiences – gaining confidence by seeing others perform

– verbal persuasion – being told we can/cannot do something

– emotional arousal – the degree to which we are mentally aroused.

Self-motivation

> **Did you know?**
> The definition of motivation is 'the drive to strive' (Cratty, 1989).

 **points**

We take part in sport for many reasons. These motivating factors might include:

*   the achievement of a sense of mastery (satisfaction at success)
*   a wish for status (being looked up to)
*   friendship (acceptance by/within a group)
*   excitement/challenge (an adrenaline rush).

Gross (1992) stressed the need for self-motivation; others can try to help, but the individual must be motivated from within.

Spence (2000), through investigation of team players, found that the motivation to win and to participate is personal; each individual has different constructs which push them.

Bidell (1984) stressed the importance of self-motivation. He suggested that although initially extrinsic motivators – money, praise, recognition, etc. – are sufficient, if an individual is to continue to participate he/she must be intrinsically motivated.

Footballers earning huge amounts of money still strive to achieve at the highest level. The extrinsic rewards have been gained, but they still strive for success and personal satisfaction.

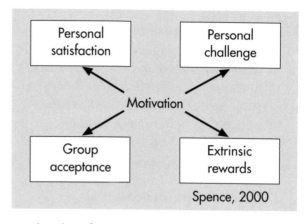

Spence, 2000

Motivational constructs

Observational learning

Bandura (1969) recognised the concept of observational/vicarious learning. He suggested that children learn both skills and behaviour through watching and copying others.

*   We watch, remember and, if we like what we see, we try to copy.
*   This shows the importance of a good demonstration when learning skills and also good behaviour from role models.
*   A beginner will learn by mimicking the demonstration.
*   Children will behave like those they see – diving, spitting or swearing at the referee.

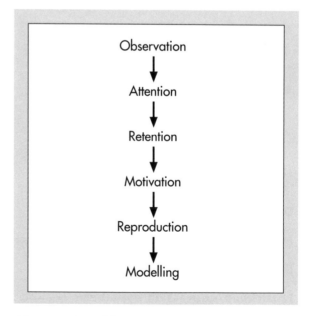

Observational learning in action

Exam tips

When answering questions you should attempt to compare different theories and always give examples.

5. The performer in action: Aggression

Fact:
Aggression is the term used to describe a range of different behaviours in sport.

Fuller information on these themes can be found in *Advanced PE for Edexcel*, pages 439–442.

Definitions

Instinct theory

Social learning theory

Frustration/aggression hypothesis

Causes of aggression

Hostile/Reactive aggression

- These are acts where the intention is to cause harm
- This will be outside the rules of the activity

Instrumental aggression

- This form of aggression involves an act where the intention is to win the ball or the point and to cause harm

Assertive behaviour

- In its truest sense, assertion is not a form of aggression
- In sport it is the use of legitimate force

Aggressive acts

Definitions

 points

Baron (1977) described aggression as the intent to harm either mentally or physically. However, Lloyd et al. (1984) viewed an aggressive act as socially unacceptable. This is why it is important to understand what is meant by aggression, in its negative form, as opposed to assertion, a positive act of 'aggression'.

Baron suggested three categories of aggressive acts:

- hostile/reactive aggression
- instrumental aggression
- assertive behaviour.

Instinct theory

- This theory is based on the work of Freud (1933), who thought that aggression is seen as an instinctive response that manifests itself in all situations.

- Lorenz et al. (1966) suggested that aggressive energy builds up and requires relief.

- It is suggested that sport is an ideal situation for the release of this energy.

Social learning theory

- Bandura (1969) suggested that although aggression may be an innate tendency, it tends to be modified or controlled by cultural factors.
- He also suggested that we learn to behave through observation and modelling; we observe the responses of others and learn to respond in similar ways.
- This has particular relevance to the way sport is portrayed in the media. Glorification of aggressive acts is likely to teach children to behave in a similar manner.

Frustration/aggression hypothesis

Many occurrences of aggression appear to result from frustration. The frustration of the participant may be the result of:

- performing badly
- a referee's decision
- losing.

The hypothesis suggests that where a performer is prevented from achieving a goal (e.g. winning), this will lead to frustration, which then builds up in the form of aggressive energy (see 'Instinct theory', page 176) and is released by an aggressive act. The more frustrated an individual becomes, the more likely it is that aggression will be displayed.

Causes of aggression

There are a large number of factors that may cause an aggressive response. These are often specific to the individual; additionally, they may cause aggression one day and not another.

Some possible causes of aggression are:

- over-arousal/stress – the pressure of the situation may lead the individual to lose control
- the venue – playing in unfamiliar surroundings is sometimes known to increase aggression; this may be due to an increase in stress
- time in the game – more aggression seems to occur towards the end of a game

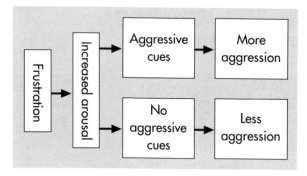

How frustration can lead to aggression

- when losing – winning teams are less likely to lose control
- perceptions of intent – if a player feels that another has intentionally hurt him/her
- social facilitation – the result of performing in front of a large crowd
- learning – teachers and coaches are sometimes responsible for teaching individuals to be aggressive rather than to control their aggression
- the rules of the game – some sports are designed to involve physical contact and this may encourage aggressive acts.

Do you know about...?

1. The theories that have been put forward to explain aggression in sport?
2. How aggression differs from assertion?
3. How instrumental/channelled aggression differs from reactive/hostile aggression?
4. Why psychologists have been used to help control aggressive behaviour in sports people?
5. How teachers can help to reduce aggressive behaviour?
6. What causes players to be aggressive?
7. How sports administrators may help reduce occurrences of hostile aggression?

Exam tips

A question about aggression in sport may not just require examples and general causes as part of your answer. You should also discuss theories, causes and applications.

6. The sporting environment

Fact:
The performer is only as good as his or her ability to cope with a given situation.

Fuller information on these themes can be found in *Advanced PE for Edexcel*, pages 442–444.

Social facilitation

Homefield advantage/disadvantage

 **points**

There are a number of situational factors that will impinge on the performance of the individual:

- social facilitation – the influence of others present during performance
- homefield advantage/disadvantage – the influence of the venue of the performance
- leadership/group dynamics.

Social facilitation

- Zajonc (1965) developed an analysis of the influence of the presence of others on performance.
- He identified the different impacts of different categories of 'others' present.
- Most previous research had focused on the impact of interactive others – those who can physically interfere with a performance.
- Zajonc also demonstrated the psychological influence of passive others through their impact on arousal levels.
- He suggested that some performers improve in the presence of others, whilst others find the pressure too great and their performance declines.
- He called this phenomena drive theory. Drive theory suggests that:

– as the level of arousal increases, so does the dominant (usual) performance
– thus an able performer will get better as arousal increases, whilst a weak performer will make more mistakes when aroused.

- The presence of passive others impacts on arousal levels (and thereby upon performance) through what Cottrell (1968) called evaluation apprehension. The performer worries that those watching are assessing the quality of the performance.

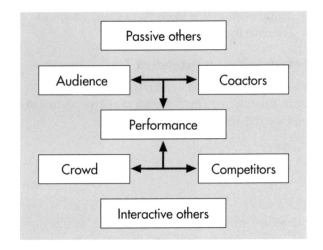

'Others' impacting on performance

Homefield advantage/disadvantage

Research and statistics have shown benefits to sports people when performing in front of a home crowd and in familiar surroundings. The research found that up to 65 per cent of games are won at home. General examples of this can be seen in a number of sports:

- football – many home teams have won the World Cup, e.g. England (1966), Argentina (1978) and France 1998
- rugby union – England have an unbeaten home record against all other major rugby nations in addition to record scores against the other 'six nations' teams; this has lead to Twickenham being christened 'Fortress Twickenham'
- tennis – Tim Henman appears to respond to the Wimbledon venue and crowds; he

has regularly performed better in this competition than in other grand slam tournaments.

This phenomenon may be explained by the impact on arousal levels as explained by social facilitation (see page 178), the inverted-U hypothesis (see page 180) and the catastrophe theory (see page 181).

Leadership

- Leadership has been shown to have an impact on team performance through its impact on team cohesion and individual motivation.

- It is important that the leader of the team is someone who is appropriate for that team and the activity.

- There is no ideal type of leader.

- Whether they are emergent, prescribed, autocratic or democratic does not matter; the important thing is that the team have direction and that they become a team rather than a group of individuals.

- When discussing leadership, you should consider the impact on social loafing, group cohesion and the Ringleman effect.

See pages 112–115 of Unit 2 Section A of *Advanced PE for Edexcel*, which investigates the different theories of leadership.

Exam tips

Answers to questions on this area will need to be related to theories from all other aspects of this unit.

---

7. Anxiety in sport

Fact:

At the top level in sport, most performers have similar skill levels, are equally fit and so on. However, some teams win more often because of their ability to deal with the stress caused by anxiety.

Fuller information on these themes can be found in *Advanced PE for Edexcel*, pages 444–447.

Inverted-U hypothesis

Cognitive and somatic anxiety

Catastrophe theory

Reversal theory

Trait/state anxiety
- Trait anxiety
- State anxiety

Key points

The terms 'anxiety', 'arousal' and 'stress' are often used interchangeably, but do differ subtly.

- Anxiety is the feeling of apprehension brought on by arousal.

- Stress is the psychological response to the stressor.

- Arousal is the physiological response to the stressor.

Theories related to anxiety include:

- inverted-U hypothesis

- cognitive and somatic anxiety
- catastrophe theory
- reversal theory.

Inverted-U hypothesis

- The relationship between arousal and performance has always been seen as one-dimensional or linear.
- Although this hypothesis has been superseded by more complex ones, it can still be used to explain the impact of arousal in simple terms.
- The theory suggests that as arousal increases, so does the level of performance. BUT, if arousal rises above an optimum level, performance is likely to deteriorate.
- It also suggests that individuals will require different levels of arousal in order to reach their optimum and that different levels are required for different activities.

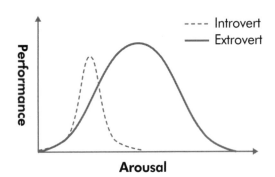

Inverted-U theory

Cognitive and somatic anxiety

More recent research has recognised a more complex relationship between arousal levels and performance.

McGrath (1970) suggested that the relationship is not linear and that it is important to recognise the difference between:

- cognitive anxiety – the psychological response, and
- somatic anxiety – the physiological response.

It is also important to recognise that cognitive anxiety (worrying about performance) will lead to a somatic response, and a performer who recognises the feelings of somatic anxiety is likely to worry about its effects.

Anxiety levels and their impact
- Cognitive anxiety leads to a decline in performance.
- Somatic anxiety has an inverted-U relationship with performance.
- Once performance begins, somatic anxiety reduces.
- Cognitive anxiety may remain high during performance.
- Cognitive anxiety levels remain relatively stable.
- Somatic anxiety levels fluctuate.

Catastrophe theory

Hardy and Fazey (1987) offered a three-dimensional explanation of the link between arousal, anxiety and performance. This is now widely accepted, and explains the relationship and accounts for sudden declines in performance and different types of anxiety.

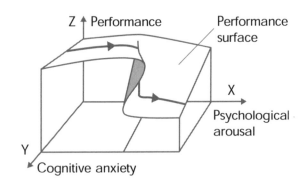

Anxiety, performance and arousal

The catastrophe theory recognises:

- the impact of small increases in anxiety on performance
- that a small increase can have a catastrophic impact
- that anxiety leads to mistakes, which in

turn produce higher levels of anxiety

- that once errors are made, earlier performance levels cannot be regained, even if the anxiety subsides
- that performance level increases with anxiety, until a point is reached where anxiety then contributes to a decline in performance levels.

Reversal theory

- Reversal theory (Apter, 1989; Kerr, 1990) stresses human individuality and recognises that we all have different preferred levels of arousal.
- In some situations we are subject to rapid changes in state. We reverse from one to another. We may be anxious before a game but as we begin to play, we reverse into a feeling of excitement and enjoyment.

Did you know?

Martens developed a widely used questionnaire-based method called the Competitive State Anxiety Test for measuring the impact of anxiety levels on performance. This is useful for analysing performance levels and the factors influencing them.

Trait/state anxiety

- Trait anxiety is an enduring aspect of personality; it is a predisposition to feeling anxious.
- State anxiety is a specific response of feeling stressed in certain situations.

Do you know about...?

1. The meaning and application of the inverted-U hypothesis?
2. The difference between cognitive and somatic anxiety? (Can you give examples?)
3. How and why catastrophe theory has superseded the inverted-U hypothesis?
4. How catastrophe theory can be used to explain sudden lapses in performance?
5. How state and trait anxiety differ?
6. The positive and negative impacts of arousal?
7. The need for psychologists/coaches to work with individuals not on team preparation?
8. How players can be taught to ignore pressure and why they need to ignore mistakes?
9. Why cognitive anxiety needs to be avoided at all costs?
10. How these theories can be linked to all other psychological issues?

Exam tips

Always explain the theory and use a range of different examples to show application.

Practise your exam technique

1. Performance in sport requires that the skills and techniques have been learnt. With reference to psychological theories, explain the process by which the skills are learnt.   (4 marks)

2. "The mind is not only a powerful part of top performance but is probably the key to the highest level of achievement." – Great Britain Hockey Coach David Whitaker (1995). Whitaker was suggesting that the mind can be the reason a team wins or loses. Explain how the performers at the top level may utilise sports psychology to help them perform in high pressure situations.   (5 marks)

3. Sport Psychologists have attempted to identify a 'sporting personality' with little success or agreement. Use one theory of personality to explain how different personalities develop.   (4 marks)

4. Many contact sports require performers to be 'hard but fair', however, many sports performers moved from instrumental to reactive acts of aggression. Explain the difference between these types of aggression with reference to theoretical concepts; and with use of practical examples explain what may lead to these aggressive acts.   (7 marks)

5. Coaches can help performers to 'control' their aggression and to channel it to be productive rather than destructive. Outline how a coach may help the player to optimise their performance and avoid acts which may break the rules of the game.   (5 marks)

Section C: A synoptic analysis of scientific principles in the development of performance

Overview

1. Introduction

2. Individual differences
- Issues relating to access and opportunity
- Differences between untrained individuals and the trained athlete

3. Short-term preparation
- Physiological considerations
- Psychological factors
- Mechanical aspects of short-term preparation
- Social factors influencing short-term preparation

4. Long-term preparation
- Physiological considerations
- Psychological factors
- Mechanical aspects of long-term preparation
- Long-term preparation: support roles and finance

5. Technology in sport
- Technology in training analysis
- Technology in training enhancement
- Technology in performance evaluation
- The concept of sports science and support
- Influence of the media on sports performance

6. Strategies for training
- The leader's role in developing performance
- The sports coach
- Cultural variations

7. Sports medicine
- Issues relating to injury prevention and rehabilitation
- Programmes for injury prevention/rehabilitation
- Nutrition and preparation
- The use of drugs in sport

Explanatory note

This section of the Unit requires you to address sporting issues synoptically. This means that you will need to draw upon the knowledge you have gained from the study of other Units in order to answer the questions set.

You should make a particular note that although this Unit occurs in the A2 part of the course, the material you studied in Units 1, 2 and 3 will be very relevant in answering synoptic questions, as will the material in other parts of this Unit.

Where a global issue is introduced into the question you may also find the material you studied in Unit 4A is useful in helping you to give examples from a culture other than the United Kingdom.

When revising you should identify the material in all the other Units that may be relevant to the topic areas in this section of Unit 6:

i)   Individual differences
ii)   Short-term preparation
iii) Long-term preparation
iv)   Technology in sport
v)   Strategies for training
vi)   Sports medicine

1. Introduction

Fact:
Synoptic analysis requires an understanding of all aspects of physical performance.

Fuller information on these themes can be found in *Advanced PE for Edexcel*, page 452.

The synoptic element of assessment brings together all previously learned knowledge, covering all the units. When answering questions, you will be expected to show a breadth of knowledge and understanding, covering physiological, social and psychological (or biomechanical) aspects of performance.

2. Individual differences

Fact:
Individual differences may be other than physical ones.

Fuller information on these themes can be found in *Advanced PE for Edexcel*, pages 452–458.

Issues relating to access and opportunity
- Age issues
- Gender issues
- Physiological differences
- Cultural differences

Differences between untrained individuals and the trained athlete
- Physiological differences
- Psychological differences
- Mechanical differences

Issues relating to access and opportunity

These including age, gender, race, disability, socio-economic background.

QUESTION: Is ability innate or is it affected by the social environment?

There is also a link here to socio-cultural issues of 'access', 'opportunity', 'provision' and 'esteem'.

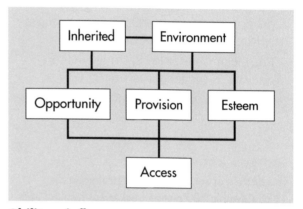

Ability – influences

Age issues
- Many world-class athletes have followed a very strict training programme from early childhood.
- Children have lower levels of concentration, tolerance and less understanding of complex terms
- Strength does not peak until around 20–30 years of age.
- Many components of fitness deteriorate with age (VO_2 max, HR, SV, flexibility, reaction time, muscle mass).
- Regular exercise slows down the ageing process.
- The UK has low level of involvement of elderly people in sport compared with USA and Australia.

Disability issues
- British Sports Association for Disabled (BSAD).
- Aussie Able Programme (Australia).
- Adaptive Sporting Programs (USA).

- Growth of disabled sport due to good role models (media attention): especially in Paralympics.
- Improved awareness as a result.
- Improved access and provision for disabled athletes.

REMEMBER Disability does not mean inability.

Gender issues

- Gender issues represent the biggest proportion of sport-related cases brought before the European Commission.
- European Charter for Sport listens to grievances on gender issues.
- The IOC considers the history of women in sport.

> **Did you know?**
> The distress of some female competitors in the 1928 Olympic 800 metres track event resulted in it being banned until 1964.

Physiological differences

- Males are stronger than females.
- Females are more flexible and metabolise fat more effectively.
- In most sports, single-sex competition counteracts this.
- Training affects both sexes equally, but lower testosterone reduces muscle hypertrophy in women.

Cultural differences

- USA and Australia have strong feminist movements which have helped increase female participation (male sport still dominates media).
- Sport in the UK is still dominated by men (especially in administration and coaching).

- Gender stereotypes still exist (but are diminishing).
- There has been a growth in female participation, e.g. Olympics and growth sports such as football.
- Religion/culture sometimes prevents women from competing, e.g. Islam.

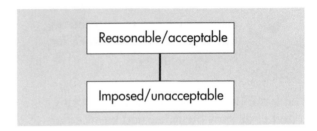

Cultural differences

> **Race**
> There is a suitability of some races to particular sports – for example:
>
> - Kenyans to running
> - black Americans to sprinting and basketball.
>
> Some 'stereotypes' are associated with certain racial groups – for example:
>
> - 'white men can't jump'
> - 'black men can't swim'.
>
> **NB Irrespective of any pre-disposition to excellence that may be present in some racial groups, economic power remains with WASPS (White Anglo-Saxon Protestants).**

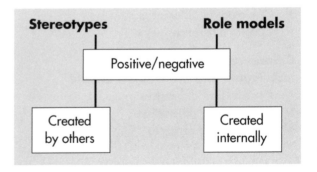

Stereotypes and role models

Socio-economic background

- Historical aspects of social and sport.
- Growth of global games, bringing plight of socially discriminated groups into the public arena, e.g. Cathy Freeman using Olympic successes to promote Aboriginal issues.
- Sport seen as an 'escape route' for the lower classes, e.g. black basketball players in the USA gaining social mobility through their sport.
- Some sports still effectively exclude lower classes from participation due the cost of participation – for example:
  - membership fees
  - cost of equipment
  - travelling.

Differences between untrained individuals and the trained athlete

There are three effective components in the differences between untrained individuals and trained athletes:

- physiological
- psychological
- mechanical.

The 'nature v nurture' debate is also very relevant.

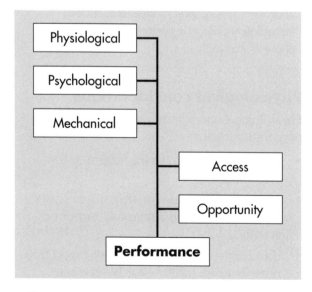

Influences on performance

Physiological differences

Physiological differences in terms of aerobic training for trained athletes compared with untrained individuals are:

- increase in size and strength of heart
- increase in SV and Q
- bradycardia
- improved muscle size and structure
- increased blood volume
- more efficient respiration
- increased Vo_2 max
- reduction in blood pressure
- reduced risk of heart disease.

There differences in anaerobic training are:

- muscle hypertrophy
- increased energy stores
- more efficient ATP-PC and lactic acid systems
- increased tolerance to lactic acid
- delay in thresholds.

Did you know?
Efficient respiration is important in both aerobic and anaerobic activity.

Psychological differences

 **points**

Regular training will make an athlete more skilful in the following areas:

- knowing what is required by the sport (cognitive domain)
- successful in reproducing movements (psychomotor domain)
- having the psychological skills to adapt to different sporting situations (affective domain).

The performance of the trained athlete will be:

- consistent
- efficient and economic
- aesthetic and fluent.

The trained athlete will have enhanced his or her innate ability, have effective selective attention, a well-developed kinaesthetic awareness and the ability to transfer skills and knowledge across activities.

The trained athlete is also likely to be:

- optimistic, courageous, outgoing and conscientious
- able to use cognitive strategies such as imagery
- able to attribute success to their own actions and failure to outside influences.

Mechanical differences

 **points**

The trained athlete will have:

- the knowledge and ability to generate effective, efficient movement
- knowledge of how to control stability
- knowledge of how to reduce negative affects of friction
- knowledge of how and why to apply spin in certain activities.

Do you know about...?

See pages 199–200, which gives a checklist of questions you should be able to answer about this section.

Exam tips

Remember that although individual differences may appear to be purely physiological, there are other, social, political and economic influences that can contribute to or detract from performance potential.

3. Short-term preparation

Fact:
Short-term preparation must be based on sound long-term foundations.

 Fuller information on these themes can be found in *Advanced PE for Edexcel*, pages 458–462.

Physiological considerations

Psychological factors

Mechanical aspects of short-term preparation

Social factors influencing short-term preparation

Short-term preparation has three aspects:

- physiological, psychological and mechanical preparations
- motivation and reward: influence of intrinsic and extrinsic rewards
- pride and passion: identification with 'institutional' or 'national' approval.

Did you know?
Short-term preparation involves that period immediately prior to a performance (competition phase of training).

Physiological considerations

Physiological considerations for short-term preparation include:

- acclimatisation (adapting/adjusting to environment)
- nutrition (maximum energy stores (carbo-loading), intake sufficient for output of activity)
- warm-up (to improve flexibility, blood flow, muscle temperature – cardio-vascular response)
- skill development.

Psychological factors

Psychological considerations for short-term preparation include:

- motivational factors including achievement, intrinsic, extrinsic
- positive mental attitude
- SMARTER goals (for goal-setting athletes)
- arousal – 'getting into the zone'
- anxiety (cognitive/somatic/relaxation techniques)
- team preparation – aiming to develop cohesion and team spirit.

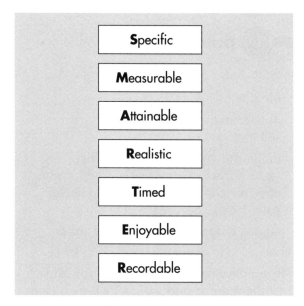

| **S**pecific |
| **M**easurable |
| **A**ttainable |
| **R**ealistic |
| **T**imed |
| **E**njoyable |
| **R**ecordable |

SMARTER goals

Mechanical aspects of short-term preparation

These include:

- playing surface and choice of equipment (to reduce/increase friction)
- equipment and sportswear (for improved performance/safety)
- technique adaptations (changing centre of mass, increasing speed of spin, spin on ball, etc.) to counter opponent's strengths and highlight weakness.

Social factors influencing short-term preparation

 **Key points**

- Sports teams develop a loyal and passionate following.
- National teams have even more passionate support.
- Honour and pride in representing country.
- Sport has been used to allow nations to develop a national identity – especially in New World and developing cultures.
- Olympic Games – walk in under national flag, national anthem at medal ceremony, national pride.
- Pride and nationalism displayed during European football championships.

Do you know about...?

See page 204, which gives a checklist of questions you should be able to answer about this section.

Exam tips

Remember that 'short-term' physical preparation includes:

'physiological'
'psychological'
'mechanical' and
'social' considerations.

4. Long-term preparation

Fact:
Long-term preparation provides the basis for short-term performance goals.

Fuller information on these themes can be found in *Advanced PE for Edexcel*, pages 462–466.

Physiological considerations

Psychological factors

Mechanical aspects of long-term preparation

Long-term preparation: support roles and finance

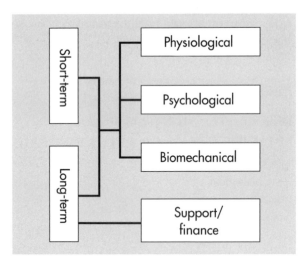

Elements of preparation

Physiological considerations

 **points**

These include:

- determining required fitness components – gap analysis

- fitness testing (to highlight strengths and weaknesses on which to base training programmes)
- training principles – progression, overload, specificity, reversibility, moderation, FITT principle
- training methods – continuous, interval, mobility, skill
- choice of training methods appropriate to sport and fitness levels (training zones)
- training periodisation – macro/meso cycle on/off season; key phase in adaptation.

Psychological factors

 **points**

These include:

- identifying needs
- long-term motivation (intrinsic, extrinsic, self-motivation)
- long-term goals (must be specific, measurable, achievable, recorded, planned, effective and reviewed – see SMARTER, page 189)
- coping strategies for stress and anxiety
- methods of developing self-confidence
- team developing/bonding, e.g. the impact of the training undertaken by British Lions rugby team before going on tour.

Mechanical aspects of long-term preparation

 **points**

These include:

- improving movement technique, e.g. moving centre of mass and applying spin, transfer of momentum
- improving or adapting equipment (technological improvements such as ergogenic aids)
- avoiding injury – by improving/adapting technique and adapting equipment, e.g. orthotics in shoes.

Long-term preparation: support roles and finance

 points

- The Soviet Union and GDR were the first to develop national programmes for identifying and nurturing talent.
- The historical divide between amateurism and professionalism in the UK and elsewhere delayed some support and finance infrastructures.
- These areas are now catered for in the UK by such organisations as Sport England, UK Sport, Sports Aid, British Olympic Association, UK Coaching and the United Kingdom Sports Institute (UKSI).
- Training camps/sports schools.
- Lottery funding and allowing athletes to train full time.

Function/role of the sports academy/institute

- Centre of excellence
- Best coaches/best facilities
- Full-time training
- Atmosphere of excellence
- Transfer of knowledge/skills/techniques
- Efficiency of funding
- Geographical factors.

Examples include:

- USA – commercial sponsorship and the media, educational system, collegiate scholarship system
- Australia – Australian Sports Commission, 'Sportsearch', Australian Institute of Sport (AIS)
- Asia – influence of ancient traditions on modern recreations
- China – heavily politicised and centralised systems of sport and recreation
- France – *Institut de Sports et Education Physicale* (INSEP)
- India – residential schooling; army boys' units.

Do you know about...?

See page 204, which gives a checklist of questions you should be able to answer about this section.

Exam tips

Remember that, as in the section on 'short-term' physical preparation, answers relating to 'long-term' preparation must also address the same considerations.

5. Technology in sport

Fact:
Technology can enhance sporting performance, but it is not a substitute for ability/preparation.

Fuller information on these themes can be found in *Advanced PE for Edexcel*, pages 466–470.

Technology in training analysis

Technology in training enhancement
- The training environment
- Training methods

Technology in performance evaluation

The concept of sports science and support
- National agencies

Influence of the media on sports performance
- The media and the individual

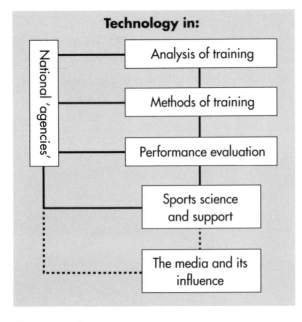

Technology in:

National 'agencies'

- Analysis of training
- Methods of training
- Performance evaluation
- Sports science and support
- The media and its influence

The use of technology

The key points to consider in technology in sport are:

- developments in techniques of performance monitoring and technical (biometric) analysis
- use of computer technology in recording and analysing performance data
- human performance analysis.

Technology in training analysis

 **points**

Internal monitoring includes:

- heart rate
- blood lactate
- brain activity.

External monitoring includes:

- video analysis for technique
- force and acceleration measurement
- muscle activity (electromyography)
- photography (stroboscopy) to analyse movement.

Technology in training enhancement

The training environment
The training environment can be considered in the following ways.

- Improved facilities for performer and spectators (retractable roofs, air conditioning, artificial heating, Astroturf pitches, artificial tracks, ski slopes and tennis courts).
- Physical and psychological disadvantage of not having access to the above.
- Use of computer design to develop improved equipment.
- Improvements in materials /techniques used for disabled athletes.

Training methods
These include:

- altitude training, environment chambers

- threshold training, plyometrics, isokinetic training
- use of heart rate monitors and training zones
- high energy foods, drinks and supplements.

> **Did you know?**
> David Beckham used an altitude tent in preparation for the 2002 World Cup competition. He slept in an oxygen deficient atmosphere in order to help maintain his aerobic capacity.

Technology in performance evaluation

 **points**

Measurements can be taken of:

- aerobic/anaerobic capacity
- strength output
- blood lactate levels.

Video analysis of technique and tactical play provides statistics.

Key examples include:

- a football 'smart shirt' that will record players' heart rate, acceleration and level of sweating
- a digital video game review system now used by Leicester RUFC (the £40,000 system enables coaching staff to use live camera images to pinpoint opposition weaknesses whilst the game is still in progress).

The concept of sports science and support

 **points**

Things to consider are:

- the role of sports science and medicine in the success of the former Soviet Union and GDR

- funding of sports science research by Sport England
- UKSI Research and Development; High Performance Coaching; ACE UK programme
- British Olympic Medical Centre
- Australian Institute of Sport (AIS)
- INSEP in France.

National agencies

The role of national agencies is:

- increasing influence of government in the provision and funding of sport and the consequent empowerment of sporting bodies
- growing acceptance that sport and politics do mix
- using technology as part of the drive for national success.

> **The use of science in nutrition and mental preparation**
> This comprises:
>
> - dieticians and nutritionalists
> - the use of anthropometry in the calculation of body fat and lean mass.

The influence of the media on sporting performance

- It influences and provides a forum for opinion.
- It puts a value on sporting performance.
- It influences the nature and scale of financial reward.
- It brings sporting performances to inaccessible places.
- It creates and broadens markets, therefore increasing finances.

The media and the individual

- There is increased media exposure of athletes' private lives.
- The media can 'make or break' sport stars.

- There are increased finances through sponsorship.
- But does improved income improve performance or simply allow clubs to buy better performers?

Do you know about...?

See pages 199–200, which give a checklist of questions you should be able to answer about this section.

Exam tips

Remember to include considerations of technology that may be involved in: training analysis; performance evaluation; and the influence of media technology on sporting performance.

6. Strategies for training

Fact:

Performance is a product of appropriate training strategy combined with motivation and leadership.

Fuller information on these themes can be found in *Advanced PE for Edexcel*, pages 470–474.

The leader's role in developing performance

The sports coach

Cultural variations
- Coaching in the UK
- Coaching in the USA
- Coaching in Australia
- Coaching in Asia

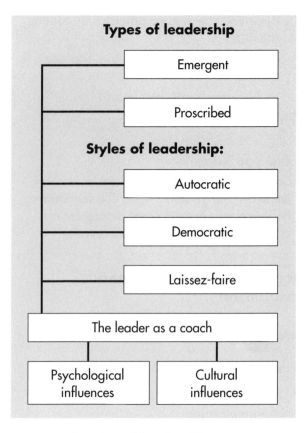

Types of leadership

- Emergent
- Proscribed

Styles of leadership:

- Autocratic
- Democratic
- Laissez-faire

The leader as a coach

- Psychological influences
- Cultural influences

Types and styles of leadership

The leader's role in developing performance

 points

- There is a variety of leadership roles in sport – for example:
  - PE teacher
  - captain
  - coach
  - manager
  - trainer.
- Leadership roles should be analysed in the context of:
  - type of leadership
  - style of leadership.

The sports coach

A good sports coach has:

- knowledge of sport – including, rules, techniques, tactics and practices

- knowledge of his/her athlete's personality, background, aims and ambitions
- knowledge of factors affecting performance – including anatomy and physiology, skill acquisition, psychology, mechanics and nutrition
- knowledge of coaching styles, methods and skills
- the ability to plan (identify the needs of the performer), conduct (know how to improve the performer through knowledge of teaching styles and learning phases) and evaluate performance (assess whether goals have been met, analysing performance).

Psychological considerations

 **points**

- Attitudes: the coach should be able to produce positive attitudes.
- Attribution: the coach should be able to help the performer attribute success to internal factors and failure to external factors.
- Self-efficacy: the coach should be able to develop self-confidence within the athlete (knowledge of Bandura's theory, see page 174).
- Aggression: the coach should aim to minimise aggressive outbursts from an athlete (knowledge of causes and theories of reduction, see pages 176–7).
- Arousal: the coach should have knowledge of and strategies to cope with over-arousal in a performer/group of performers.
- Cohesion: the coach should know how to develop team cohesion, thus ensuring that the team plays to its potential.

Did you know?
Psychological well-being is now considered to be of prime importance in the preparation of élite sporting performers.

Cultural variations

Does the type or style of leadership vary according to the nature of the activity? Or are there political/cultural considerations that might also influence such matters?

Coaching in the UK
- Oxbridge 'melting pot' and recreational ethic versus win at all coasts ethic (USA, Lombardi).
- Historically, coaching was a voluntary, unpaid activity.
- We have seen the development of National Coaching Foundation (1983), now 'UK Coaching'.
- There is a High Performance Coaching programme.

Coaching in the USA
- Lombardi's 'win at all costs' ethic reflects capitalism and frontier spirit.
- Commercialisation of sport – professional attitude to coaching at every level.
- The coaching profession has high status, but coaches are readily sacked if not successful.
- There is extensive use of statistics and technology.

Coaching in Australia
- Australian Coaching Council (ACC); centralised system.
- There is a High Performance Programme.
- The UK system of amateur coaches is being replaced by the US-style approach.
- The best coaches are head-hunted to work at the Australian Institutes of Sport (the state pays).

Coaching in Asia
- There is a male versus female dominance in Asian cultures.
- There are problems over access to sport and especially coaching.

Do you know about...?

See page 204, which give a checklist of questions you should be able to answer about this section.

Exam tips

Training strategies may be influenced by the type of leadership/coaching, and this in turn may reflect the cultural and/or political circumstances in which they exist.

7. Sports medicine

Fact:

Sports medicine is the application of medical knowledge to the preparation and rehabilitation of sports performers.

Fuller information on these themes can be found in *Advanced PE for Edexcel*, pages 474–478.

Issues relating to injury prevention and rehabilitation

Programmes for injury prevention/ rehabilitation
- Principles of injury prevention
- Principles of treatment
- Therapeutic modalities

Nutrition and preparation

The use of drugs in sport

Issues relating to injury prevention and rehabilitation

 **points**

- Is sport really good for you?

- There is increased risk of injury in contact sports and adventurous activities.
- Governing bodies and control over rules, playing areas, equipment and age categories in relation to safety.
- There is increased pressure on winning and use of 'medicine' to relieve/hide pain.
- The increased pressure on winning involves longer and harder training regimes, putting more pressure on the body.

Did you know?
Injury is a physical hurt or damage occurring during sport.

Programmes for injury prevention/ rehabilitation

 **points**

Rehabilitation goals include:

- education and conditioning to prevent injury
- the return to the same level of competition as soon as possible after injury.

Principles of injury prevention
These principles include:

- warm up/cool down, use of equipment, mobility training, correct technique
- correct equipment, surface, training, recovery, relaxation and diet.

Principles of treatment
These include:

- tailoring treatment to athlete, not the injury
- minimising damage
- reducing pain and swelling
- maintaining overall fitness during recovery
- actively rehabilitating to help early return to sport
- reducing likelihood of re-occurrence.

Traditionally, rehabilitation follows treatment of injury, but now commercial pressures and advances in science mean that aggressive rehabilitation is encouraged.

> **Did you know?**
> Rehabilitation is the restoration of an injured athlete to pre-injury level.

Issues include the following.

- Are all injury prevention methods 'ethical' and in the best long-term interests of performers?
- Do commercial interests hasten a return after injury – to the detriment of the performer (e.g. 'burn-out' in women's tennis; premiership footballers returning from injury in 'record time')?

Therapeutic modalities

 **points**

These include:

- short-wave machines, which increase heat
- ultrasound, which produces heat and helps repair soft tissue
- TENS (Transcutaneous Electrical Nerve Simulation), which is an electrical current that stimulates contraction of muscle and ion movement, thus reducing pain
- laser therapy, which lowers pain and swelling.

Techniques of reconditioning

This includes:

- isometric, isotonic and isokinetic training
- flexibility and endurance training
- manual therapy, to increase mobility.

Nutrition and preparation

 **points**

- A balanced diet and carbohydrate content is very important.
- The diet is adjusted around competition, e.g. carbo-loading to ensure sufficient energy stores for performance.

- There is concern over eating disorders in sports, especially for gymnasts and jockeys.
- Modern thinking is that most athletes follow full-time carbo-loading.
- Use of supplements to enhance athletes' diet, e.g. creatine monohydrate increases PC stores in body, so raising threshold of alactic system.

> **Did you know?**
> A carbo-loaded diet needs to contain 70 per cent complex carbohydrates.

The use of drugs in sport

 **points**

- Issues here are both scientific (medical) and ethical.
- Drugs created by 'chemists'.
- Drugs associated with medical ethics.

> **Drugs associated with cheating/the use of drugs – some prompts**
> - History of use of drugs at all levels of competition (including Olympics).
> - Medical justification of use of some drugs and not others.
> - Current developments in use of sports science, e.g. environment chambers versus blood doping.
> - Possible future developments through science.
> - Drug testing and 'masking'.

> **Did you know?**
> The current IOC interpretation of an unacceptable substance includes those that will give unfair advantage and that might also cause harm to the performer (Jacques Rogge, interviewed on UK TV, June 2002).

Do you know about...?

1. The differences between untrained individuals and trained athletes?

2. The issues in modern sport related to age, gender, race, disability, socio-economic background?

3. The specific issues that affect short-term preparation for competition?

4. The specific issues that influence long-term preparation for competition?

5. How the nature of access, provision and opportunity affect participation at both grass-roots and élite performance levels?

6. The developments in technology that have changed both the nature of sporting performance and the nature of its potential audience?

7. The growing impact of media technology in interpretations of sporting performance and values?

8. The role of the leader/coach/manager in the preparation of élite performers?

9. How differing cultural values influence access, provision and opportunity and the interpretation of 'sporting ethics'?

10. Sports medicine and its use and misuse in the sporting arena?

11. The importance of nutrition in the preparation of élite sportsmen and women?

12. The use and misuse of drugs in sport and the ethical questions associated with this issue?

Exam tips

Remember that references to sports medicine can include the purely functional (prevention, treatment etc.) and 'ethical' issues (e.g. blood-doping; the use of drugs).

Practise your exam technique

These essay questions are also marked out of 50, with marks being given for relevant points and examples – within the board's mark bands. (See below – these mark bands also apply to questions set on Unit 4B)

1. What role does technology play in the preparation of elite performers?
2. How can individual differences affect the type of global games a person takes part in?
3. Discuss the ideal preparation for an élite athlete preparing for a global competition in a week's time.
4. 'Drugs are Illegal – Supplements are OK'. Explain this apparent contradiction.

Answers and mark schemes for sample exam questions

Unit 1A

a) *early PE programmes*: 3 marks for any three of:
the need for military recruits; obedience; quick response to commands; the need to improve basic fitness levels; to introduce military discipline at an early age

b) *exclusion of girls*: 3 marks for any three of:
girls had no military purpose; girls were too weak; it was unladylike; would make them fit for motherhood; medical opinion changed; outcry by pioneers of 'equality'

c) *characteristics of games*: 3 marks for any three of:
character-building; physical conditioning; leadership qualities; loyalty to the team/house; preparation for future life

d) *governing bodies of sport*: 4 marks for any four of:
recreational ethic; fair-play; honour; integrity; playing to the rules; taking part more important than winning OR winning more important than how you play; loss of integrity; growth of professionalism; 'gamesmanship' rather than sportsmanship

e) *social changes*: six marks for any six of:
slow improvement in wages; reduction of working hours; increased free time; increase in the number of large population centres; exclusion policies of amateur sports bodies; growth of mass spectatorism; increase in general literacy; improved travel; working class identity with 'honest professionalism'; local 'celebrity' conferred upon sporting heroes

f) *UK Sport*: Max of two marks for 'structure'; two marks for 'function' and two marks for 'relationship':
structure: any two of: independent body; funded by Gov't and National Lottery; HQ in London; national network; runs UKIS
function: responsible for 'UK/GB' teams; in charge of coaching/preparation; élite performer identification; Coaching UK is 'coaching arm'
relationship: senior sports body; works closely with four 'home' sports councils; utilises 'network centres'

Unit 1B

These 'essay-type' questions are marked on the basis of 'quality' and 'content'

The quality of the essay is marked according to 'bands' set by Edexcel. e.g.:

Mark Band	Quality
21–25 marks	Well structured continuous prose showing evidence of planning. Covers all aspects of the question and highlights points with practical examples. There is evidence of analysis, appropriate technical terminology and engagement with/debating of issues.
17–20 marks	Evidence of structure and description and some analysis of the relevant issue(s). Use of appropriate language and examples in most cases. All points may not be covered or the answer may not be balanced.
13–16 marks	A descriptive account that may lack balance and technical terminology. Some points may not be supported at all and practical examples may be missing.
12–14 marks	Predominantly descriptive but with some valid points. Little analysis and/or effective

Mark Band	Quality
	structure. Poor use of practical examples and some points not developed.
9–11 marks	A series of isolated/unconnected statements showing some understanding but with a low level of language. May include vague assertions and fail to answer the question directly
5–8 marks	Disjointed prose, and much inaccuracy or irrelevance. Statements show a failure to grasp the issue(s) relevant to the question.
1–4 marks	Too brief and an incomplete answer. Lacking breadth and accuracy and failure to identify or address the topic. There is little material that is relevant to the question.

Criteria such as the above will apply to all questions in Unit 1B.

'Content' might be marked as below, and is specific to each question.

1. What changes have caused the rise in the number of Olympic competitors from Africa and Asia since the mid-1960s and why has this happened?

Changes: rise in numbers, first of men, then of women competitors; gradual shift to local control of National Olympic Committees; development of wider participation opportunities for ordinary people; development of own coaching structure; improvement of PE/sports programmes in schools/universities.

Reasons: many of these countries were formerly colonies of UK or other European countries; the 1960s saw the granting of independence to many of these countries; local people had increasing control over NOCs as former ex-patriate officials returned home; some ex-patriates stayed behind and provided the basis of teaching/coaching expertise in a newly developing infrastructure; freedom to develop PE etc. programmes of their own; Commonwealth grants/VSO etc. assisted in this; indigenous male competitors replaced former ex-patriate representatives but in increasing numbers; female numbers increased due to slowly improving opportunities AND as a result of the global trend towards equal opportunity for women; greatest increase in events requiring the least level of financial investment (emergent nations) – give examples.

2. The Paralympic movement is now becoming increasingly accepted as part of the Olympic movement. Briefly state the history of the movement and identify what you consider to be critical points in that history.

History: foundation (Stoke Mandeville etc.); broadening of interest/number of countries; number of competitors/number of events/classifications; summer/winter games; foundation of IPC; 'three teardrops'; Samaranch; increasing inclusion in main Olympic programme.

Critical points: forcing the issue (the acceptance that people with disabilities could/should play sport; disagreement with/rejection by Samaranch; foundation of the IPC; reasons for the 'three teardrops'; poor provision at some Olympiads (e.g. Atlanta); change of heart by the IOC; growing acceptance; the success of Sydney 2000.

Unit 3
Indicative Mark Scheme:
1. Continuous training:

The question is for three marks and so three points would probably be all that are required.

A common mistake is to see the term "***principles***" and then to relate it to an exercise or training type question, assuming that you are being asked to recall the "Principles of training". That is not what this question is asking. It is specifically asking for the characteristics (principles) that set continuous training apart from other methods of training. Marks would be awarded on the basis of one mark each for up to three of the points below:

Long distance
Constant intensity
Long duration
Aerobic activity.

2. *Structural and functional adaptations*:

This question is asking for a more detailed response (hence the 6 marks) but it can be answered just as specifically as the previous one.

The main word is '**and**'. This tells us that the question is looking for answers related to two areas and so it would be fair to assume that 3 out of the 6 marks are available to each area.

We are looking for 3 changes to the structure and 3 changes to the function of the cardiovascular system resulting from endurance exercise. The examiner would probably award one mark each for up to three of the points below:

Structure
- Bigger left ventricle of the heart / hypertrophy
- Increased strength of cardiac muscles
- Increased capillarisation of the cardiac muscle
- And of the working muscles
- Increase red blood cell levels / blood volume

Functional
- Bradycardia / lower resting heart rate / below 60bpm
- Increased Stroke Volume
- Cardiac output is constant at rest

- Greater Max Cardiac Output
- Lower working heart rate for a given workload
- Quicker return to resting heart rate post exercise / quicker recovery / greater efficiency
- Greater O_2 carrying capabilities
- Greater venous return

3. *VO_2max*:
The question is worth four marks. You are asked to define one term. There will be one mark for the definition and then further marks for identifying factors that effect it – from:

- maximum amount of oxygen that can be taken in <u>and used</u> (must have "and used") in a minute per kg of body weight.
- gender / sex
- age
- level of fitness
- type of fitness
- RBC count / health / social habits
- asthma

4. (i) *Use of a variety of different training methods*:
The opening statement refers to the term **variety** and 'methods' is **plural** so it is referring to **more than one** method of training.

You are asked to identify a sport of your choice. You would be unlikely to score a mark for simply naming a sport BUT if you fail to name a sport you could fail to score any marks at all. The rest of your answer should be related to the sport that you use.

Having listed the different methods (of training) you have to explain why they would be used – relating your answer to the physiological benefits derived from each method.

Marks would be awarded for:
- naming a sport that accommodates subsequent answers   (2 marks)

- two <u>appropriate</u> methods of training
  (1 mark for each method)
- two benefits of each method
  (1 mark for each benefit)

4. (ii) Identify and explain the principles...
Again the word 'and' appears – so you know that you are looking for two things. **Principles** of training is the main topic.

You will not get marks for simply listing the principles of training, the question asks you to **explain** them.

Consequently, you know that you will have to identify 4 principles and that each should be explained relative to the example you gave in part (i).

One mark would be awarded for up to four <u>appropriate</u> principles of training with an accompanying brief explanation (e.g. one sentence).

Unit 4A
Indicative Mark Scheme

1. *high school and professional sport in the USA* (4 marks)

   One mark each for up to four of:
   - In USA high school sport acts as the nursery for professional sport
   - There is only one route to the top in US sport – school / college / professional
   - Good school performers are recruited to colleges/colleges act as the intermediary
   - Best players are given scholarships to help them train and continue their education
   - Aim of college players is to get into the annual draft
   - The draft system recruits student players into professional teams

2. *the draft system present in US sport* (4 marks)

   One mark each for up to four of:

   - Draft is the annual recruitment of college players into professional teams
   - Every college game is analysed/players are ranked according to ability and performance
   - Worst team from season before gets first pick
   - Reflecting equal opportunity/land of opportunity
   - Ranking reflects win ethic/win at all costs attitude

3. *elements of 'Frontier Spirit' in North American sports* (3 marks)

   One mark each for up to three of:
   - competitive element/win-at-all-costs attitude clearly evident
   - reflected in macho approach/survival of the toughest in sport
   - survival of the fittest team/much emphasis on fitness/muscle
   - Frontier and sport dominated by men/women have only supporting roles

4. *historical and cultural background of America shaping sport* (4 marks)

   One mark each for up to four of:
   - most sports can be traced back to UK/European roots
   - early independence from Britain led to new image / adoption of sports to suit new culture
   - Isolationist policy led to separate US sports/ cut off from expansion of British sports
   - mention of specific examples/American football/baseball/ice hockey as adaptations of old world sports
   - Invention of new sports to reflect new image/basketball/volleyball

5. *historical and cultural background shaping sports in New World cultures* (4 marks)

   One mark each for up to four of:
   - most sports can be traced back to UK/European roots

- rugged terrain/bush culture led to domination of rugby
- sports played an important role in link to mother country/importance of cricket
- some sports adapted to suit the new culture/Australian rules
- some sports invented/adapted from indigenous people/ to reflect new environments

6. *outdoor education and recreation – popular in New World Cultures* (4 marks)

One mark each for up to four of:
- closeness of bush/country side
- need to teach about outdoor safety and survival skills in school
- vast range of environments easily accessible
- link to Olympic sports and possible success
- outdoor sport central to culture

7. *New World cultures and development of élite sports programmes* (4 marks)

One mark each for up to four of:
- visited centers around the world – especially Eastern Bloc
- Imported sports science and programmes
- adapted these to suit culture
- use of foreign coaches and techniques
- AIS/ NZ sports academy/ invite best young performers from around the world
- Adapted sports selection system into 'Sports Search'

8. *emergent cultures* (4 marks)

One mark each for up to four of:
- poor economies/poverty
- use of limited/available natural facilities
- based on limited/available natural talent
- little or no base of coaching expertise
- cannot afford expensive technological developments

- focus on success in a limited/affordable area
- limited access to sport for ordinary people

9. *European/global influence on sport and recreation in Asia*:

One mark each for up to two of:
Historically:
- Colonial influence
- Religious/missionary influence
- Military officers
- Trading influence

One mark each for up to two of:
Currently:
- Enduring colonial/missionary influences – now established sports
- adopting European global sports to show development against 'western nations'
- the role of global media/television
- the development of professional sport offers career/marketing opportunities

Unit 4B

These 'essay-type' questions will be marked out of 50 – on the same basis as those in Unit 6C. You will be expected to make a number of relevant points and give examples but overall marks will be awarded in 'bands' laid down by the exam board. (See 'mark bands' below the Mark Scheme for Unit 6C.)

1. *use of global games for protest*
- MUST give examples of use of global games for protest (e.g. Apartheid protest at rugby games; 'black power salute' etc.)
- to bring world attention to a cause/issue/injustice
- to discredit a regime/philosophy
- systematic/non-systematic
- platform for propaganda
- to hold governments to ransom (e.g. terrorism)

2. *global games and the promotion of sport amongst minority/disadvantaged groups*
   - opportunity to reflect broadened access both politically and in sport
   - can also highlight lack of access to certain groups (e.g. some Muslim women)
   - élite performance requires 'grass-roots' provision – some groups are denied access
   - political philosophy/human rights issues can prevent access to global games
   - rich countries have distinct advantage of poorer ones

3. *the drive to win and the erosion of sporting ethics*
   - origin of 'win-at-all-costs'
   - influence of professional sport
   - old-fashioned amateurism was behind the times
   - Huge rewards influenced 'sporting' standards
   - Influence of eastern bloc philosophies
   - Influence/pressure of global media

4. *global games and amateur/professional rules*
   - became increasingly difficult for 'genuine' amateurs to compete on an equal level with full-time professionals
   - eastern bloc performers were in effect full-time professionals
   - Olympic acceptance of payment to performers/trust funds
   - Increasing levels of professionalism forced global games to accept that 'top' performers were no longer amateurs
   - Brought clarity/transparency to a traditionally 'grey area' of under-the counter payments
   - Amateur sport was attracting increasing criticism for its 'double standards'

Unit 6A

Indicative Mark Scheme

1. *maximal muscle contractions:*
   One mark for either:
   - 'all or none' law
   - muscles contract maximally or not at all

   One mark each for up to three of:
   Force of contraction is controlled by
   - wave summation
   - frequency of the recruitment of the stimulated motor units
   - gradation of contraction
   - recruitment of more motor units

2. *motor unit transfers neural impulse into muscular contraction*:
   One mark each for up to NINE of:
   - impulse detected at the motor neurone pool
   - dendrites conduct the impulse into the cell body
   - the now concerted impulse travels away from the cell body along the axon towards muscle fibres
   - the impulse is protected and speeded up by the presence of the insulating myelin sheath
   - the action potential at a given point in the axon produces a diffusion of Sodium ions ($Na+$)
   - this enables further transmission of the impulse
   - the message travels along the neuro muscular junction to the motor end plates
   - these connect the motor neurone to the muscle fibres and complete the motor unit.
   - the arrival of the neural action potential produces a release of Calcium from the "T" vessels which results in a $Ca++$ charge
   - the two main proteins within the muscle fibre are Actin & Myosin
   - they are attracted to each other

- a globular protein (tropomyosin) is wound around the actin
- troponin is in turn attached to the tropomyosin and this prevents the actin & myosin from attaching
- the now present Ca++ attracts the troponin
- at the same time the heads of the myosin become activated by ATP
- the removal of the troponin now allows the actin & myosin to form a temporary bond and pull towards each other.
- this is called a cross bridge
- this bond is immediately broken and then reformed as the process is repeated

3. *the concept of the energy continuum:*

One mark each for: (2 marks max.)

- energy continuum refers to the fact that all 3 energy pathways are always working but one will be dominant at any given time.
- the dominant pathway will be determined by the intensity and to a lesser extent the duration of the activity.

One mark for relevant example:

- example can be any speed/endurance event, e.g. 1500m track, 200m swim.

One mark each for up to four of:

- start – lactic acid
- mid race – aerobic
- final stages – lactic acid
- finishing effort – ATP PC / alactic
- approx. 45 % of energy from ATP – CP system (beginning and end of the race)
- approx. 60% from the aerobic system – (mid race)
- lactic acid system – overlapping with the ATP-CP system at the beginning and the end of the race

4. *build up of lactic acid:*

One mark each for up to three of:

- as the lactic acid accumulates, muscle fatigue and pain occur.
- lactic acid = greater acidity in the muscle.
- low pH within the muscle cells inhibit enzyme action in the cell mitochondria, which normally promotes the change of glycogen into energy.
- hence the effect of lactic acid fatigue is to inhibit muscle action so that physical performance deteriorates.

Unit 6b(i)

1. Distance is actual ground covered, displacement is shortest route possible from A to B.

   MUST USE SPORTING EXAMPLE

2. Scalar quantities have size/magnitude only – e.g. distance, speed, mass, volume

   Vector quantities have size and direction – e.g. force, acceleration, velocity, displacement

3. a) steady speed b) accelerating c) steady speed d) stationary

4. **One mark** for correct formula: momentum = mass × velocity;

   One mark for correct calculation of momentum before collision

   Club = $0.7 \times 5 = 3.5$ kgms; Ball = $0.075 \times 0 = 0$ kgms

   Momentum after collision: Club = $0.7 \times 2 = 1.4$ kgms

   One mark for **use of formula**: Total momentum before = total momentum after

   One mark for **correct values**: $3.5 = 1.4 + 0.075 \times v$; $3.5 - 1.4 = 0.075v$; $0.075v = 2.1$

   One mark for **correct answer**: Must use units

   $$v = \frac{2.1}{0.075} = 28 \text{ ms}$$

5. therefore: v = u + at   (1 mark)

    $12 \text{ ms}^{-1} = 0 \text{ ms}^{-1} + a \times 4s$

    $a = \dfrac{12 - 0}{4} = 3\text{ms}^{-2}$ (1 mark)

    Now apply to F = ma   (1 mark)

    $F = 60 \text{ kg} \times 3 \text{ ms}^{-2}$ F= 180 N   (1 mark)

6. *Magnus Effect*

    Hitting ball with side spin

    Causing pressure differential on either side of ball

    Ball swerves in direction of spin

7. *MUST USE EXAMPLE*

    Spin faster by bringing body parts closer to axis of rotation e.g. arms in for skater/trampolinist, tucking for divers/gymnasts; Spin slower by moving body parts away from axis e.g. arms out for skater/trampolinist; Straightening out in somersault for diver/gymnast.

    1 mark for each correct explanation, 1 mark for suitable examples.

Unit 6B(ii)

The questions are designed to test both your theoretical knowledge and understanding and your ability to apply it to practical examples. Below is a suggestion of the theoretical content required and marks that might be awarded for answers to the questions above.

1. *Learning process*:
    -   Outline of why learning is needed: 1 Mark

    One mark each for up to three of:
    -   the learning process
    -   stages of learning
    -   different theories of learning: (e.g. 'associationist' ; 'cognitivist'
    -   (with some explanation/examples)

2. *High pressure situations*:
    One mark for reference to the fact that pressure has an impact on performance.

One mark for identifying the relationship between performance: arousal, anxiety and stress.

Up to three marks for:
-   an explanation of the theories linking performance and arousal – or
-   an explanation of how the coach can help prepare performers to cope with and avoid the negative impact of stress and to optimise performance.

3. *Sporting personality:*
    One mark for a satisfactory explanation of personality.

    One mark for reference to perspectives (e.g. Psychoanalytic, Interactionalist, Humanistic).

    Up to three marks for use/explanation of ONE perspective AND mention of the 'nature v nurture' debate.

4. *Reactive/Instrumental aggression:*
    Up to three marks for an explanation of the difference between reactive and instrumental aggression.

    Up to two marks each for up to *two* examples explaining the occurrence of aggression in sport. (e.g. Instinct theory, Social learning theory, frustration/aggression hypothesis).

5. *Control of aggression*:
    Explanations of how the coach can help reduce aggression:

    One mark each for up to five of:
    -   reference to any of the theories referred to in (4) above
    -   reduce arousal
    -   teach the performers to focus
    -   utilise the feelings of frustration to improve performance
    -   use rewards to encourage non-reactive responses
    -   act as a positive role model

Unit 6C

1. *technology in the preparation of elite performers:* (credit given for specific examples)

   - improvements in training equipment – computerised etc.
   - better clothing/personal equipment
   - technology allows better/more efficient methods of plotting/recording and predicting performance gains
   - better medical diagnosis/care lessens the risk of injury in training
   - better rehabilitation speeds recovery
   - technology/wireless links allows second by second monitoring of physiological changes
   - athletes/coaches have greater access to scientific information

2. *individual differences affecting participation:*

   - tendency to stereotype according to body-type
   - tradition/expectation
   - valid for some sports – e.g. high jump; basketball; events by weight classification
   - political/racial overtones (issues of access)
   - self-perception
   - ability level
   - tradition of limited provision for (e.g.) disability groups

3. *ideal preparation for an élite athlete :*

   - credit for: 'physiological'; 'mechanical'; 'psychological'; 'social' (aspects of preparation)
   - diet; accommodation; travel; relaxation
   - maintain 'peak'; training warm-up facilities; drills to stay sharp
   - mental rehearsal; focus; relationship with coach; maintain motivation; interaction with other team members (if appropriate)
   - avoidance of media intrusion; maintenance of daily routine

4. *'Drugs are Illegal – Supplements are OK':*

   - some definition/explanation of 'drugs' and 'supplements'
   - context (e.g. not ALL drugs are illegal – SOME supplements MIGHT be illegal)
   - why are these substances taken?
   - supplements refine/enhance diet – maximise potential
   - drugs artificially boost/aid performance
   - some performers have genuine medical reasons for taking drugs (medication)
   - some supplements have illegal (sometimes hidden) ingredients
   - essence of contradiction: drugs are mostly illegal but need not be – supplements are seen as acceptable but may not be

Band	Quality
43–50 marks	Continuous prose well structured with evidence of planning. Covers all aspects of the question using practical examples to highlight points. Evidence of analysis, correct use of technical language. Debates and challenges issues covered in the question in detail. Synthesis of all aspects of study. In depth and factual use of data/quotations. Candidates make a number of original statements showing knowledge of subject material. Accurate use of spelling, punctuation and grammar.
36–42 marks	Structured description with some analysis of the issue. Use of practical examples and correct language to support most of the points. May lack balance and not fully cover all parts of the question. Range of examples given from global games. Brings in many aspects of subject material and applies knowledge from a range of cultures. Factual information backing up most of points made. Candidates identify links between sport and wider society. Accurate use of spelling, punctuation and grammar.

Band	Quality
29–35 marks	A fundamentally descriptive account with good use of points. There is some use of technical language but points are not always supported. Factual information used to support some of the points made. Limited synthesis from a range of study aspects. Satisfactory use of spelling, punctuation and grammar.
23–28 marks	Valid points but predominantly descriptive. Little level of analysis or linking parts of answer together. Limited use of practical examples and points only partially developed. Concentrates mainly on the use of Olympic examples. Satisfactory use of spelling, punctuation and grammar.
17–22 marks	Mainly isolated statements. Limited points suggesting some understanding but poor use of language. Bland assertions and failure to answer the question set directly. Errors in spelling, punctuation and grammar.
8–16 marks	Disjointed with limited number of points. Considerable inaccuracy or irrelevance. Mainly statements that highlight a lack of grasp of what is relevant. Many errors in spelling, punctuation and grammar.
1–4 marks	Very brief and seriously incomplete narrative answer. Lacks and accuracy. Failure to identify correct topic. Little material relevant to question.